fotofeis

foto

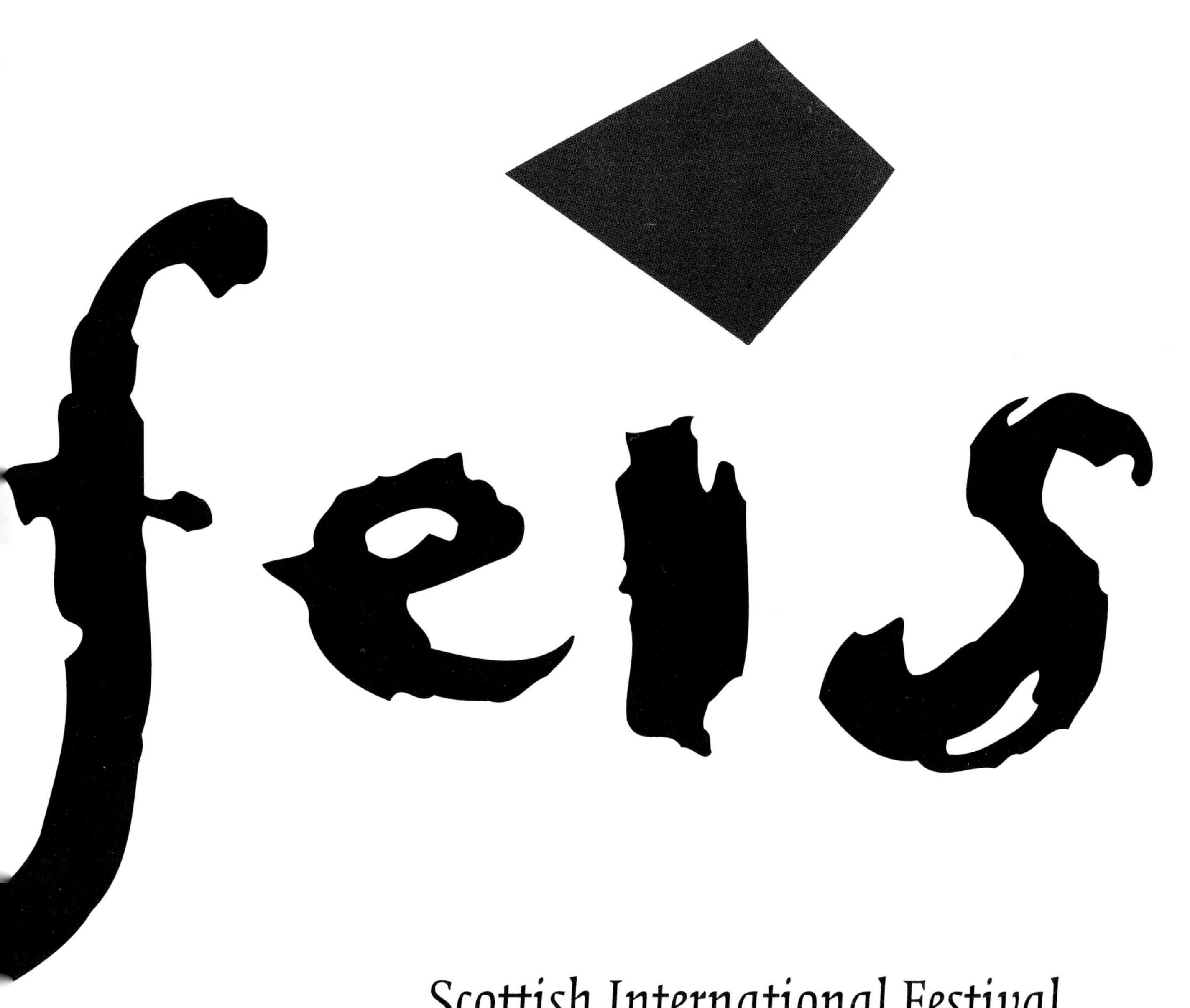

Scottish International Festival of Photography

PUBLISHER

Fotofeis Ltd
58 Timberbush, Edinburgh EH6 6QH
First edition of 3,000 copies
published May 1993
ISBN 0 9521396 0 X

DISTRIBUTION

Art Data, Unit U03, Acton Business Centre
School Road, London NW10 6TD

CATALOGUE

Edited by Alasdair Foster, Ken Gill,
Jackie Shearer and Geraldine Coates
Designed and typeset in FF Quadraat by Dalrymple
Cover illustration by Blue Peach / Colin Gray
Fotofeis logo by Tayburn Strategic Design
Printed by BAS Printers Ltd, Over Wallop

FESTIVAL STAFF

Alasdair Foster *Director*
Anne Dana *Administrator*
Ken Gill *Programme Coordinator*
Jackie Shearer *Information Officer*
Fleur Buckley *Press Officer*
Juliet Dean *Education Coordinator*
Lesley Shearer *Education Assistant*
Fiona Rankine *General Assistant*
Sylvie van den Berg *Placement Scheme*

FOREWORD

'Unique', admittedly, is a word much over-employed by the journalistic classes. Yet it is an accolade richly deserved by Fotofeis, given the scope of its remit, and the number of innovations it has sought to bring to the global world of photographic festivals.

From a personal perspective, the most exciting aspect of this month long event has been the fact that from the beginning it has viewed itself as pan-Scottish. Neither is this a tokenistic commitment involving the odd parachute jump into those parts of our nation which have been culturally less well nourished than others.

The very fact of the permanent features being overlaid by a rolling four week programme encompassing events, exhibitions, conferences, and seminars each specific to four regions of Scotland, makes Fotofeis truly a national International Festival.

Chair of the Fotofeis board is the perfect vantage point from which to witness a massive project such as this evolve from something I once rashly described as "a mildly demented gleam" in the eye of its director, to the multi-faceted programme launched on 4 June. For the chair's responsibility is shared, the commitment minimal in relation to the extraordinary workload taken on by the staff, and the pride and the pleasure virtually limitless.

This catalogue seems an appropriate place therefore to record my heartfelt appreciation of the prodigious efforts of everyone concerned with the setting up of the world's first nationwide photographic biennial. It is difficult enough running a festival when the template has been drawn by others, and the programming is the only function which must be started from scratch. In this instance Alasdair Foster and his team began with that most alarming of visions ... a blank sheet of paper.

That they have filled it so imaginatively will ensure that a, yes, unique, idea is made flesh in a way which will give considerable pleasure to the widest possible public. I need hardly add that the fact Fotofeis is happening in Scotland is a source of particular pride: further proof, if any were needed, that small countries can sustain big ideas.

RUTH WISHART

Chair, Fotofeis

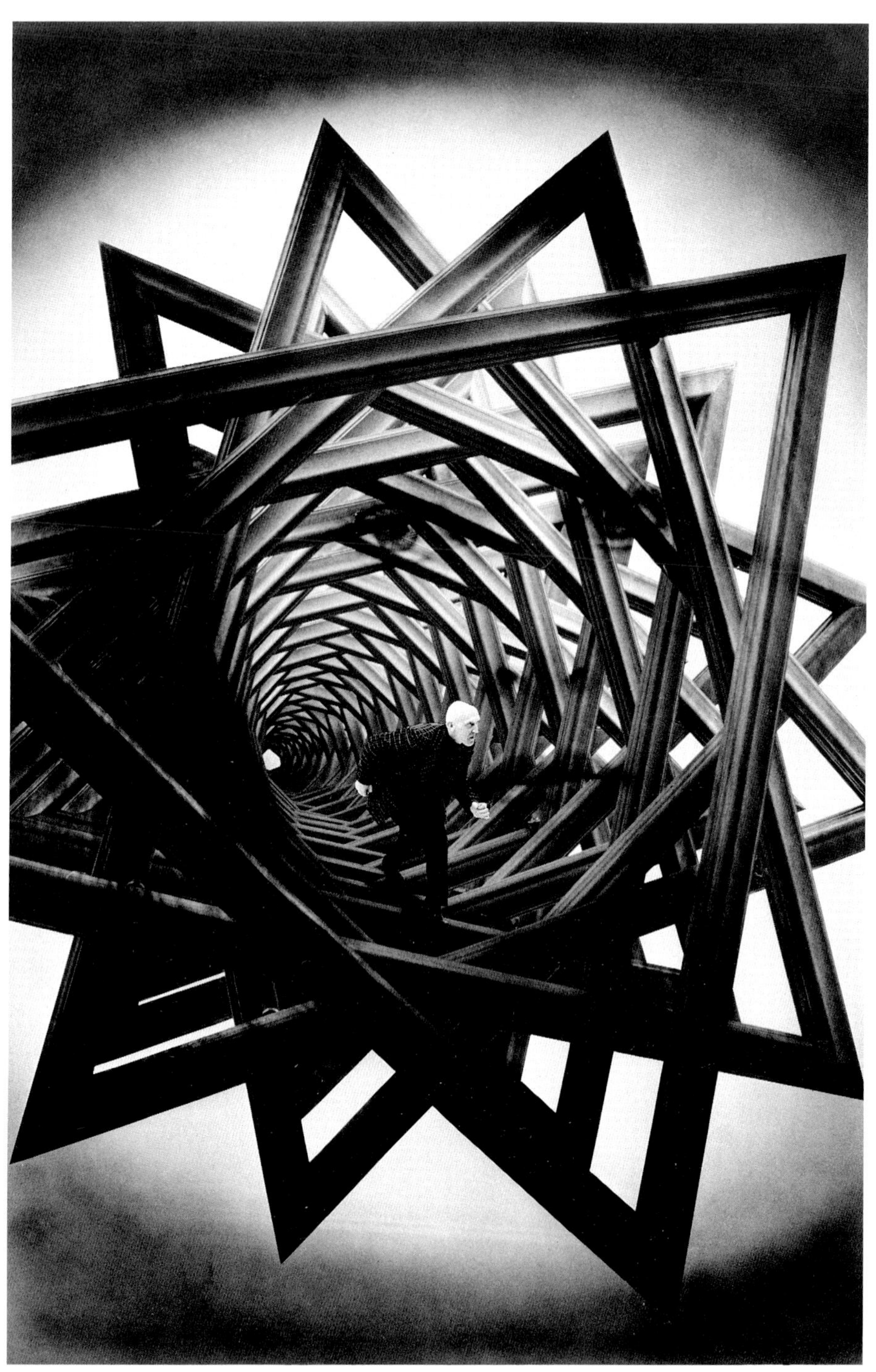

Alex Vermuelen The Senses Apart *photoprint*

CONTENTS

WELCOME TO FOTOFEIS

Fotofeis is the first of a new kind of photographic festival – over one hundred exhibitions and events spanning the whole country, from Dumfries in the south west to Wick and Thurso on the northern coast; from the Western Isles to easterly St. Andrews – it is a month-long celebration of the medium in its many and diverse forms.

Such an original concept required a suitably individual name – so one was invented. Fotofeis (it's pronounced 'foto-fayshe') is a hybrid word, bringing together the most common European prefix for Photography with the Gaelic word for a festival – the name itself implies the integration of the global with the local which is at the heart of this festival. For Fotofeis is not simply a showcase for pre-packaged foreign touring shows (though a number are premiered), but the focus for specially created thematic exhibitions, for international artist exchanges resulting in new commissioned works (some site specific and permanent), for developing activities across and between communities, nationally and internationally, and for the drawing in of the very best of independent photography.

Perhaps the easiest way to understand how, and indeed why, Fotofeis came into being and the reasons for its innovative format, is to consider its genesis. The idea of a festival began in 1989 as a response to the great diversity and quality of photographic exhibitions and activities which were staged as part of the 150th anniversary of the medium's invention. The question was straight forward: if all of that could be achieved simply because we were all, independently aware of a significant anniversary, why not harness this expertise and energy to create a festival?

There followed a series of meetings of interested parties, facilitated by the Scottish Arts Council, at which it was soon agreed that, 'yes' we want a festival, and 'no', it should not follow the single city format of so many other biennials, but rather it should exploit to the full the diversity of skills to be found across Scotland.

I became involved during the development stage and was immediately struck by the potential of such a festival. Firstly, it would create in the UK a forum in which a wide range of international photographic practice (especially that which comes from beyond the USA/Western European axis) could be experienced and discussed; secondly, it could integrate several strands of photographic activity in this country which, historically, have tended to remain separate and autonomous – the national and municipal museums, the contemporary art and photography galleries, the burgeoning community arts sector, and the long tradition of salon photography. It is a great personal pleasure for me that in this, the first Fotofeis, we have succeeded in encompassing such a wide array of work both within the country and from far afield. To pick four exhibitions at random from our programme, there are, at the Smith Art Gallery in Stirling the exquisite Mayan portraits of Guatemalan photographer, Luis Gonzalez Palma; in a woodland outside Inverness, an exhibition of 'virtual imagery' by Manual; at the Peacock Artspace an exhibition of photographs modified with flame by the German artist Kain Karawahn staged alongside *Burner*, a video installation by Stewart Wilson; and from Castlemilk in Glasgow, Womanhouse have undertaken a riotous photographic exploration of the phenomena of sex and stress.

In a world so heterogeneous and diverse we cannot assume that photography has a single canon of excellence. We must learn to recognize quality *of its kind* and to value each area of practice on its own terms. The notion of 'centres of excellence', so fashionable in previous decades, tended to concentrate everything in one locality and to construct a restrictive framework for excellence. While this no doubt makes cultural activity easier to administer, and creates the comfortingly illusion that what is good is containable, and by inference, knowable, it does little to reflect the reality of the medium's vigorous diversity. Photography is the most egalitarian of the visual arts. Applied, appropriated or abused by everyone, it can never remain a fixed unity, but is evolving in a multiplicity of directions. Eschewing the inbred perfection of the self-perpetuating, it is the happy mongrel of the arts, strong and healthy in its chaotic pedigree, ubiquitous, but always, in each and every manifestation, unique.

One need only look at the range of exhibitions on show at Scotland's three specialist photography galleries to see this illustrated. At Portfolio in Edinburgh, a major retrospective of the work of American photographer Ralph Eugene Meatyard whose oeuvre can be seen as the precursor to such stars of the contemporary art world as Richard Prince, Cindy Sherman and Jeff Wall. In contrast, Street Level in Glasgow has commissioned a special exhibition of work from the Baltic States, where the recent political upheavals are allowing new levels of communication with the West. Curated by artists from within Estonia, Latvia and Lithuania and imaginatively staged within the architecturally renowned Cottier (a building itself in transition), it is the first opportunity for 50 years to see the photographic art of this region. In a hugely ambitious project Stills, Scotland's oldest photographic gallery, has collaborated with the Institut Français d'Ecosse to organise *Public and Private: Secrets Must Circulate*. Involving work by some of the brightest new stars of British, French and Dutch photography, this mammoth enterprise takes in three galleries, two churches and numerous other sites across the city of Edinburgh.

The festival has four themes, each different in its approach: one is based on subject-matter (*Family*), one on the changing nature of the medium (*Photography Plus*), a third theme explores a topical development (*New Imaging*) and the final theme offers a platform to work from different geographic and cultural backgrounds (*Views from the Edge*). Each theme is located in a different area of Scotland. Each area has at its hub, a city (Glasgow, Edinburgh, Aberdeen and Inverness), but exhibitions and activities are also taking place in suburban and rural locations and in other towns and cities in the area.

Fotofeis is the first photographic festival in which the centre is mobile. The Fotofeis Roadshow will visit each area in turn for one week of the festival: a social centre within each city will be the focus for lectures and discussions, portfolio viewings and seminars, making plans and conversation. Other educational activities, such as the community and schools projects happen away from the centre, reaching out to involve new audiences from different localities.

Fotofeis makes no attempt to be the summation of contemporary photographic practice, nor does it address itself simply or solely to a specialist audience. In locating its elements across the whole of the country, the festival actively encourages the involvement of not one, but many local audiences, while, at the same time, drawing on a wider experience and practice. Visitors and those travelling from other areas experience the many exhibitions and events in a wide range of contexts and landscapes. There is no single view, no monolithic hierarchy of good taste. Instead, form is found in the theme for each area. Within this shared theme, many and diverse photographic practices can be viewed across a wide range of venues.

This decentralized approach, with its philosophy of 'access to excellence' will continue to evolve and adapt. It celebrates yet is not uncritical. In encompassing a wide range of practice we still seek out excellence of its kind. In embracing diversity the festival is not without structure. For, perhaps particularly in the case of photography, art is about the communication of ideas, experience, perception. In each area a single thematic idea passes, like a golden thread, through the exhibitions and events, drawing them together.

A festival should be more than the sum of its parts and addressing themes across such a diverse array of practice, allows not simply a discussion of that thematic idea, but the juxtaposing of one area of practice with another. It is an opportunity to expand patterns of viewing, to make new comparisons.

No one could accuse Fotofeis of a lack of ambition. That it has, in its first year, achieved so much is a tribute to the many artists, organisations and venues who have contributed so much energy and talent to making it a success, and, in no small measure, to the dedication of the team it has been my pleasure to work with on this project. It is also testament to the generous support of the Scottish Arts Council and the Arts Council of Great Britain, of the Scottish Local Authorities; and of the many other national and international funders and sponsors who have enabled us to create the first Fotofeis. But money is not everything, and I would particularly like to thank the staff of the Scottish Arts Council for their continued encouragement and advice.

Fotofeis is the result of the effort and talents of an enormous range of people across Scotland and from around the world. It is their collective energy and imagination which have made this festival possible.

Enjoy!

ALASDAIR FOSTER
Director, Fotofeis

The Fotofeis Roadshow

EDINBURGH, FIFE, BORDERS AND LOTHIAN REGIONS

8 – 12 JUNE

ABERDEEN, TAYSIDE AND GRAMPIAN REGIONS

15 – 19 JUNE

INVERNESS AND THE HIGHLANDS

22 – 26 JUNE

GLASGOW, CENTRAL, STRATHCLYDE, DUMFRIES & GALLOWAY REGIONS

29 JUNE – 3 JULY

One of the most innovative aspects of the festival is the Fotofeis Roadshow whose personnel and vehicles bring a travelling exhibition, social centre, related education events and talks to areas of Scotland where the four festival themes are located.

The Scottish Arts Council's Travelling Gallery exhibition provides an overview by including work from all four of the Fotofeis themes. The show is rich and diverse both in the working methodology of the artists and in their differing uses of the medium of photography.

Berlin artist, Joachim Schmid takes an analytical approach to the ubiquitous snapshot. Having spent years collecting photos from flea markets, the artist has classified and selected groups of images that not only analyze the conventions of amateur photography but celebrate them in wry groupings. In contrast, American artist Amy Jenkins uses computer-generated and real imagery to create photographs which defy classification as either electronic imaging or conventional still-life.

Africa Guzman's atmospheric and intriguing landscapes explore the industrial hinterland found at the edge of the city. Taken at twilight, they present an other-worldly vision of deserted territories most of us pass by without looking at twice. Luis González Palma's work centres on the indigenous Mayan people of Guatemala, originally marginalised by the Spanish Conquistadors. In borrowing the symbolism of their culture, more commonly seen on the popular lottery tickets, Palma's works are rich and powerful. Scottish photographer Colin Gray makes work which is deceptively whimsical. Yet these works cleverly present an intimate study of his parents.

Over the four weeks of the festival the focus of attention will shift week by week to a different area and theme. Integral to this is a centre of activity where artists from the locality and members of the public can meet with photographers from overseas. A programme of lectures, seminars and events punctuates each week.

Outreach work beyond the social centres in the outlying areas will bring artists and workshops to communities living too far away from the principal exhibitions, and will also provide valuable opportunities for artists to work with new groups.

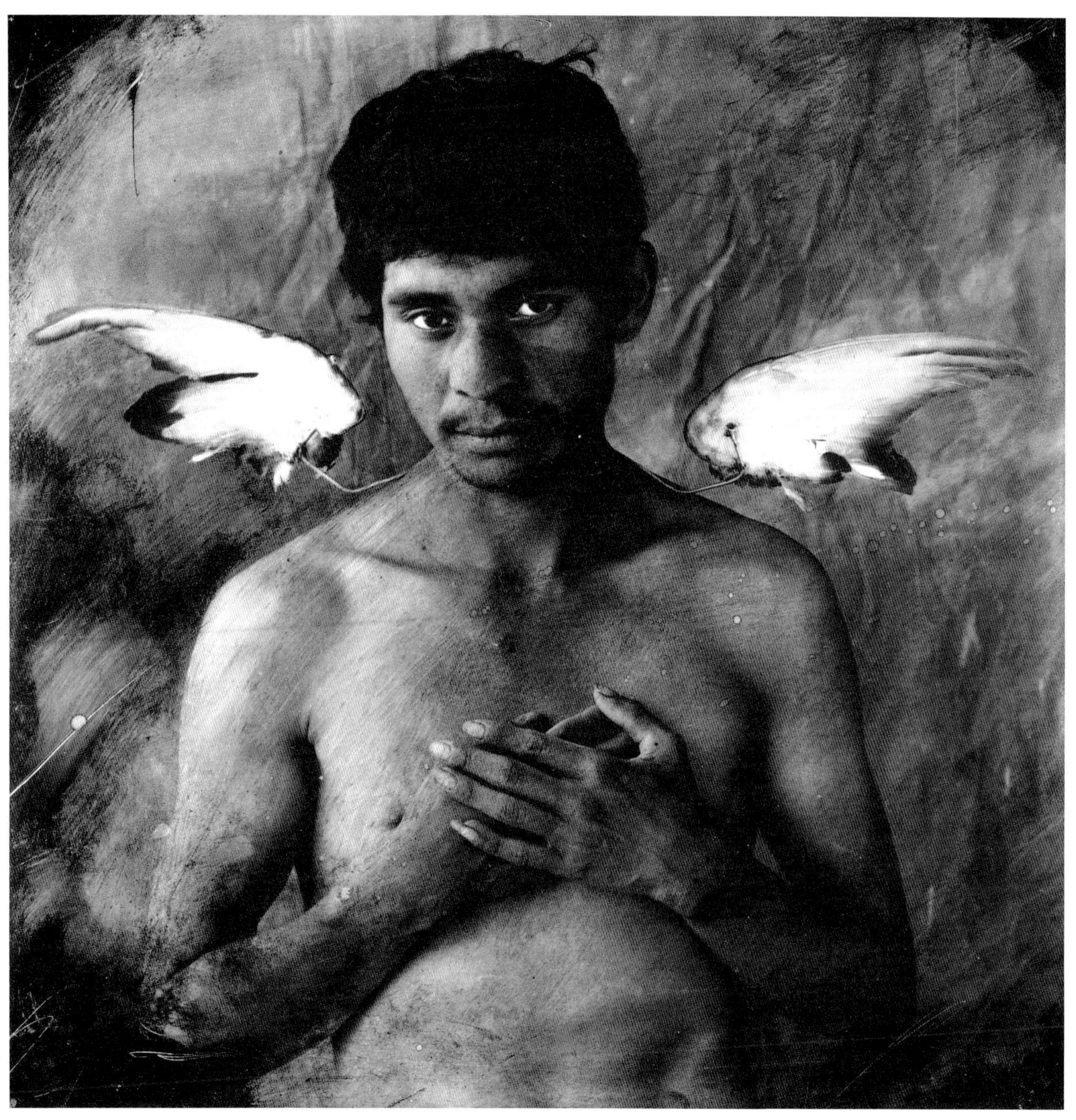

Luis González Palma Angel *mixed media (original in colour)*

Family

EDINBURGH AND THE
SOUTH EAST

LOOKING AT THE FAMILY

Shirley Read

The family is the central institution of modern British society, a major preoccupation of our times. Whether or not we live as part of a family unit, the idea of family is a daily reality which pervades and shapes our lives. Photography, in its many private and public uses, is bound closely into our ideas and experiences of family.

A fairly random sampling of my day finds the word family used three times on the front page of the newspaper and five of the twenty photographs inside related to family issues. My breakfast cereal packet provides the image of a smiling family meal. Walking to the bus stop I pass a building which houses the African Caribbean Single Parent Family Project and Nursery. At the library the computer catalogue under family is too large to be scanned through quickly but it starts with five novels by different authors, all called *Family Affairs*. A glance at the television programme schedule reveals *The Addams Family* and assorted family dramas. I know I have only to turn the radio on to hear politicians speak of 'family values'.

When we speak or write of 'family', we know that our use of the word will be understood immediately and we assume a single meaning for it. It does, however, have a multiplicity of different meanings; anthropologists, historians, politicians, church leaders, sociologists and journalists are all describing different concepts of blood ties, property arrangements, sexual, reproductive, socialising and other domestic functions and structures.

In the narrowest of anthropological usages 'family' means a woman and her dependent children. This is both because of the perceived primacy of the mother/child bond and because, in a number of cultures, the father is not present as part of the family unit. Family can also be used to describe a wider arrangement of consanguineous relationships and a range of joint land and property ownership agreements.

At its broadest, in humanist terms, 'family' describes the human 'community' in which birth, death and all individual experience between the two are seen as part of the universal and unifying family experience of humanity. One can also speak of the family of workers, the oppressed, or the family of God. Members of a church, trade union or political group who call each other 'Sister' or 'Brother' are referring to the sharing of experience and belief rather than to blood ties. In the Roman Catholic church a member of the priesthood is addressed as 'Father' and his parishioners seen as his children.

This multiplicity of meanings generally remains unquestioned because most people tend to assume that their experience of family life is the norm and that most families are similar to their own. Tolstoy's dictum that "all happy families resemble each other, each unhappy family is unhappy in its own way" (*Anna Karenina*) is only one example of the assumption that the family is the natural, inevitable and only way of organising society.

If, however, the family is seen as natural and inevitable then it is also likely to be regarded as fundamentally unchanging. The rapid changes which have affected the family in this century have therefore come to be seen as a threat to the institution rather than part of an acceptable, though shifting, pattern of family structures.

The myth of the family as an unchanging institution, essentially the same from the industrial revolution until this century, is in part based on a romantic historical notion and in part drawn from the observation of contemporary peasant cultures which are seen to provide universal truths about the family.

In this idealised version of history, the extended family, before industrialisation and urbanisation reduced both its size and its social role, was a sprawling, multi-generational and economically interdependent unit. Within the family, land was owned and worked, the sick and elderly were taken care of, the young were educated. In this more caring world, life was simpler and each individual member knew his or her place and function in the family unit. While urbanisation brought change, the key nurturing role of the family remained undiminished until two world wars changed society for ever, breaking up families by sending the men away to fight and the women out to work. The Welfare State was then seen to remove the final remnants of power from the family and hand them to the State. It only remained for divorce to be made easier and the Pill to become widely available for the family to be seen as under threat.

Some historians would argue that, overall, the institution of the family has changed remarkably little in the last seven centuries. What has changed this century is the diversity of its forms, not the popularity of the institution itself. The speed and extent of change in this century is what leads us to accept the view that the family is threatened.

In fact, statistics show that the family is now a more widespread, if changed, institution than at any previous time. More people marry, they marry younger, live longer and have smaller families which are completed earlier. In 1911, for example, only 55 per cent of women of marriageable age would marry compared to 73 per cent in 1951. The increase in divorce, brought about when the 1945 Legal Aid Act made divorce possible for couples who would have been unable to afford it before, is matched by an increase in the rate of re-marriage. Single parent families and unmarried couples with children in long term relationships are just two of the new and widespread family patterns.

The family is also perceived as more private and inward looking with a greater interest in the home and close relatives than before. However, the importance of maintaining strong ties with the wider family group is still seen as crucial in contemporary society.

From its very beginnings, photography has been involved in recording and creating images of the family. The first photographically illustrated book, Fox Talbot's *The Pencil of Nature* (1844–46), in itself partly a family history and documentation of the home, commented that once only the rich could own portraits of their nearest and dearest but that, with the invention of photography, it would soon be possible for anyone to purchase a portrait cheaply. Photographic portraiture and the arrival of the first portrait studios grew in the later part of the century and now every High Street has its window full of smiling faces, of romantic weddings and cute children.

This has meant that the marketing of photography has also been directed at the family. The development of simple and cheap camera technology has been central to the development of the photographic industry, with the result that most families now own a camera.

Photographs of the family, originally taken for the private domain, have now passed into the public sphere as we begin to look at shared memories and at the greater communities formed through workplace or geographical area.

One such collection has been made by the Island History Trust on the Isle of Dogs in East London. The Trust is an oral history archive with a collection of some 4000 family photographs gathered from the largely working class community living around the Docks from the 1880's to the present day. Crucially it sees itself functioning in both a public and private way to the local people, acting as a sort of giant family album for a community irrevocably changed by the closing of London's docks and the subsequent redevelopment of the area.

The collection reflects the way in which family photographs are taken to mark special occasions rather than to document daily life. Its categories include schools, sports, weddings, outings organised by churches, pubs and workplaces, coronation and street parties, hop-picking and holidays at Southend and Margate.

As is often pointed out, photographs show the appearance of things, not the underlying truths. What is missing from this and other similar collections is the ordinariness of family life, the dramas of domestic interaction which characterise any family. To fill out their meaning the Trust has collected a great deal of oral history information to accompany the photographs. But the photographs are still marked by absence. What for instance is one to make of this photograph, taken in the 1930's, of a large wedding party? They are packed into a backyard, a shower of rain has just made the yard slippery and bride, groom and bridesmaids sit on chairs placed on a small piece of carpet. The guests and family crowd around them, someone in a pinny holds a child still, someone else raises a glass to the camera, young men mock wrestle. The photograph is scratched and creased and, shockingly, the bride's mouth has been scratched out or covered over. What story remains untold here?

Although old photographs raise more questions about relationships and interactions within the family unit than they can answer, they frequently do tell us a great deal about the economic and social climate of their time. Compare, for instance, photographs of two middle aged married couples taken in the 1930's and in the late 1980's. In the earlier photograph, taken in a studio, the couple stand, self conscious and stiff, about two feet apart without touching. Both are small and slight and appear to be dressed in their best clothes, both wear hats. The second photograph was taken outside the local supermarket and the couple stand close together, arms round each others waists. They are plump, smiling, relaxed, dressed in velour track suits; they radiate intimacy, physical and financial self sufficiency and confidence.

The other pair are photographs of young women taken in 1916 and in the late 1980's. In the first, a young woman, stands at an angle to the camera holding the back of an ornately carved chair. She wears a check dress edged with velvet and neatly buttoned to the throat, a watch and a locket and her hair is carefully pinned back behind her ears. She gazes impassively out past us into the future. The picture was taken at her workplace. It was apparently common practice for factories to set up a club into which members paid a small amount weekly. A draw would then decide which member would have her photograph taken.

In the recent picture, again taken outside a supermarket, the young woman is in her early twenties. She leans forward directly claiming our gaze, smiling provocatively. Her jeans are tight, the top of her shirt is unbuttoned and her long hair loose. Once again we see that she is accustomed to being photographed and that she takes on the pose dictated to her by the social conventions of her day, influenced more by the families in Dallas or Dynasty than by traditions within her own family.

There are, of course, numerous ways in which photographs of the family are used. It's a photographic cliché now that the stereotypes of family provided for us by the advertising industry – white, middle class, two children, car and home owning, a loving family in which the father goes out to work and the mother nurtures – create an image of a perfection by which we are all bound.

But how do we use our own family photographs? For most of us photographs are a sort of reassurance about our place in the world. They stop or mark time for us; every Christmas I receive a card from the United States which shows only the two young sons of the family. Every year I am reminded of the passing of time since I last saw them by noting how much they have grown, by the changes in their hairstyles, their T-shirts, the appearance or disappearance of baseball bats and evidence of newer hobbies.

Our habit of keeping family photographs on display marks our passage through life, making it visible to others and ourselves and keeping memory alive. My uncle, killed in the Second World War, is real for me even though he died before I was born because his photograph – of a young man in his twenties in uniform – has always been present in the family home. A neighbour prominently displays his parents' wedding photograph, despite their later divorce, he says as "a memory of happier times".

In looking at why adults carry photographs of their families around with them, psychologist Robin Skynner, in his book with John Cleese, *Families and How to Survive Them*, makes the connection with the childhood stage of carrying soft toys. These, known in psychology as transitional objects, and exemplified for us by Linus's security blanket in the *Peanuts* cartoon, represent our need as adults to hold onto the internal confidence that we can handle the changes that life throws at us and keep moving on.

Society has the same need to hold on to such certainties to retain its self confidence. When the marriage of Prince Charles and Princess Diana broke up, *The Guardian* chose to use a famous Snowdon portrait of the couple, titling it 'Public faces, not so private anguish'. The carefully posed photograph makes direct reference to Gainsborough's painting, *Mr and Mrs Andrews*. In the painting the squire and his wife, with hunting dog and gun, are placed in the English landscape. She sits on an ornate bench in front of an oak tree on the edge of a cornfield; he stands behind her, casually resting an arm on the back of the bench. In the Snowdon photograph the Prince and Princess, accompanied by their children, a pony and a picnic, are also posed in a rural setting in front of an oak tree. She sits on an ornate bench and he stands behind, one hand casually resting on her shoulder, the other on the shoulder of one of the young Princes who holds the bridle of the pony. The table which holds the picnic is a reference to the entire history of still life painting.

The message of the photograph is clear, it speaks of the unchanging nature of English family life, of a monarchy with its roots deeply embedded in tradition exemplified by the rural setting and the English oak.

It is nearly forty years since the photographer Edward Steichen organised what is still probably the best known, and was the most widely toured, exhibition of all time. *The Family of Man* drew on photographs from all over the world and was put together for the Museum of Modern Art, New York, in 1955, as a giant family album for the human race. Whilst showing the diversity and contrast of peoples' lives, its central theme was the universality of human experience. Although it was criticised for its sentimentality and naïve idealism, we can view it now as a response to the trauma of a world divided by war.

In the 1990's, approaching the millennium, what will these more recent examinations of family, brought together for Fotofeis, show us? Hopefully they will open up a space for questioning the idea of the family in modern Britain. And, by looking at the new realities of family in a changed and changing world, they will free us from the static idealisms which control our dreams of the everyday.

Shirley Read is a lecturer, writer and researcher on photography. She was a founder member of Camerawork and former Curator of Photography at The Island History Trust, Isle of Dogs, London.

INTIMATE LIVES:
Photographers and their Families

City Art Centre

2 MARKET STREET
EDINBURGH

PREMIERE

5 JUNE – 24 JULY

KORS VAN BENNEKOM *Netherlands*

NAN GOLDIN USA

COLIN GRAY UK

JACQUES-HENRI LARTIGUE *France*

SALLY MANN USA

JULIE MILLOWICK *Australia*

MAUD SULTER UK

ANNE TESTUT *France*

The eight photographers in this exhibition have used their own families, closest friends, lovers and confidants as the basis for an exploration of the institution of the family from within. These images of domestic beauty and pain, comfort, security and conflict, cause us to consider afresh that most intimate of human relationships – the family.

Jacques-Henri Lartigue first began taking photographs in 1902, aged 7. His earliest images were of his close relatives, and these pictures of a French bourgeois family at the turn of the century have come to epitomise an age long past. In the same field, Kors van Bennekom is well-known in his native Netherlands for his relaxed, life-affirming photographs which document with great tenderness the natural cycles of birth, growth and maturity.

Sally Mann has gained an international reputation for her sensuous photographs of her children, which examine with honesty the contradictions and dualities of childhood innocence and self-awareness. Using the camera as a searchlight, Nan Goldin's *Ballad of Sexual Dependency* chronicles her extended family of friends and lovers over more than a decade in a deeply personal, intense and uncompromising way.

In Julie Millowick's recent *Familiar Stories*, she combines image and text to produce photo narratives which dramatically reconstruct the darker side of family life.

Colin Gray's photographic series, *The Parents*, explores his relationship with his mother and father and their relationship with one another. Amusing and poignant, these theatrical reconstructions, often based on childhood memories, examine the physical and mental changes in his parents over the past thirteen years.

Much of Maud Sulter's work is concerned with questions of sexual and racial identity. Here we preview new work which centres upon her immediate family.

Anne Testut's formal compositions have a surreal and mysterious quality about them. Posed, like waxworks, her photographs employ symbolism and allegory to deliberate upon the changing fortunes of her well-to-do family.

Subsidised by the
Scottish Arts Council

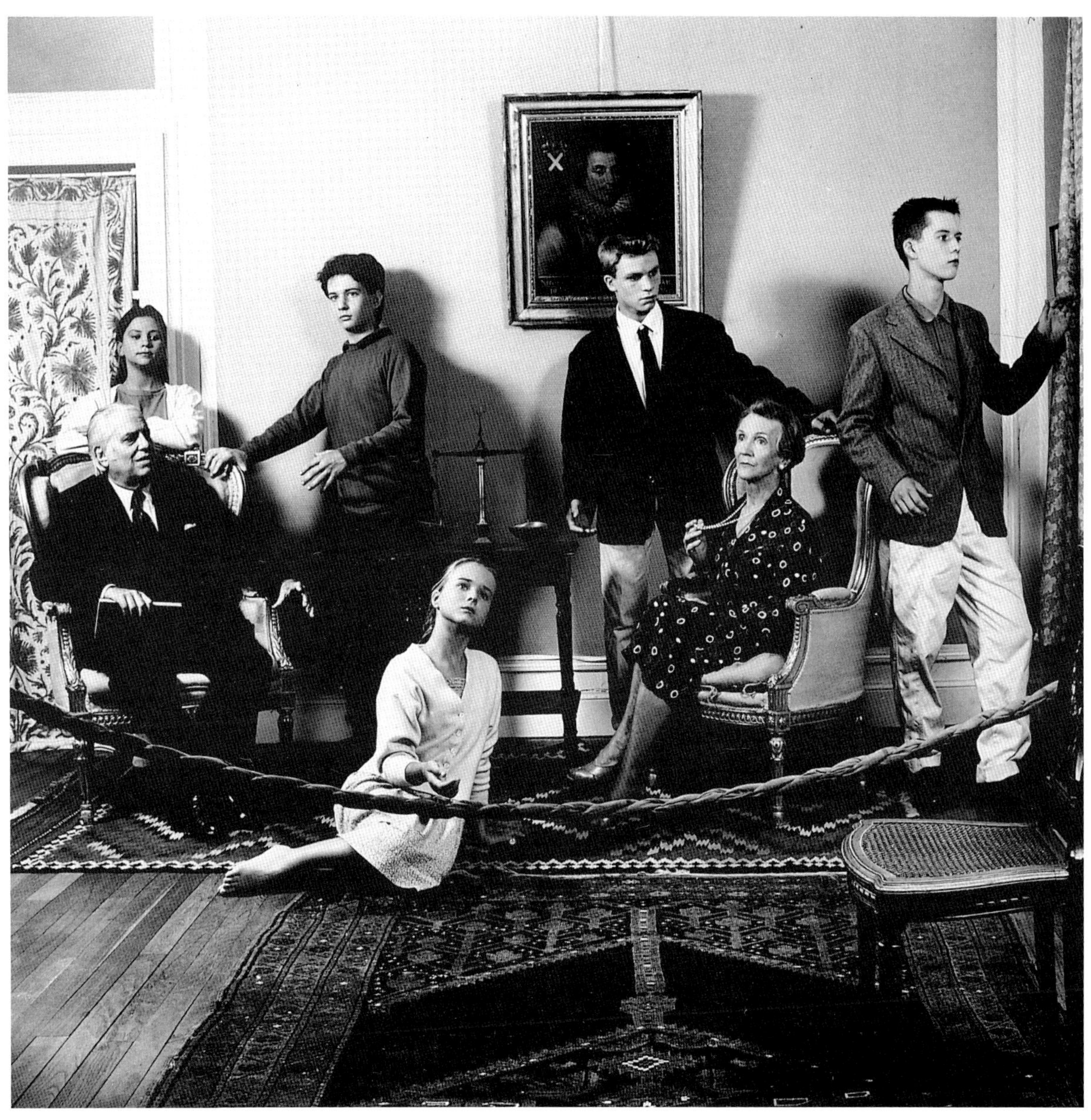

Anne Testut Le Musée Grevin *silver-gelatin print*

OWEN LOGAN UK
Bloodlines – Vite allo specchio

Crawford Arts Centre

93 NORTH STREET
ST. ANDREWS

PREMIERE

11 JUNE – 11 JULY

Exhibition organised by the Photographers' Gallery, London and the Istituto Italiano di Cultura, Edinburgh

Owen Logan was born to a Scottish father and an Italian mother. His work reflects this background and is the result of a three year project about Italian migration.

Alasdair Foster writes, "Logan does not simply take elegantly crafted, eloquently constructed images, he also understands how to link one image to the next to create, in this case, two convergent resonant and highly articulate sequences..."

These two sequences each chart a lifespan amongst culturally related but geographically divided communities in Italy and Britain. In the photographer's own words, "My interest was in emigration, my ideas were focused upon the cultural difficulties of emigré communities. I hoped to produce a body of work which examined the ambiguous face of emigré culture through a kind of photographic mirror. I use the word 'mirror' carefully and it may need explanation. The mirror is one that is constructed through a series of photographs which are divided into two halves. The division denotes a change of location between a homeland and a new country. The two sides can, with varying degrees of clarity, reflect one another."

Today we see Europe's external borders being fortified. Ideas about Europe, its lands and people have often been voiced by representatives of the state using connotations of soil and blood. These are two elements which bring together notions of both personal and national identity. Yet, personal ties and values based on kinship have been and continue to be problematic for industrial society.

In order to appreciate the position of new migrant groups in Europe, we would do well to question the foundation of our collective European identity. In order to understand the nature of present conflicts arising from Europe's new borders, Logan has looked at Italian migration in a way that encompasses its difficult history, aware that the future is rooted in the past.

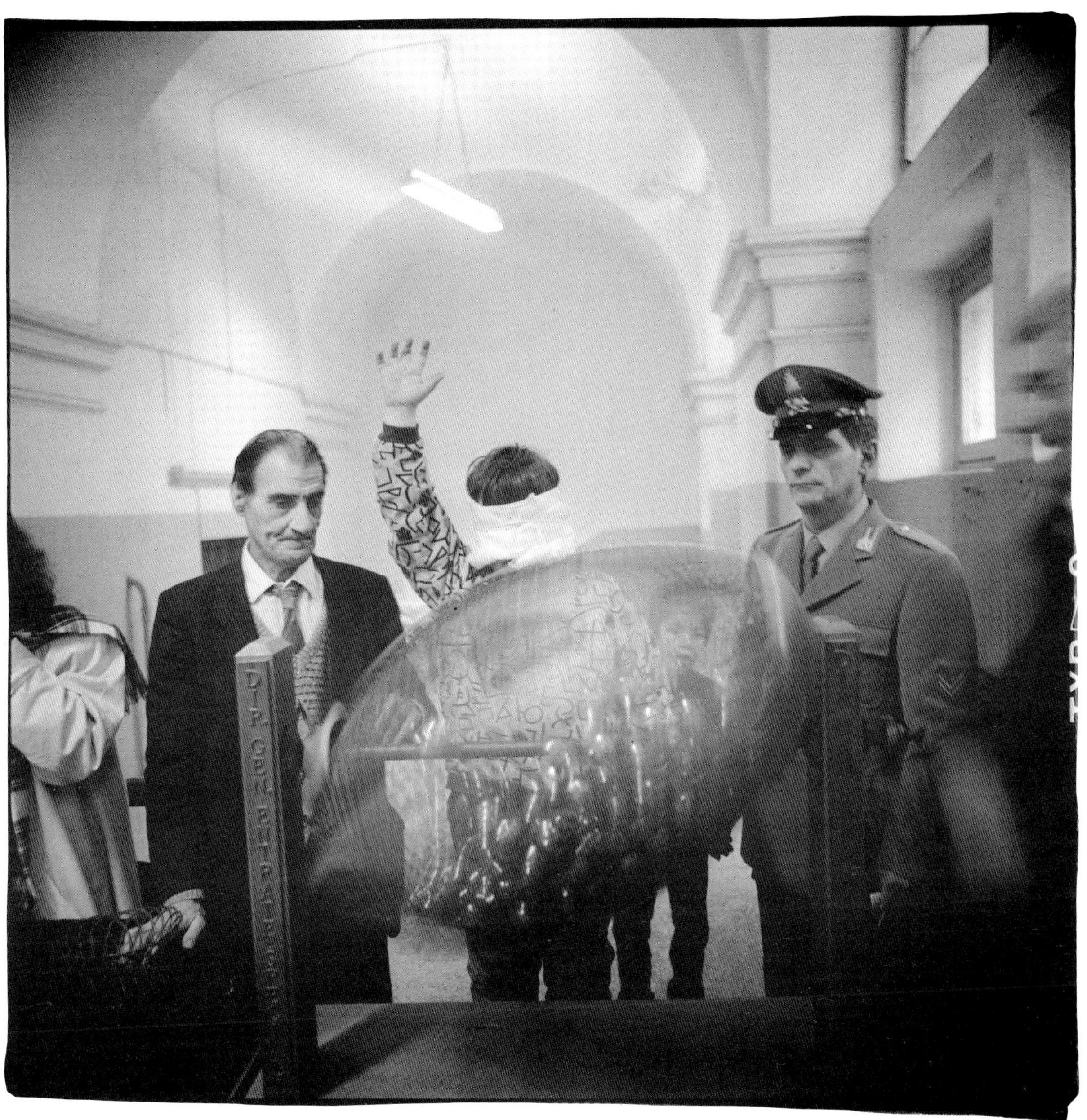

Owen Logan The Draw *silver-gelatin print*

RALPH EUGENE MEATYARD USA
Retrospective

Portfolio Gallery

43 CANDLEMAKER ROW
EDINBURGH

UK PREMIERE

5 JUNE – 3 JULY

This exhibition marks the current re-appraisal of the work of the American photographer Ralph Eugene Meatyard (1925-72), which had only marginal status in photographic histories written during his lifetime. Meatyard drew not only upon the work of historical and contemporary photographers, but upon sources and ideas from poetry, literature, art theory, the philosophy of Zen, and his technical training as an optician. His fabricated photographs involved strategies now seen in the fictional dramas of a number of contemporary artists, including Cindy Sherman, Richard Prince and Jeff Wall.

The exhibition features Meatyard's most enigmatic series, *The Family Album of Lucybelle Crater*, his figurative works, and some of his early experimental series which oscillate between abstraction and reality in an exploration of perception as experienced by the camera rather than the human eye.

Using the devices of ambiguity and paradox, Meatyard created a series of 'romances', stories where derelict buildings, dime store masks and everyday objects are transformed into disturbing surrealist dramas. He understood the ritualised nature of relationships and believed that masks transform, disguise and conceal.

However, it is the meaning of his final series, *The Family Album of Lucybelle Crater*, which has divided critics. According to Barbara Tannenbaum, curator of Ohio's Akron Art Museum's retrospective *Ralph Eugene Meatyard – An American Visionary*, the Lucybelle Crater series is Meatyard's summary of his life. "He chose not to show the places he had been or the things he had done, this man whose life was most real in the realm of the imagination. Instead he presented his kin, whether related by blood, marriage, or friendship ... The *Lucybelle* series, like all of Meatyard's work, has several faces, several layers of meaning. It is personal and universal, erudite and folksy, tragic and witty. Behind Meatyard's work lay a profound spirit, one that delighted in the often contradictory nature of his art and his very existence."

Portfolio Gallery is grateful to Christopher Meatyard for providing prints for the exhibition and acknowledges the invaluable assistance of the Howard Greenberg Gallery, New York, in presenting this exhibition.

Exhibition sponsored by Jackson-Wilson

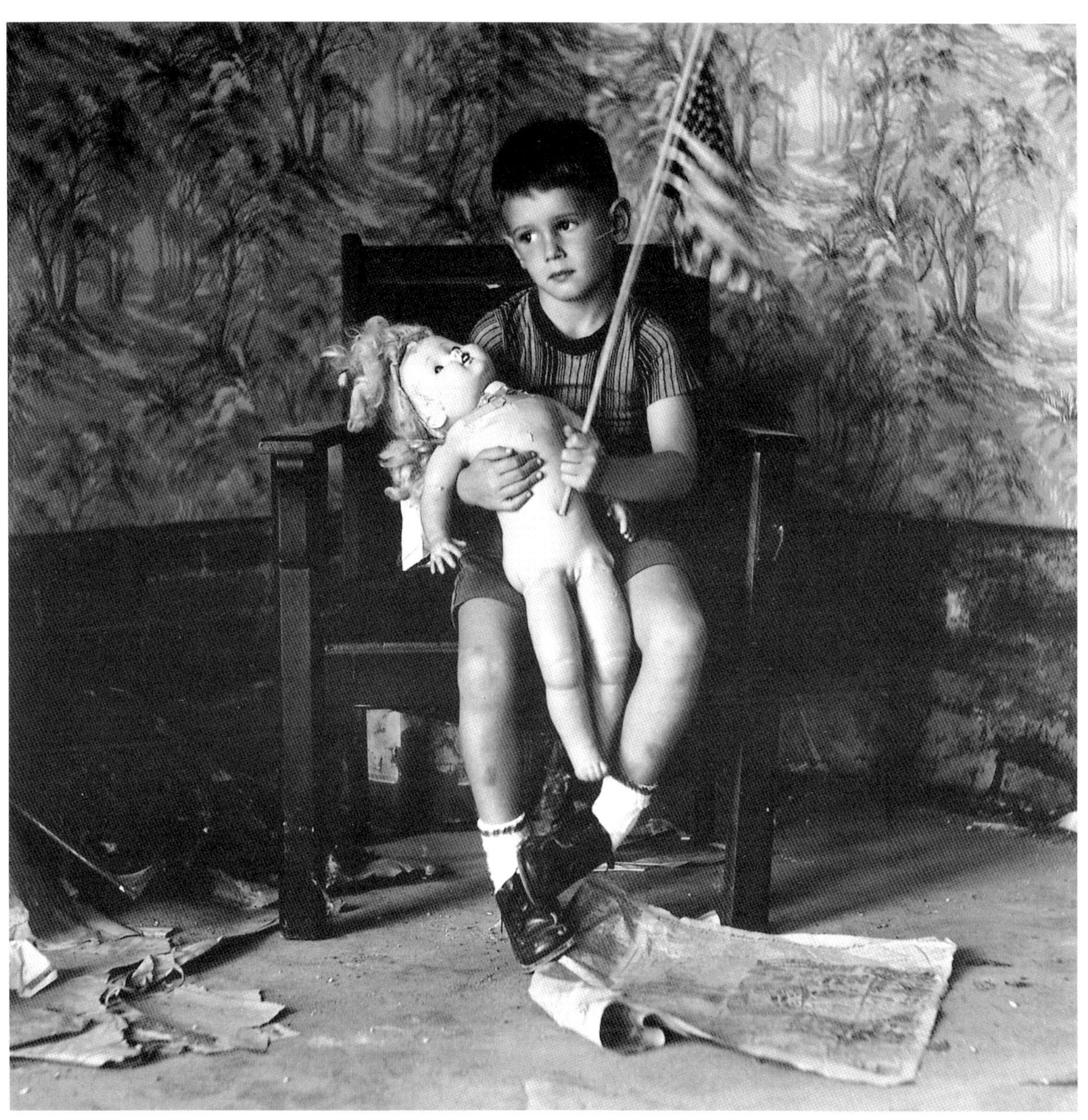

Ralph Eugene Meatyard Untitled (Boy holding flag and doll) 1959 *silver-gelatin print*

WYNN and EDNA BULLOCK USA
Faces and Figures

Talbot Rice Gallery

UNIVERSITY OF EDINBURGH
OLD COLLEGE
SOUTH BRIDGE, EDINBURGH

EUROPEAN PREMIERE

5 JUNE – 4 JULY

"Wynn Bullock was one of the most widely respected photo-artists of our time. And yet, in many ways, he was one of the least understood. Wynn became well known for his evocative and striking photographs of trees, nudes in nature, and moving water but, in order to appreciate the scope of his creative life and work, it is important to know that in addition to being a gifted image maker, Wynn was also a deeply inspired and intellectually curious man." Thus Chris Johnson begins his appraisal of Wynn Bullock's life and work in *Contemporary Photographers.*

Wynn Bullock was a man of many talents. He started his professional career in the 1920's as a concert singer, spent several years managing family real estate, and then, in the late 1930's, longing to be more creative, he turned his hobby of photography into a way of life. His photographic career spanned more than three decades from 1941. His work has been featured in over a hundred one-man shows and his prints in the permanent collections of more than eighty museums and galleries around the world.

Though Edna Bullock spent thirty years of married life in a household imbued with the practice and philosophy of photography, she did not take up the camera until six months after Wynn's death in 1975. In her sixties, she returned to school to learn the technical skills of the medium. In her seventies, she is building a reputation for her black and white photographs of nudes in natural surroundings.

Wynn Bullock and his work have been the subject of two documentary films and six books. This year, in acknowledgement of his life and photography, the Aperture Foundation in New York is launching a multi-faceted project which will include a special monograph, a limited edition portfolio, and a major retrospective exhibition. In 1994 Capra Press in Santa Barbara will be publishing a book of Edna Bullock's nudes, with a text by her daughter, Barbara. The exhibition at the Talbot Rice Gallery, specially arranged for Fotofeis in collaboration with the Bullock estate, is an opportunity to preview and contrast their work.

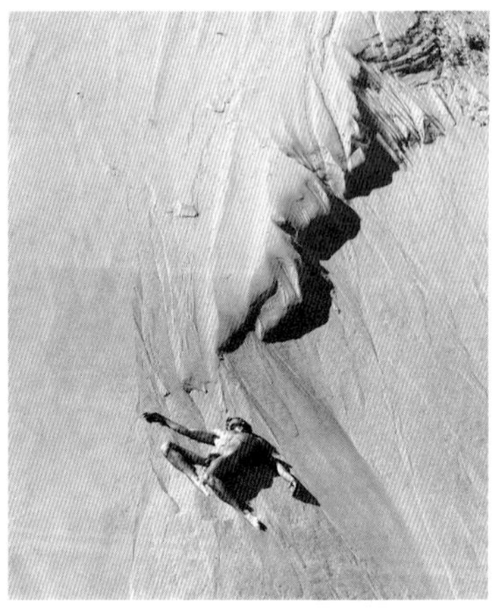

Edna Bullock David at The Point *(detail)*
silver-gelatin print

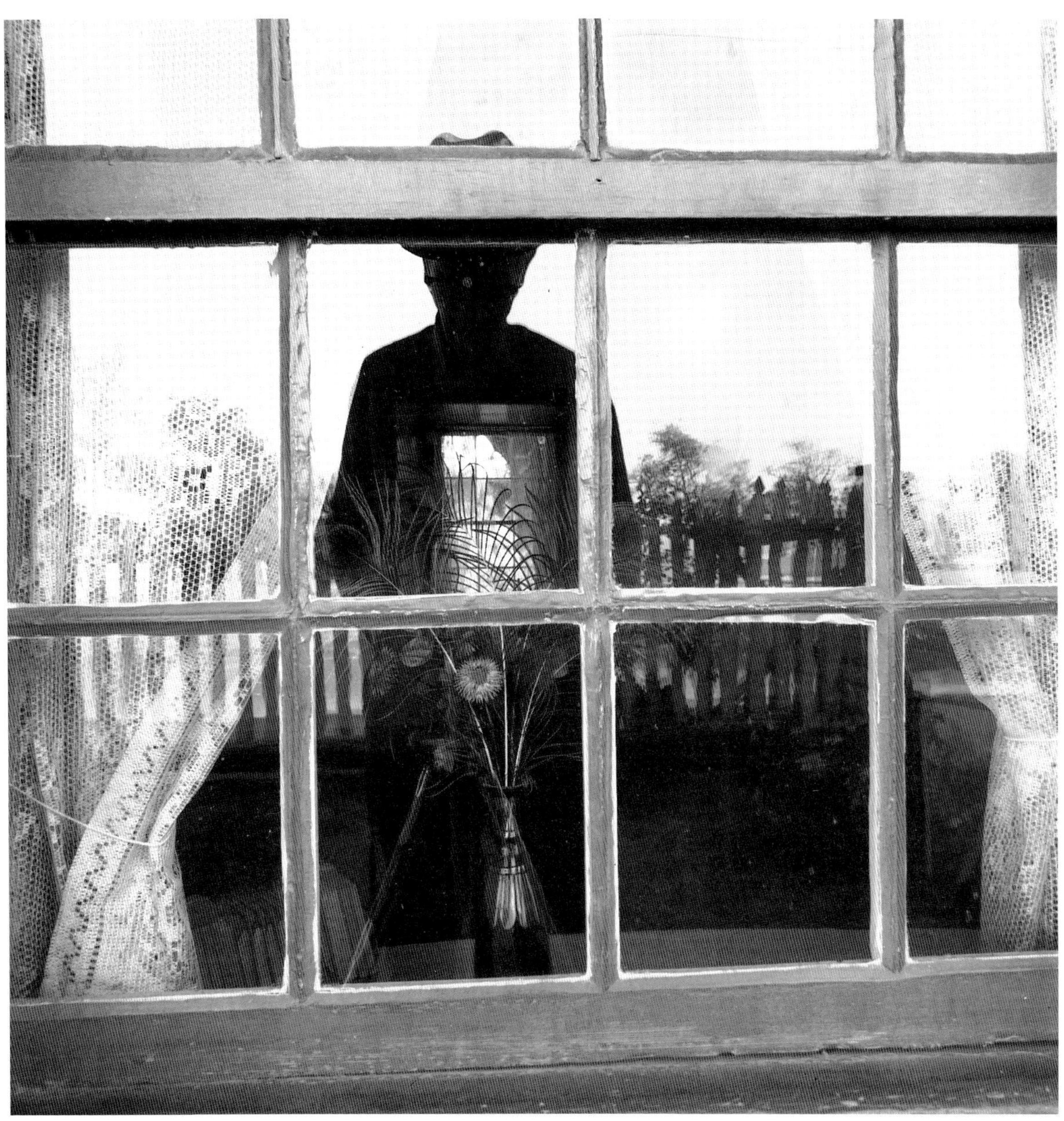

Wynn Bullock Self-portrait, 1971 *silver-gelatin print*

JOACHIM SCHMID *Germany*

Taking Snapshots: Amateur Photography in Germany from 1900 to the Present

The Queen's Hall

CLERK STREET, EDINBURGH

PREMIERE

6 JUNE – 3 JULY

This exhibition deals with the artistically unassuming, everyday 'snapshot photography' which developed during the last quarter of the 19th century and was quickly taken up by large numbers of people. Its photohistoric appreciation is in reverse proportion to the quantity of pictures produced. This multitude of photographs, which is only partially visible, can be used as a kind of raw material for the historiography of everyday life. At the same time, it has its own aesthetic which results from the naïve act of 'snapping'. The carefully chosen examples presented in this exhibition show the visual richness as well as the sociological potential of the family snapshot.

The individual photographs were selected according to main subjects and aesthetic characteristics and then arranged in groups. Together, they present a kind of classification of snapshot photography. These analytical arrangements are complemented by groupings of individual examples which cannot be classified – relics of some kind of 'snapping orgy' – and complete pages from photo albums.

The exhibition (comprising about 140 framed groups, each measuring 40 cm x 50 cm) has been conceived as an open, modular system: the frames can be combined in different ways, and each combination allows a different reading of the pictorial mosaic.

Joachim Schmid lives and works in Berlin. His earlier projects include his (in)famous portfolio *Masterpieces of Photography, The Fricke and Schmid Collection* which presented, with disturbing persuasiveness, anonymous snapshots found in the flea markets of Europe, masquerading as the lost images of some of the great names of photography.

Taking Snapshots was organised by the *Institut für Auslandsbeziehungen, Berlin* and it is the first time they have premiered an exhibition outside Germany.

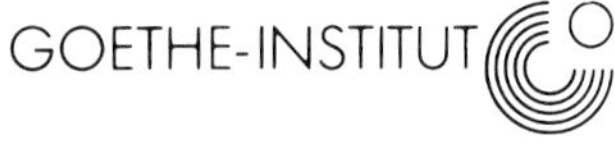

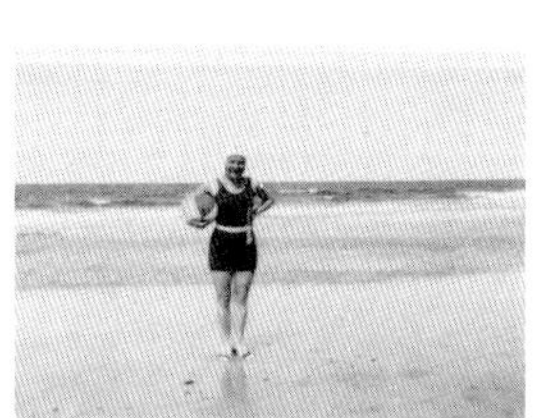
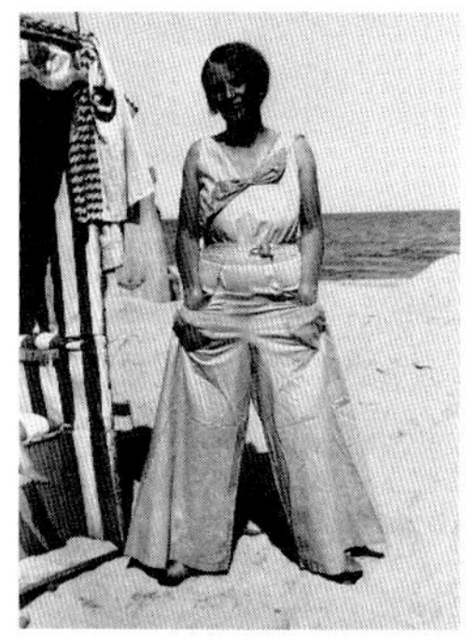
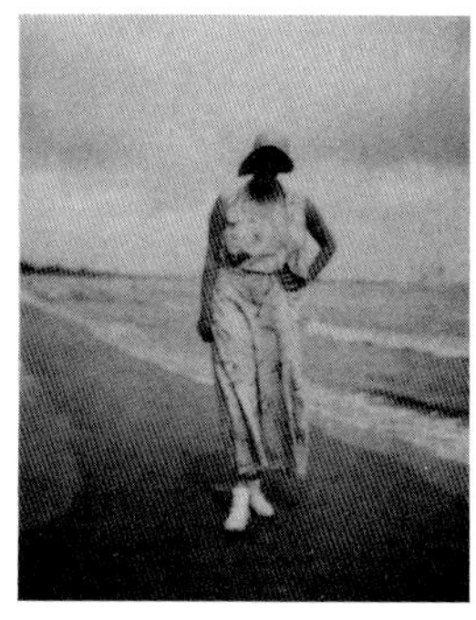
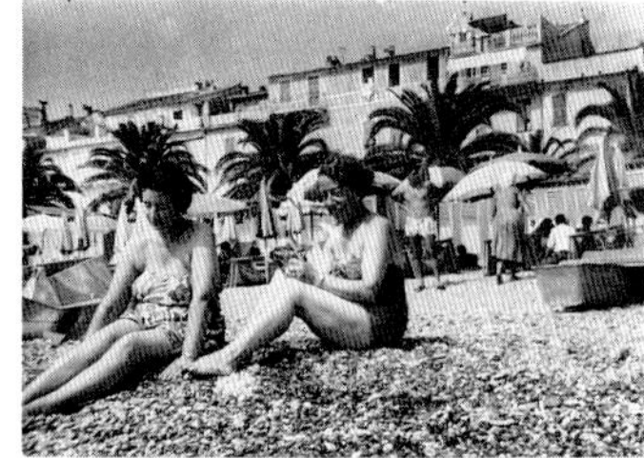
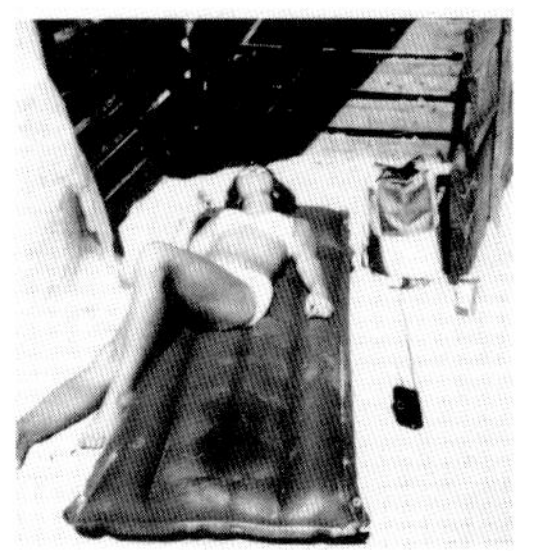
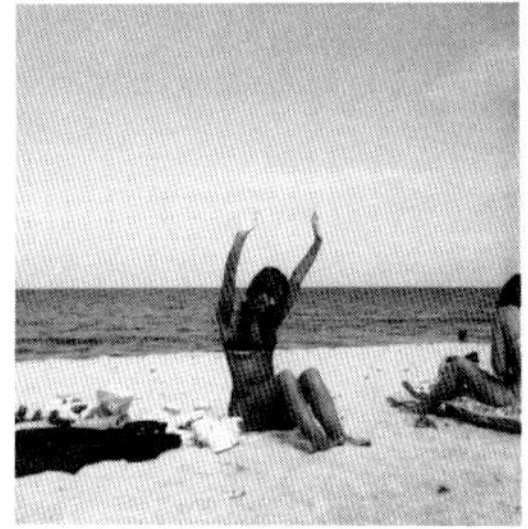
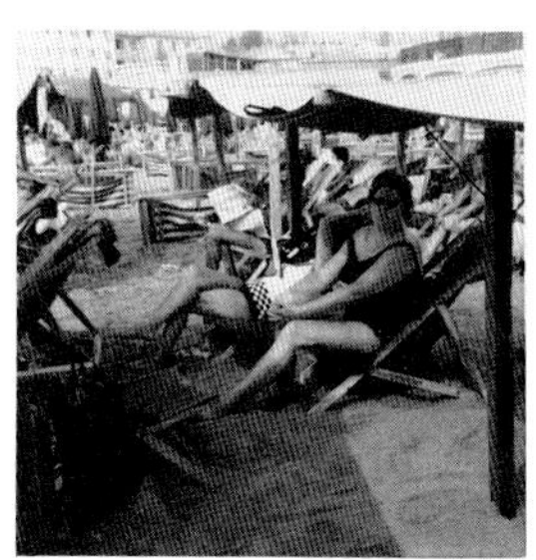
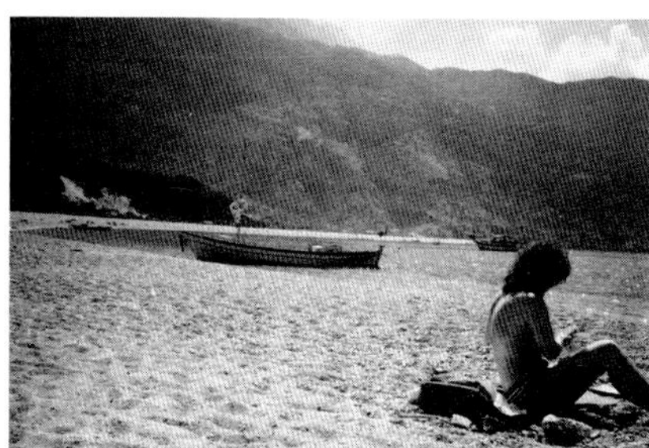

Joachim Schmid Frauen am Strand 20er bis 80er Jahre *(Women on the beach from 1920s to 1980s) assemblage of found photographs*

TON HUIJBERS *Netherlands*

Intimate Statues

KJP Gallery

NAPIER UNIVERSITY
61 MARCHMONT ROAD
EDINBURGH

4 JUNE – 26 JUNE

There is something deceptively simple about the work of Ton Huijbers. Small, exquisitely printed silver prints arranged in modest suites, show himself and his family 'at play'. But there is a seriousness to these games, they are performed with the concentration a child might bring and, from this investment, take on a mystery of their own.

The pyramid of naked bodies – father at the bottom, then mother, then children, the smallest at the top – speaks not only of that happy intimacy which finds in mutual nudity neither embarrassment nor innuendo, but simply trust. Nor is it merely a parable on paternal responsibility, the weight of family life falling heavily on the photographer as though he were some prostrate Atlas. There is something enigmatic about these images which makes us look again, and again.

Willem K. Coumans has described Ton Huijbers' photography as "not only an irreplaceable document of his family, but also a fascinating self-portrait of a photographer ... [His] most important drive is to photograph the strangeness of human existence which can be experienced as a mystery, or as a dream that one cannot escape, that demands to be visualised in such a way that more will be evoked than just that which is perceivable."

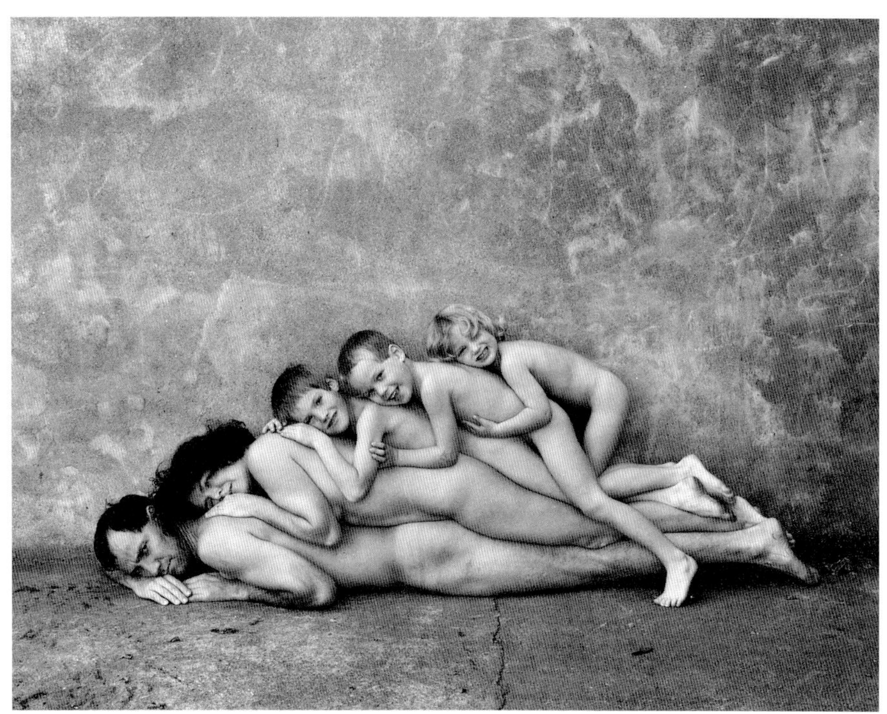

Ton Huijbers The Family *silver-gelatin print*

PUBLIC AND PRIVATE:
Secrets must Circulate

Institut Français d'Ecosse

13 RANDOLPH CRESCENT
EDINBURGH

Stills Gallery

105 HIGH STREET
EDINBURGH

Talbot Rice Gallery

UNIVERSITY OF EDINBURGH
OLD COLLEGE
SOUTH BRIDGE, EDINBURGH

Tron Kirk

HIGH STREET, EDINBURGH

Bellevue Church

EAST LONDON STREET
EDINBURGH

PREMIERE
4 JUNE – 18 JULY

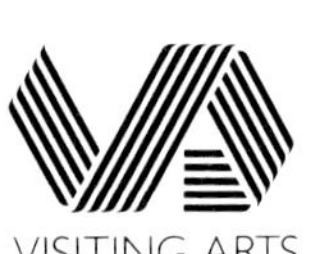

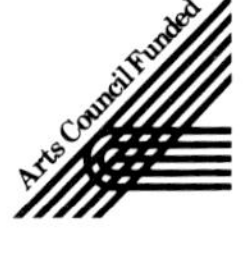

Subsidised by the
Scottish Arts Council

Organised by Stills and the Institut Français d'Ecosse, and curated by Alain Reinaudo (France), this major new exhibition is staged in gallery and non-gallery spaces across the city of Edinburgh. It features artists from France, Britain and the Netherlands whose work spans a diverse range of photo-based practices from straight photography to photo-installation, among them Helen Chadwick, Dany Leriche, Jochen Gerz, Jan Hendrickse, Sharon Kivland, Pierre Molinier, Pierre et Gilles, Bernard Plossu, Patrick Raynaud, Lydia Schouten and Stephen Willats. Many of these acclaimed artists are showing in the UK for the first time. Specially commissioned new works have also been created by Matthew Dalziel, Louise Scullion and Jane Mulfinger.

The theme of the exhibition is the fundamental dichotomy between what is 'public' and what is 'private'. This is a question particularly relevant to the medium of photography, which almost always presumes a subject (the photographer and viewer) and an object (what is photographed or looked at). The exhibition begins by exploring that most intimate, yet universal grouping of individuals, the family, and the role of the media; comparing public cynicisms with the experience of private individuals. It encompasses the theme of voyeurism, where the photographer (and therefore the viewer) penetrates an individual's private space, with that of exhibitionism, where the relationship between viewer and viewed is reversed and the object of the photograph takes control.

Public and Private does not intend to be a comprehensive inventory of artists whose work happens to be relevant to the exhibition theme, nor is it a didactic essay on the politics of representation. Rather, it has been conceived to provide "a space open to the subjective interpretation of the viewer, giving almost free rein to the enigma" (Alain Reinaudo). It highlights the fundamental paradox surrounding meaning and interpretation inherent in all art but particularly relevant to photography; a medium which has the superficial appearance of truth but an infinite capacity for deception.

This exhibition is supported by the Association Français d'Action Artistique.

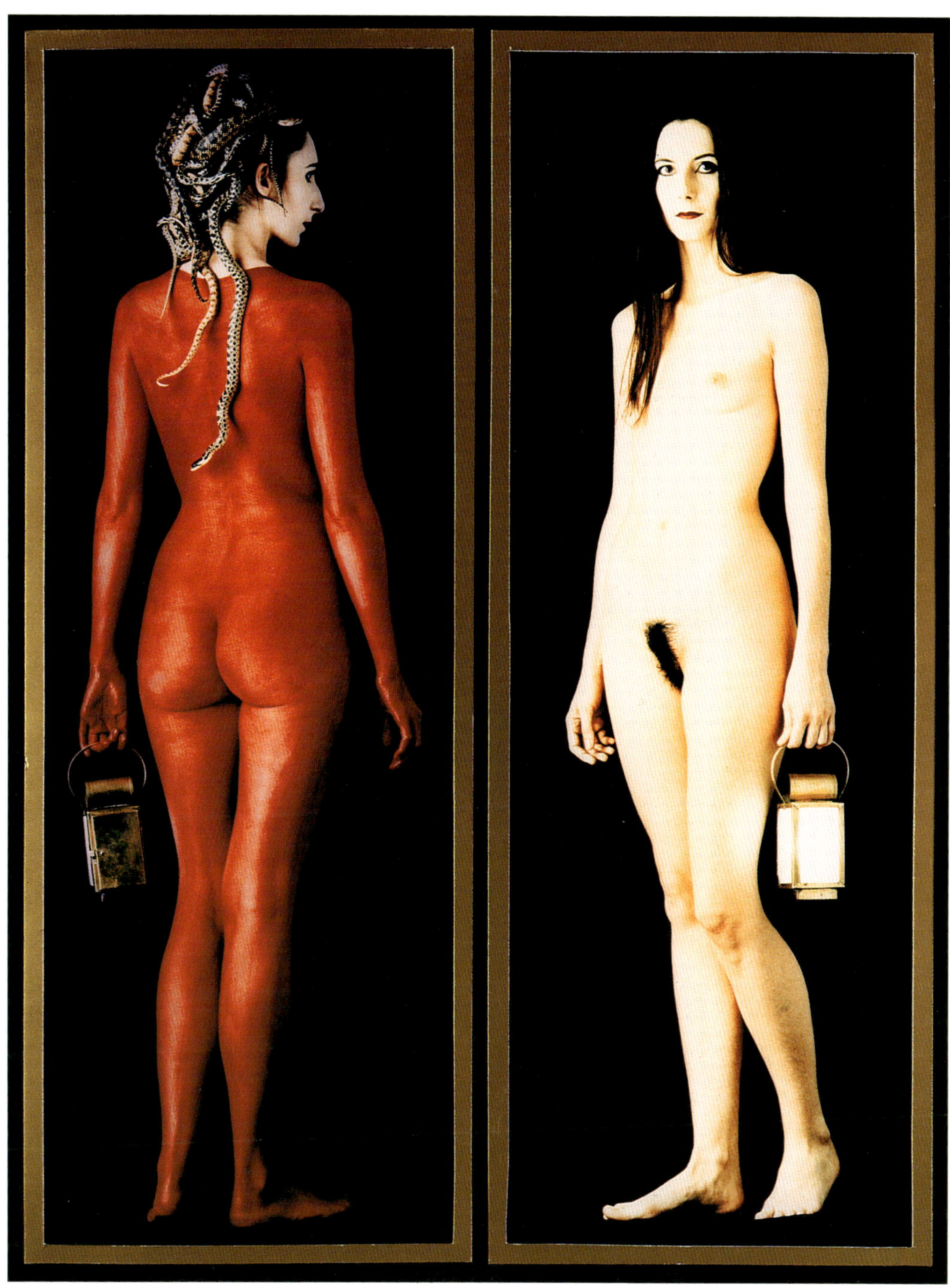

Dany Leriche Portraits sous influence 'Elizabeth' *colour diptych*

FLESH & BLOOD
Photographers' Images of Their Own Families

Kirkcaldy Museum and Art Gallery

WAR MEMORIAL GARDENS
KIRKCALDY

EUROPEAN PREMIERE

5 JUNE – 4 JULY

Curated by Alice Rose George, Abigail Heyman and Ethan Hoffman.

Exhibition presented in association with The Picture Project, New York

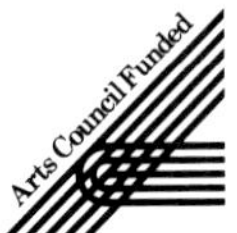

Subsidised by the
Scottish Arts Council

Sixty-six leading international photographers, including Elliott Erwitt, David Hockney, Sally Mann, Duane Michals, Sylvia Plachy and William Wegman reveal some of their most personal works – pictures of their families. In a kaleidoscope of images *Flesh and Blood* explores and celebrates the family. Picture by picture, it challenges our conception of what a family is, provoking vivid emotions of joy, humour, curiosity and grief. Ultimately, we feel we know these people and, as one moment in a life is frozen forever, we can, through our imagination, speculate on the rest of the story.

These photographs include privileged moments – a Paris honeymoon morning or the discovery of the death of the photographer's father – as well as the more everyday activities of eating, bathing, watching TV or simply day-dreaming. The exhibition movingly conveys the many facets of family life, from the relaxed security that can only be seen within families to the tensions that can spring up in their relationships.

From New York to Cairo, from Kentucky to Prague, we glimpse a diverse range of lifestyles. The privileged elegance of Tina Barney's feminine enclaves, all rose chintz, pink walls and mirrors, housemaids and wide lawns contrast with the bitter, scrappy environment of Marc Asnin's Uncle Charlie who supported five children alone on Social Security. His lined face in the photograph evokes the price paid: "... what I could have been ... no one knows: there was a distinct maybe".

Here, the link between the generations is revealed through the expression, pose or gesture of children, their parents and their grandparents. Whether highly stylised or casual, these photographs hold the kernel of a glorious and terrible truth.

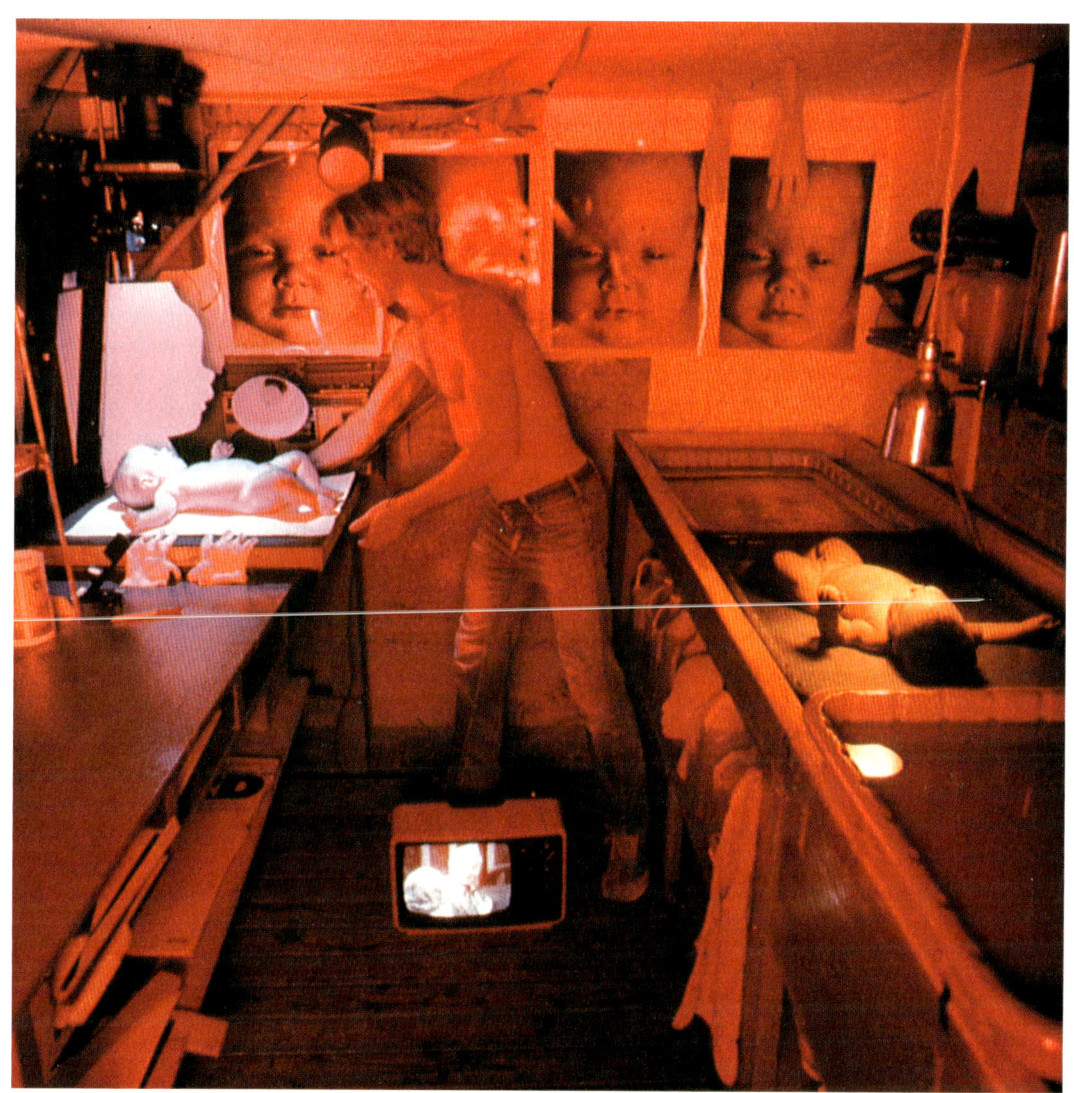

© *Vance Gellert* Untitled *from the series* 'Carl Vision' *colour print*

JOACHIM SCHMID, COLIN GRAY, ALEXANDER HAMILTON, SCOTT RUDDOCK, CHRIS MORRIS and SUSANNA PIERATZKI

Fife Art Bus

TOURING THROUGHOUT FIFE

PREMIERE

7 JUNE – 2 JULY

Fife Art Bus appears courtesy of

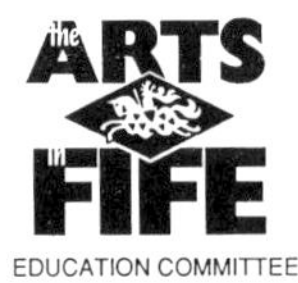

This survey brings together the work of six artists who are exhibiting in the south east of Scotland during Fotofeis. Each approaches the theme of *Family* from a very different perspective, and together they convey not only the great variety of photographic talent on display during the festival, but the diversity of meaning that the word 'family' can encompass.

The Berliner, Joachim Schmid, has spent many years collecting old family snaps in the flea markets of Europe. He has found in their infinite variety patterns which illustrate how, despite our individual differences, we tend to focus on certain occasions and ways of presenting ourselves when we pick up a camera. Schmid has carefully selected his images and mounts them in groups which illustrate these patterns of behaviour.

Also from Germany, Susanna Pieratzki has created a series of simply staged yet poignant images in which her parents play out their own life histories – from wartime camp to retirement. Scottish photographer Colin Gray also stages scenes in which his parents are the protagonists, but his lush colour images are altogether more whimsical, though no less poignant, in their acknowledgement of the imperturbable process of aging.

Scott Ruddock addresses himself to the rather different question of children who, through force of circumstance, are required to mature early and take on the mantle of adult responsibility. These photographs are taken from a photographic essay documenting the life of 12 year old Marie from Cardiff, who, like more than ten thousand other children in the UK, finds herself responsible for caring for her younger brothers and sisters.

Finally Alexander Hamilton and Chris Morris remind us that the family is not the sole preserve of us humans. In a series of exquisite cyanotypes which record the delicate structure of each pressed flower, Alexander Hamilton traces the genealogical roots of the Peace Rose, while Chris Morris presents a touching and amusing portrait of life among a family of monkeys.

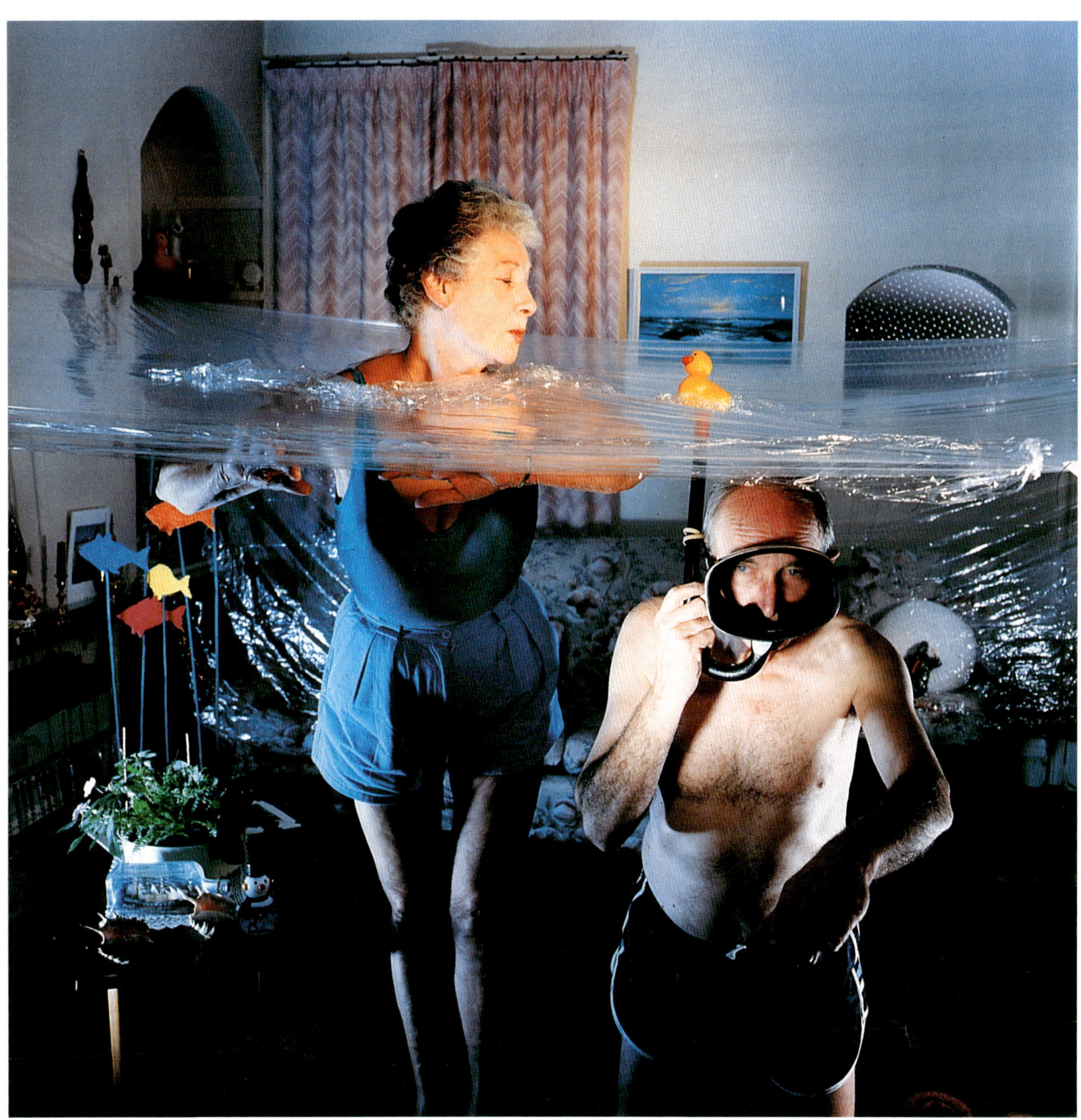

Colin Gray The Parents *colour print*

SANDRA SEMCHUK in collaboration with Martin Semchuk *Canada*

Coming to Death's Door

Kirkcaldy Museum and Art Gallery

WAR MEMORIAL GARDENS
KIRKCALDY

EUROPEAN PREMIERE

5 JUNE – 4 JULY

Supported by
The Canada Council

My father suffered a serious heart attack in July, 1988. In *Coming to Death's Door*, he and I look together at the event which led to my helping him escape from the hospital. In the photographic images I trace my own responses to my father and to his mortality. This investigation occurs within the simple experiences of moving from the tent where I slept separate from my father's home, overlooking a lake in northern Saskatchewan, and of situating myself in his bedroom. I use the camera gesturally as a way of sustaining the experience from the inside, and of leaving a trace as an outside observer. The fragmented image, like the broken self, hastens the processes of reconstruction and synthesis.

Many of the lines of text are excerpts from a dialogue with my father. He also helped me edit the images.

I am grateful to my father for sharing with me his experience of coming to death's door. Although one can never truly be prepared for the death of a parent, this visual and verbal dialogue has engendered in each of us an awareness of the links between life and death. We, in turn, hope that by sharing these experiences with you, you will not feel so isolated in your own attempts to come to terms with the paradox of death-in-life.
Sandra Semchuk

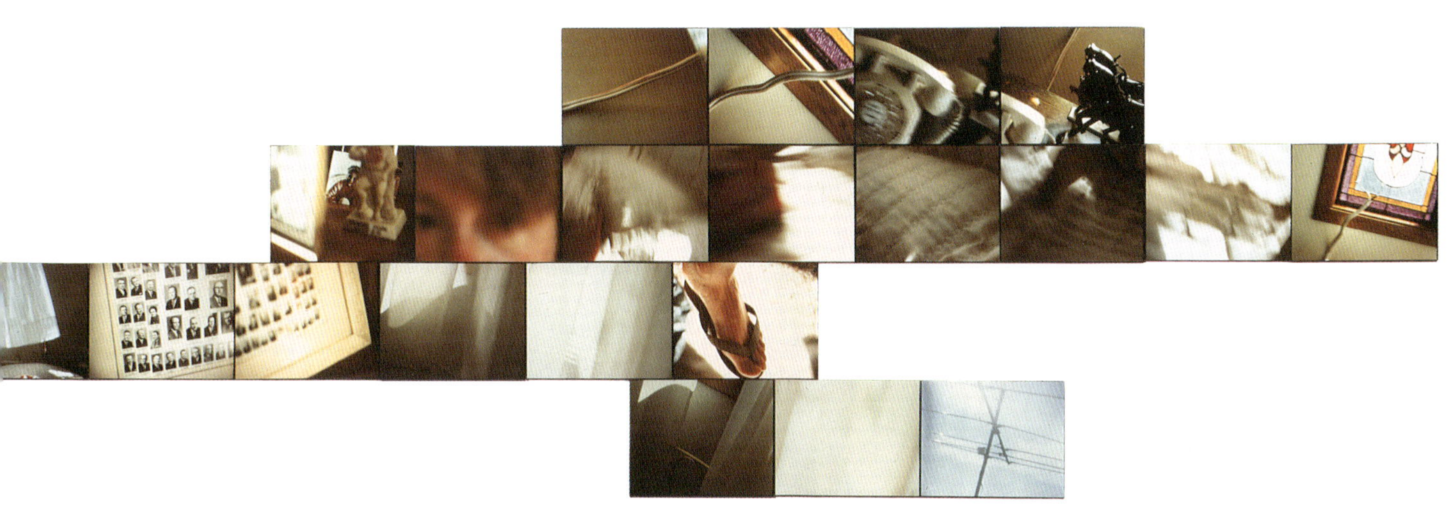

Sandra Semchuk and Martin Semchuk Coming to Death's Door *(detail)* *cibachrome prints*

ALEXANDER HAMILTON UK
In Pursuit of Perfection

Falkland Town Hall

MAIN STREET, FALKLAND
FIFE

PREMIERE

4 JUNE – 4 JULY

This work explores the concept of 'the pursuit of perfection'. It is based on the genealogy of the Peace Rose which is considered to be one of the finest hybrid tea roses ever created. This rose traces back its family members for at least two hundred years and is the result of the efforts of several generations of rose breeders, united in the common goal of creating the perfect rose through controlled selection.

Using the cyanotype process, a unique record is made of roses selected from the Peace Rose family tree. Cyanotype images are in direct contrast to commercial catalogue photography in that they eschew colour. Instead they reveal the structural form of each rose while at the same time registering its unique physical presence as the flower indents and stains the paper.

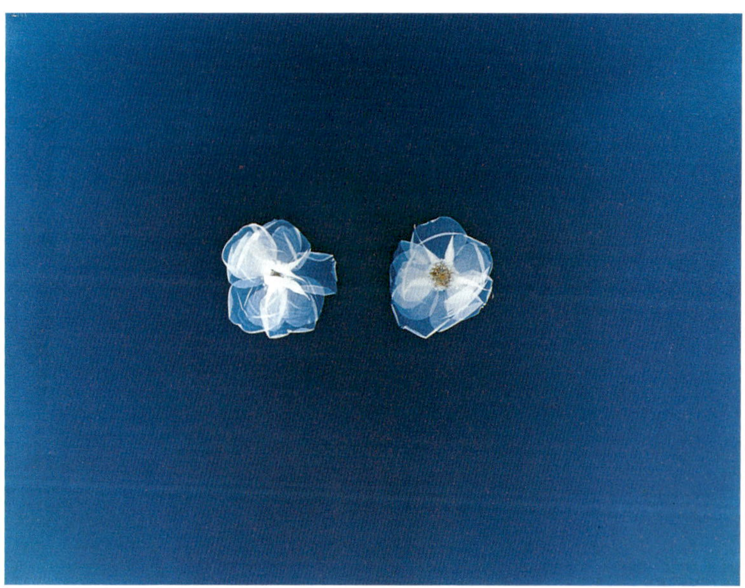

Alexander Hamilton Peace Rose *cyanotype*

BOAZ TAL *Israel*
Works

The Traverse

10 CAMBRIDGE STREET
EDINBURGH

UK PREMIERE

7 JUNE – 26 JUNE

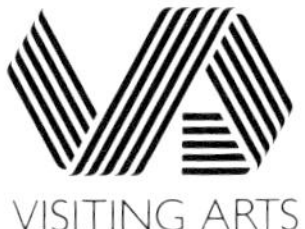

Supported by the Centre for Technological Education, Holon

"We take a lot for granted. Our lives are layer upon layer of expectation, cliché and tradition. Using simple gestures, a minimum of props and without professional models, Boaz Tal peels back these layers, poses questions and reveals much."
Marianne Fulton, Associate Curator, The International Museum of Photography at George Eastman House, Rochester.

The photographs of Boaz Tal create a deliberately artificial and, at times, uncomfortable world in which the aspirations of high culture collide with the banality of everyday family life. Tal is the actor/director arranging himself, his friends and members of his family in tableaux which sometimes quite directly mimic a specific painting or sculpture, at others merely hint at a genre or period from art history. But this is art with the artifice stripped away. Nothing is hidden, nothing is smoothed over or perfected. Even the apparatus of making photographs – the lamps, tripods and wires – lie around in clear view.

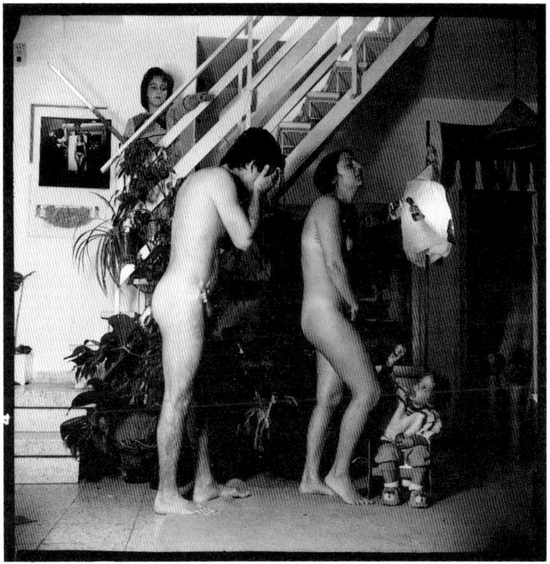

Boaz Tal The Expulsion *silver-gelatin print*

NATIONAL GALLERIES OF SCOTLAND

Photographing Children

Scottish National Portrait Gallery

1 QUEEN STREET
EDINBURGH

PREMIERE

29 MAY – 3 OCTOBER

This exhibition is designed to explore the way we portray children and draws on the work of both great and hack photographers in the last 150 years. It is, significantly, only with the invention of photography that adults have been free to picture children as individuals – to express, or seek for, the intimate love and affection of the adult-child relationship.

The studio photographer's wrestling match with childhood has involved a desperate bid to take a picture of a girl or boy held still and on miraculous, rare occasions, looking pleasant. The amateur snapshot camera, with its customary speed of 1/125, gives most of us the chance to miss the child's inherent charm 124 times per second. The problems of capturing action and emotion, the mercurial shifts of character and disconcertingly short attention span are severe problems for pictorial expression. The world of a child is immensely complicated and fast-moving. The desperate adult pursuit of childhood zipping past continues, with the children well ahead.

Adults tend to concentrate on attempting to photograph the admirable side of childhood – innocence, beauty, charm, uncomplicated happiness. We are spurred on by the ever-hopeful grown-up notion that children are sweeter than we are, which leads us to the optimistic conclusion that they will also be tidy and quiet. Only rarely in photography are the doubtful, threatening, critical or anarchic sides of childhood tackled head on.

Photographing Children presents a more balanced picture of childhood: from anarchy to its saccharine opposite. It will be hung at two heights, one for adults and one for children to encourage the comments of a smaller audience.

Sponsored by
EAE Communications

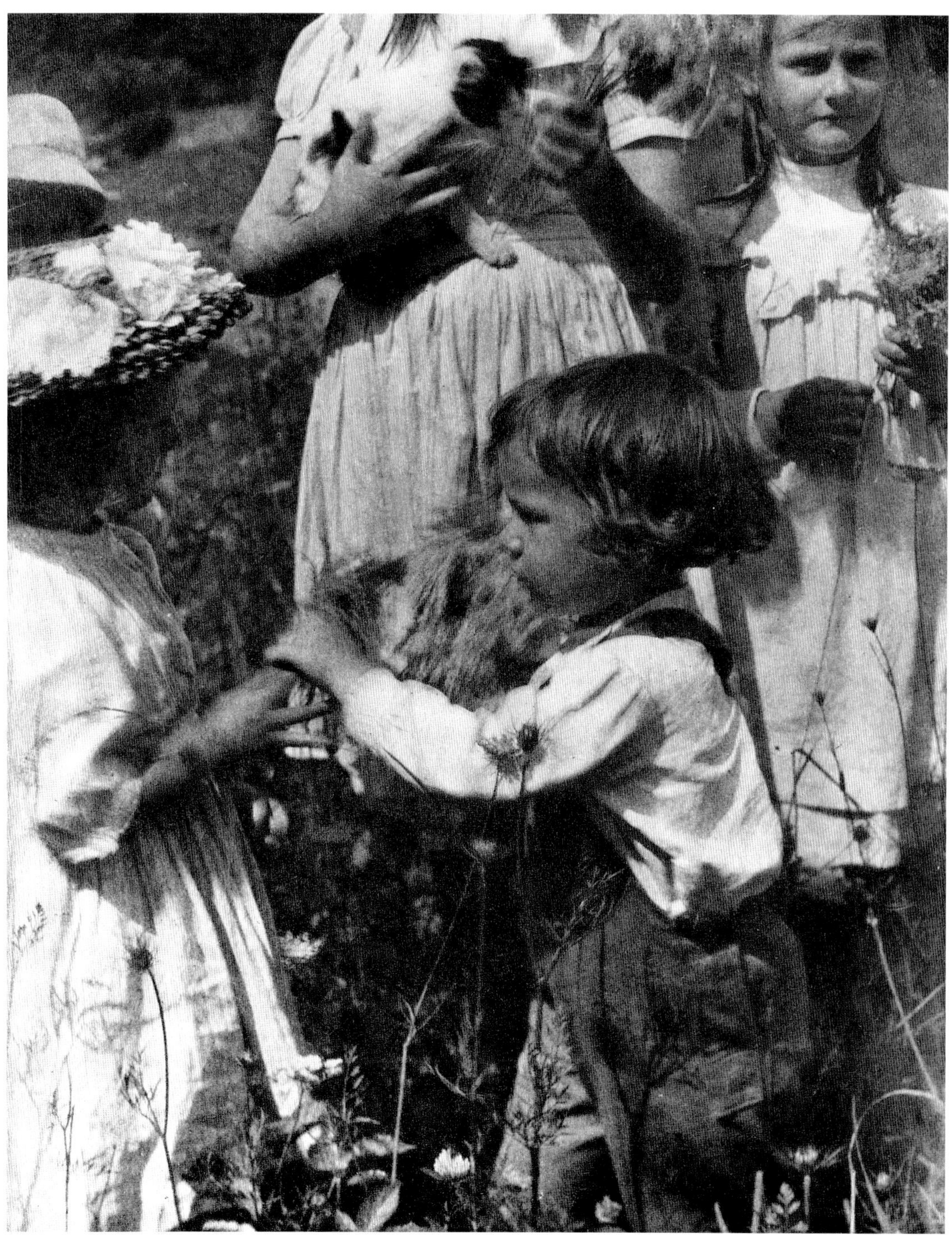

Gertrude Käsebier Happy Days 1905 *photogravure*

NANNA BISP BÜCHERT and TINA SCHWARZ *Denmark*

Family Stories

The Danish Cultural Institute

CARLSBERG HOUSE
3 DOUNE TERRACE
EDINBURGH

UK PREMIERE

4 JUNE – 2 JULY

Originally made for exhibition at The Museum of Photographic Art in Odense, Denmark, Nanna Bisp Büchert's suite of twenty images draws on authentic family photos and letters from the thirties and forties written by the photographer's mother to her mother in Iceland. Images and texts are arranged together with fossils, fruits and the dried remains of plants to form delicate assemblages, which are then photographed. The resulting images evoke repressed memories and show the fate of a family inexorably taking shape.

The work of Tina Schwarz concerns a woman's discovery of what it means to be a mother and to have her own family. It describes a moment when she understands that she does not know how to be simultaneously a mother, a wife and an individual. All she sees is that what she knew does not accommodate what she experiences.

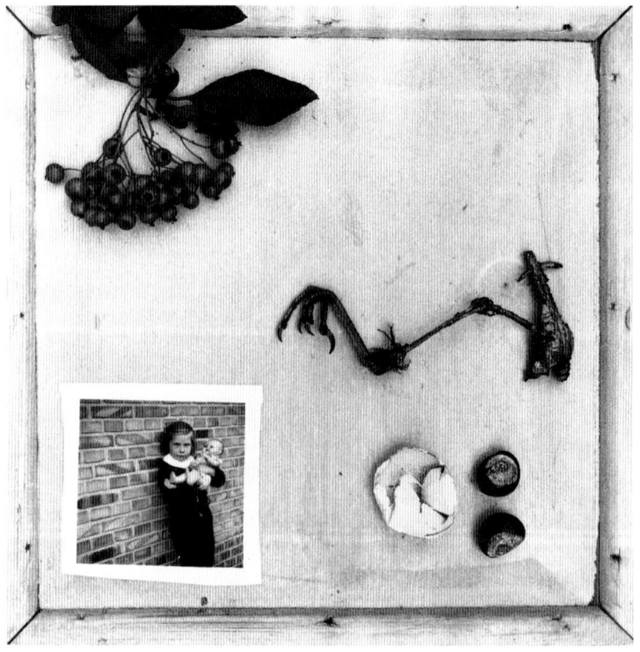

Nanna Bisp Büchert Untitled *silver-gelatin print*

LEIF LINDBERG *Sweden*

Writing of History

Pittencrieff House Museum

PITTENCRIEFF PARK
DUNFERMLINE

UK PREMIERE

4 JUNE – 21 JUNE

Helge and Leif Lindberg's Writing of History aims right at that diffuse zone between personal and collective history. The source of the imagery here is his father's [Helge Lindberg] photo album from which Leif Lindberg has chosen photographs spanning the years from 1930 to 1960. These decades, with their curious blend of wartime nationalism / conservatism and the growth of the social democratic welfare system, mark the birth of the Swedish model state.

Method is here intricately linked with content. Each selected image is presented as a gumprint; a small fragment is also enlarged and printed. These visuals are then literally sewn together. Cool analysis and soft-spoken nostalgia join hands in this peculiar meeting of family album with the annals of cultural history. History is brought to life and yet distanced by the very same gesture. These images thus show us how personal and political, private and public, culture and self, are unremittingly interlaced.
Jan-Erik Lundström

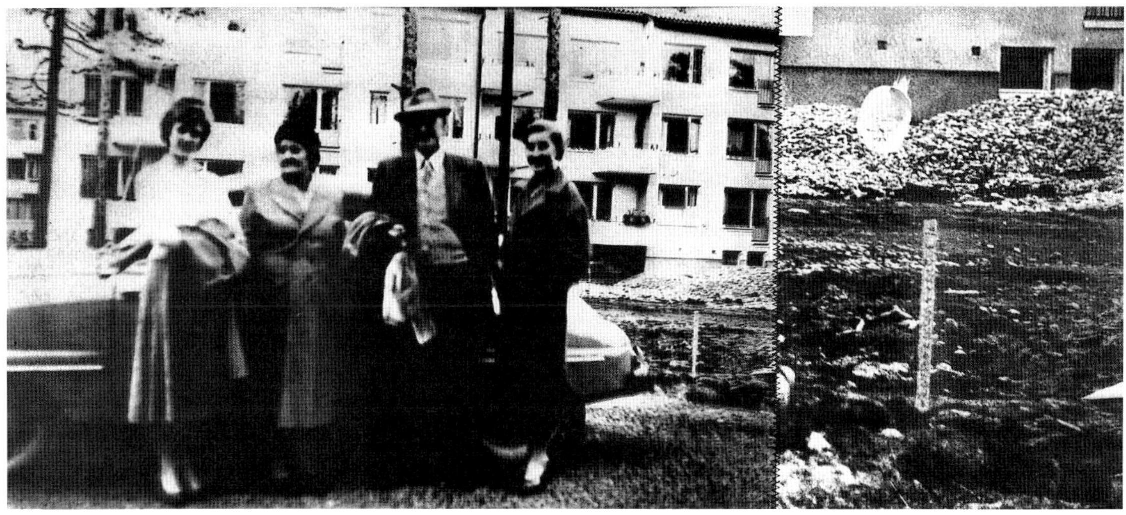

Leif Lindberg Untitled *gum print and stitching*

ADRIANA LESTIDO *Argentina*

Adolescent Mothers

Theatre Workshop

34 HAMILTON PLACE

EDINBURGH

EUROPEAN PREMIERE

4 JUNE – 4 JULY

These photographs were taken in a home for adolescent mothers called *Nuestra Sra. del Vallo* which is funded by the *Comisión Nacional de Políticas Familiares y de Planificación.* Some 30 or 40 unmarried teenage girls from poor backgrounds who are pregnant or have children live there because they have no families of their own to care for them.

At *Nuestra Sra. del Valle* the girls are given a primary education and can take classes in work-related activities. The home is structured, the girls cannot come and go freely, they must be granted special permission. On Thursdays and Sundays they are allowed to receive visitors and take phone calls from the fathers of their children.

It is estimated that 2,000 teenage girls in Buenos Aires live in homes like this.

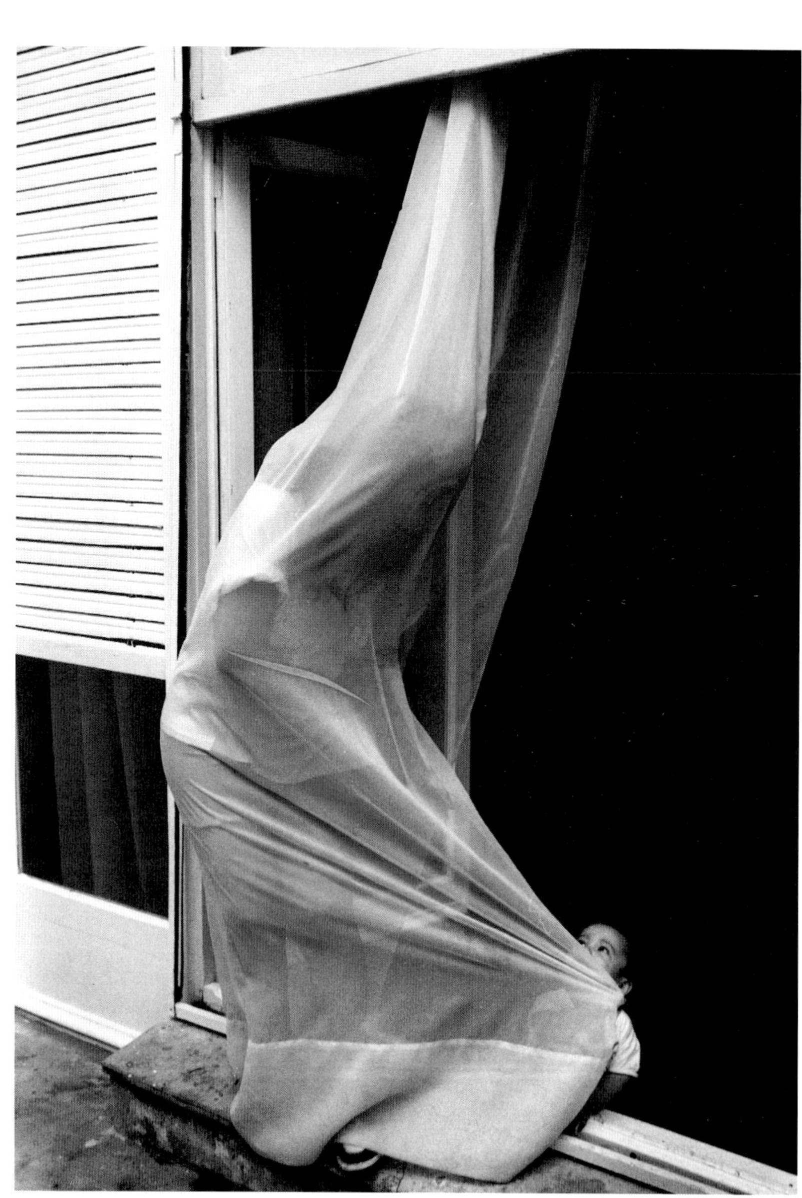

Adriana Lestido Untitled *silver-gelatin print*

SUSANNA PIERATZKI *German*

Parents

The Cameo

38 HOME STREET
EDINBURGH

PREMIERE

4 JUNE – 4 JULY

Family snapshots tell your friends that you have *been there, done that*. They are social documents, rarely about an individual's character. I had been photographing my parents for some time before I thought about doing an entire series about them. As I was to discover later, it was my way of dealing with their mortality. When I began, I only knew that I wanted to portray them as they really are, without imposed social clichés.

The photographs combine extracts from my parents' biography with my personal childhood memories and certain fantasies. The opening photograph marks the end of World War II and their survival of the Holocaust. Each image deals with an aspect of their journey through life. They are not shown as a couple, an entity, but as two separate beings with their own strengths and weaknesses.

Now the project is complete I realise that what started out as being about my parents has, in truth, turned out to be a voyage towards myself.
Susanna Pieratzki

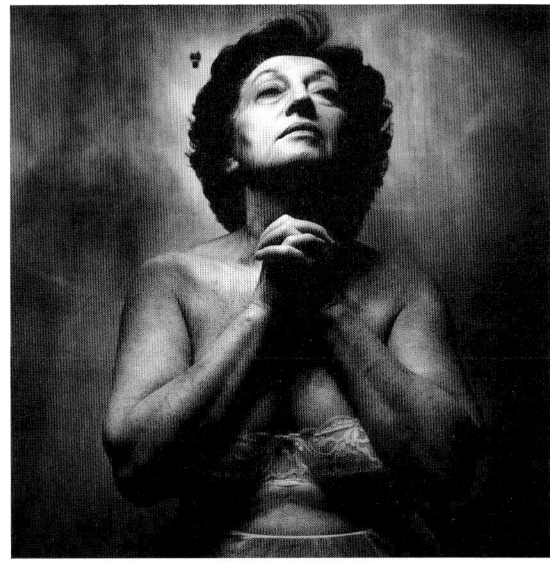

Susanna Pieratzki Mother *silver-gelatin print*

ELISABETH BROEKAERT *Belgium*

Babies Behind Bars: The story of women being pregnant, giving birth and taking care of their babies whilst in detention.

Edinburgh Unemployed Workers Centre

103 BROUGHTON STREET
EDINBURGH

PREMIERE

4 JUNE – 4 JULY

Askham Grange, an open prison near York, has one of only three mother and baby prison units in the whole of Britain. It is the only one allowing children to remain up to the age of 18 months.

The Unit is a totally self-contained new block within a large country house. Opened in 1973, it has its own ante-natal ward, surgery (with 24 hour cover), kitchen, laundry, bathrooms and, most importantly, a nursery where the mothers can feed and play with their babies.

The Home Office ruling is that no child can remain once it is 18 months old, and the child then has to be looked after by relatives or placed in care. The Unit has its own specific rules and daily routine. The day begins at 6am and continues with education classes, gardening, cleaning the house, feeding baby, washing, making beds ...

Elisabeth Broekaert

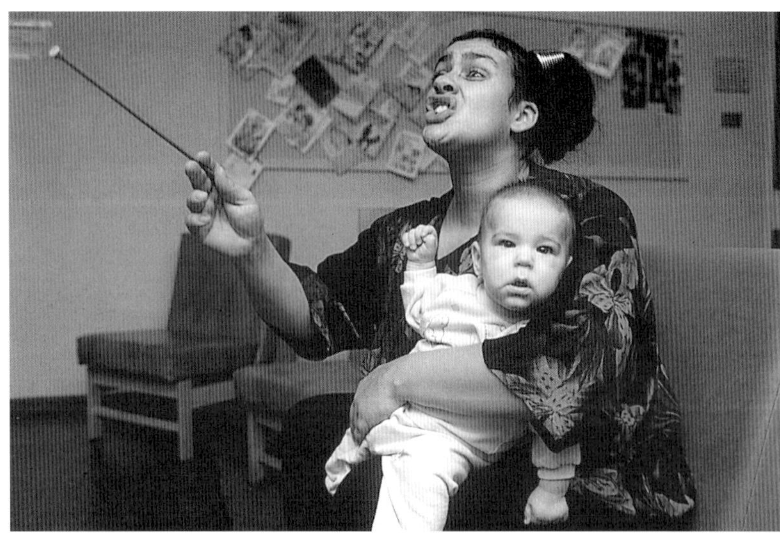

Elisabeth Broekaert Untitled *(original in colour)*

DAVID BARNETT, JOHN CONNOLLY, IAN FRASER, IAN LYON BILLY McARTHUR, EVELYN RAMSAY UK

The Creation of a New Self-Image

The Collective Gallery

22–28 COCKBURN STREET
EDINBURGH

PREMIERE

11 JUNE – 3 JULY

This Artlink initiative has been made possible by financial assistance from: Charity Projects, Scottish Post Office Board and EUCREA.

Working with a small group of people with different experiences of disability but a common purpose, Artlink in collaboration with artist Brian Jenkins, have created a platform for individuals to express themselves, voicing their feelings and aspirations through their control of the creative process of image construction and manipulation.

Within the language of photography, charity advertising is the form by which disabled people are most often seen, portraying them not as individuals but as stereotypes of a medical condition.

This exhibition is the culmination of a year long Artlink initiative aimed at constructing more positive images of people with special needs, and beyond that, to encourage each individual to explore their own sense of self.

An associated poster campaign along Princes Street (Edinburgh's main shopping area) is aimed at increasing awareness and breaking down the negative stereotypes of people with disabilities.

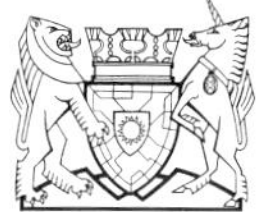

Lothian Regional Council

Subsidised by the
Scottish Arts Council

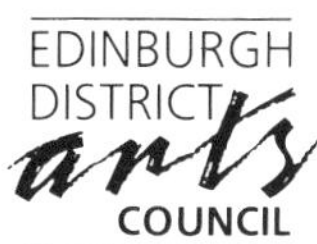

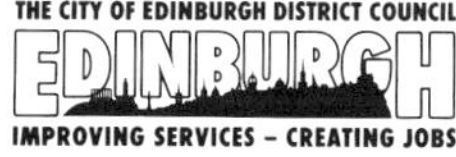

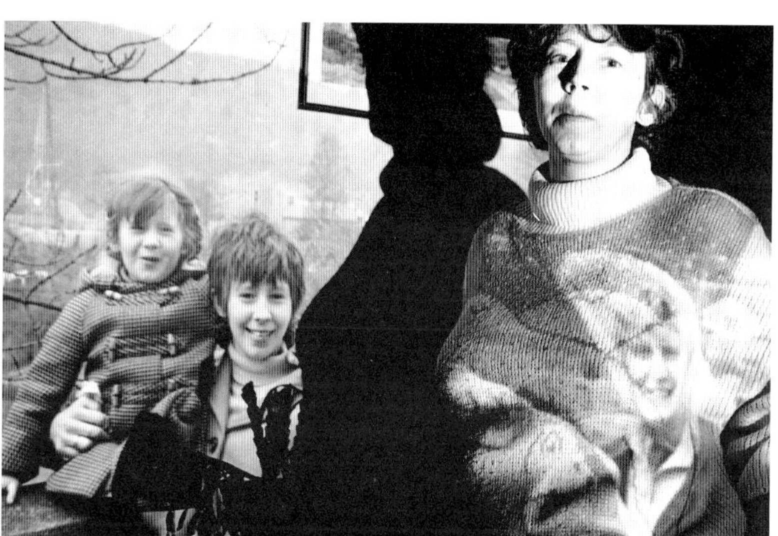

Evelyn Ramsay Untitled *silver-gelatin print*

SCOTT RUDDOCK UK
Childhood Postponed

Lochgelly Centre

BANK STREET, LOCHGELLY
FIFE

PREMIERE

31 MAY – 21 JUNE

Children today are under increasing pressure, through the media and peer influence, to grow up quickly. However, this induced transition from child to adult can sometimes come about through real necessity. In Britain today it is estimated that ten thousand children are responsible for caring for one or more members of their family. Expert opinion is that the true figure is much higher.

This series of photographs was taken at the Cardiff home of 12 year old Marie and spans a six week period in 1991. Following an emotionally debilitating and unstable time in her life, Marie's mother found that the task of caring for her six children was becoming too much for her to deal with alone. As the eldest, Marie automatically took on the role of second parent, providing both practical and mental support.

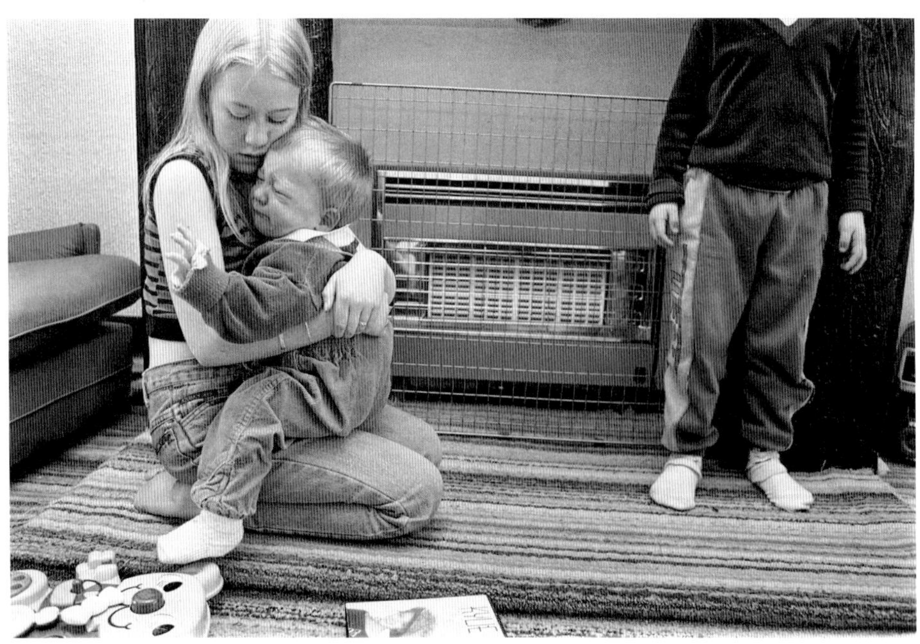

Scott Ruddock Marie and James, Grangetown, Cardiff *silver-gelatin print*

TRICIA MALLEY UK
Tremendous Reality

Crawford Arts Centre

93 NORTH STREET
ST. ANDREWS

PREMIERE

11 JUNE – 11 JULY

Our relationship with other people is determined by many factors; there are those who are born to be our family and those we choose to be part of our lives. The family is one of the strongest ties especially when it is chosen by design not birth.

I have documented a group of people who have chosen to spend their lives as part of an extended family – the Cistercian Monks at Sancta Maria Abbey, Nunraw. For those of us outwith religion it is sometimes difficult to understand why people lock themselves away in a commune given to Christ. By spending time with the monks, documenting everyday life, work, activities, worship, and their interaction with one another, I wanted to discover the tribal need of humans to be part of a family, the desire to belong.

Tricia Malley

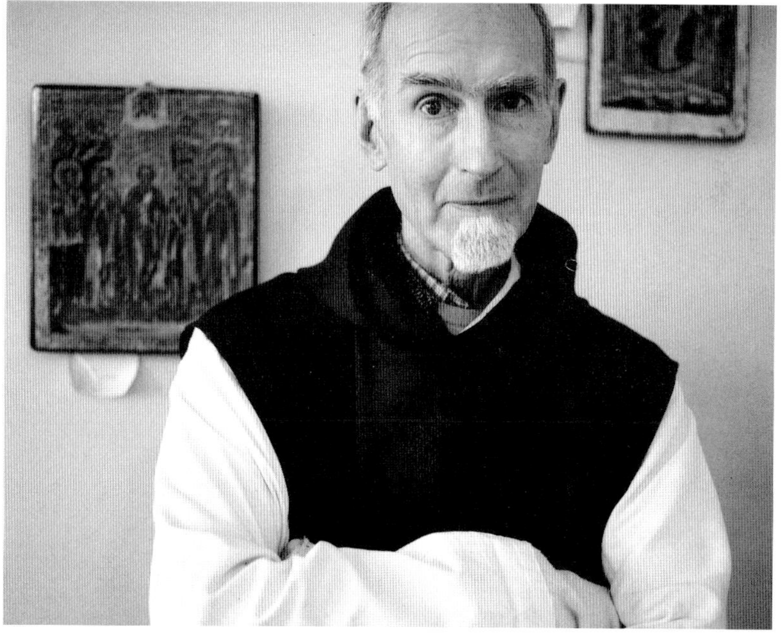

Tricia Malley Father Stephen *silver-gelatin print*

IAIN STEWART UK

Voices in a Small Room

Institut Français d'Ecosse

13 RANDOLPH CRESCENT, EDINBURGH

PREMIERE

4 JUNE – 8 JULY

Voices in a Small Room is a very personal piece of work about a private experience. Dealing with death, family bereavement and the subsequent adjustment to loss, the work combines image with text in an attempt to re-create memories, rekindle emotions and remember places. *Voices in a Small Room* can, of course, offer no solution to the emptiness of loss – only the cold light of a new day and the bitter comfort of life's continuance.

Iain Stewart Untitled *(detail) silver-gelatin print*

GORDON DODDS UK

Mothers' Daughters

Castlecliff Workshops

25 JOHNSTON TERRACE, EDINBURGH

PREMIERE

5 JUNE – 3 JULY

In many societies there is a fundamental importance placed on mothers being responsible for the religious and social education of their children. Hence their daughters can have a close affiliation, as one day they will be expected to fulfil that family role.

In today's society, when the individual woman decides to deviate from the foundations laid down by her family or the role provided by her mother, problems can arise. Gordon Dodds explores these and other issues in this exhibition.

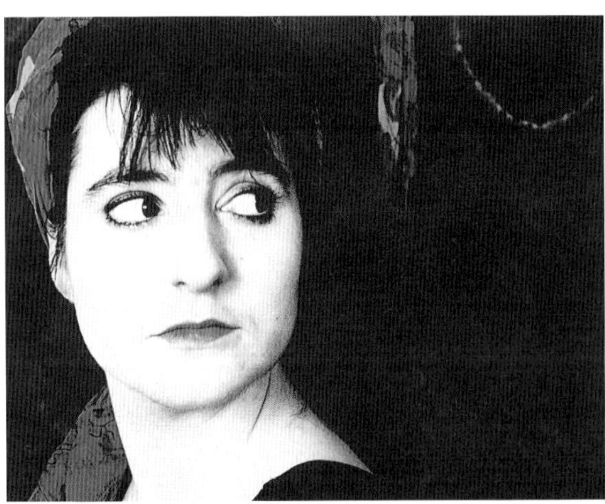

Gordon Dodds Lynn *C-type print (original in colour)*

SUE EVANS and TIM ROBINSON (ffOTO FICTIONS) UK

A Day in my Life

Maison Hector

47 DEANHAUGH STREET
EDINBURGH

PREMIERE

4 JUNE – 4 JULY

A *Day in my Life* is a parody on the quotidian grind of family existence. The series follows the central female character through a day of frenetic activity in which she attempts to encompass the many roles of mother, worker, carer, lover. In doing so, the series addresses the bizarre nature of much of the daily, unrecorded routine of life. The series was created by Sue Evans in collaboration with Tim Robinson.

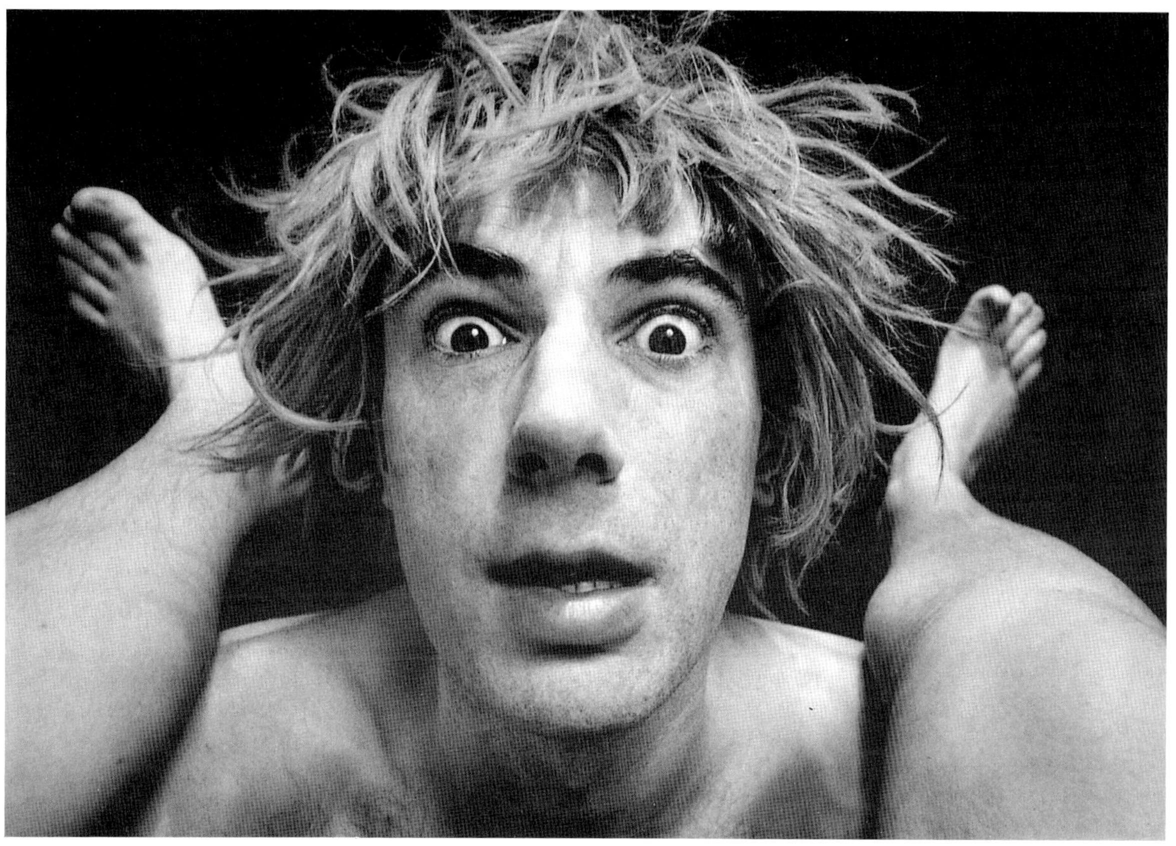

Sue Evans and Tim Robinson from 'A Day in my Life' *tinted silver-gelatin print (original in colour)*

CHRIS MORRIS UK
Parallel Lines

Corridor Gallery

FIFE INSTITUTE OF PHYSICAL
& RECREATIONAL EDUCATION
VIEWFIELD ROAD, GLENROTHES

PREMIERE, 1 JUNE – 30 JUNE

Families come in all shapes and sizes – and species. Chris Morris' photographs are both a serious study of a colony of monkeys and a humorous comment on the 'universal' nature of family life. It is difficult to look at these close cousins in the animal world, without making an anthropomorphic leap of imagination: without thinking, 'I know how that feels'.

DUNFERMLINE PHOTOGRAPHIC ASSOCIATION UK
Families

Dunfermline District Museum

VIEWFIELD TERRACE
DUNFERMLINE

PREMIERE, 4 JUNE – 3 JULY

The Dunfermline Photographic Association meets regularly and its membership spans the district. *Families* brings together the membership's personal response to the theme, an exciting and diverse range of photography from the area. This local show can be viewed in juxtaposition with the exhibition at Pittencrieff House by the Swedish photographer, Leif Lindberg.

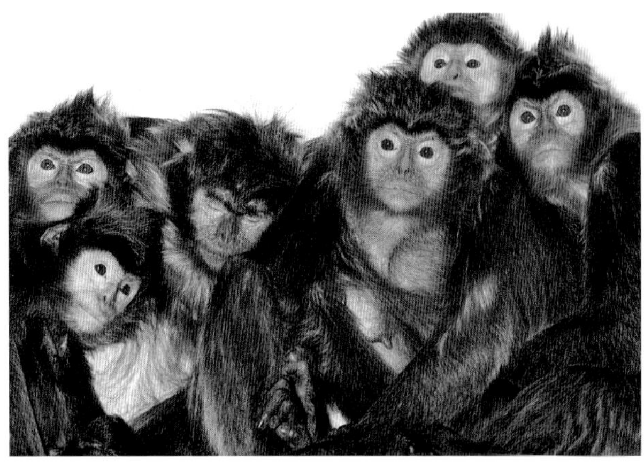

Chris Morris Untitled *silver-gelatin print*

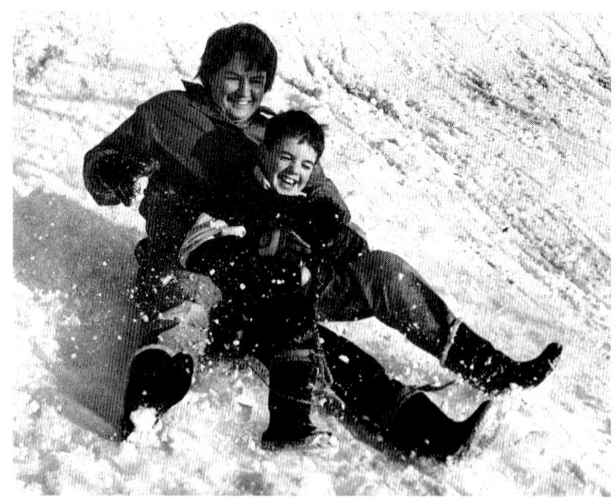

Jim Honeyman Glissade *silver-gelatin print*

GRINDLAY COURT CENTRE
Asylum

Grindlay Court Centre

GRINDLAY STREET COURT
EDINBURGH

PREMIERE

7 JUNE – 19 JUNE

LYNN BEVERIDGE

KEITH BRAME

MARGARET CAMERON

MICHELLE COZZI

WILLIAM DONALDSON

DAVID HOLLOWAY

FIONA MacPHERSON

PAT WILSON

Asylum is the result of a series of workshops which took place in the first three months of 1993. The project involved two professional photographers, Keith Brame and Fiona MacPherson, working alongside six people from Grindlay Court Centre: Michelle Cozzi, Lynn Beveridge, David Holloway, Pat Wilson, Billy Donaldson and Margaret Cameron. Grindlay Court Centre provides a service for people with learning disabilities, aiming to help them to take their place as adult citizens in the community.

The theme of *Family* presented the group with interesting and challenging possibilities. Whilst the experience of family for people with learning disabilities is, of course, as rich and diverse as for anyone else, there are elements of 'difference' which lend themselves to investigation.

The title *Asylum* challenges the preconceptions which surround the lives of people with learning disabilities. Despite the new use of the word 'asylum' – a place of refuge – many people still equate the word with its old meaning – a mental institution.

Subsidised by the
Scottish Arts Council

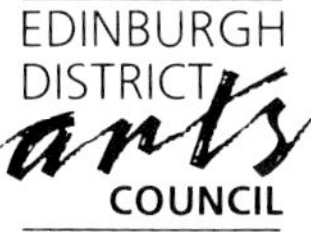

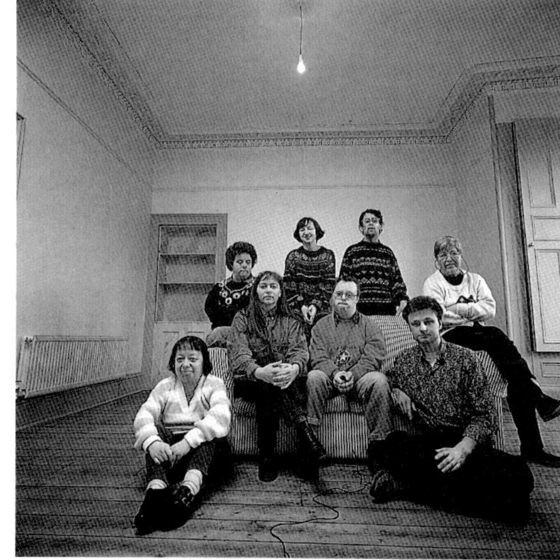

David Holloway Workshop participants

Leith Library

28-30 FERRY ROAD

4 JUNE – 4 JULY

Edinburgh Room Gallery

CENTRAL LIBRARY

GEORGE IV BRIDGE

24 MAY – 2 JULY

Craigmillar Library

7 NIDDRIE MARISCHAL GARDENS

4 JUNE – 4 JULY

Fountainbridge Library

137 DUNDEE STREET

4 JUNE – 4 JULY

Gilmerton Library

64 GILMERTON DYKES STREET

4 JUNE – 2 JULY

Central Lending Library

GEORGE IV BRIDGE

4 JUNE – 2 JULY

McDonald Road Library

2 MCDONALD ROAD

14 JUNE – SEPTEMBER

FOTOFEIS IN EDINBURGH'S LIBRARIES

A number of Edinburgh libraries are staging exhibitions and events during Fotofeis with the aim of involving as many groups and individuals as possible from around the city. In their variety and imagination, they demonstrate the many diverse ways in which photography can be used to create understanding, awareness and a sense of identity within and between communities.

Children from the Himalayan city of Khatmandu are mounting an exhibition at LEITH LIBRARY in conjunction with children from Fort Primary School in Leith. Taken by the children themselves, the images focus on the way in which they see their own families, and highlight the breadth of family experience across both cultures.

The resulting photographs form part of an ongoing cultural exchange between the children. The schools twinning scheme was established in 1992 by the photographer Kenny Bean, following a visit to Nepal. It involves the exchange of drawings and photographs which express many aspects of the everyday lives of the children themselves. *This exhibition is funded by Edinburgh District Arts Council and Jessops Photocentre.*

In the EDINBURGH ROOM GALLERY of the CENTRAL LIBRARY is an exhibition of the work of several generations of the Inglis family – *Photographs from Rock House*. In 1948, a substantial gift of glass negatives was presented to the Library by the firm of Francis Caird Inglis and Son, Photographers, Rock House, Calton Hill. A long established family business, it had occupied the Rock House Studio (originally set up by David Octavius Hill and Robert

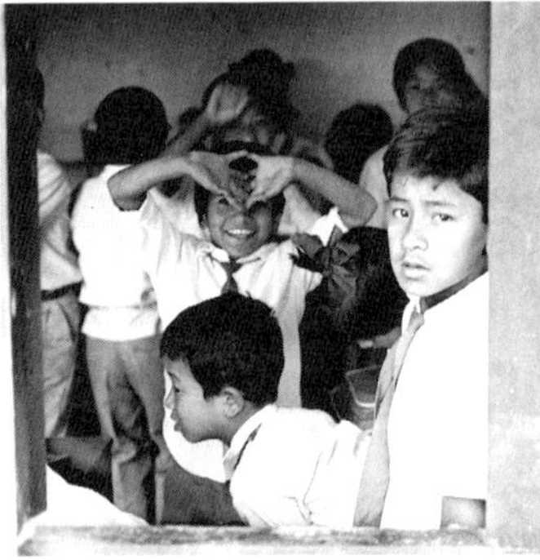
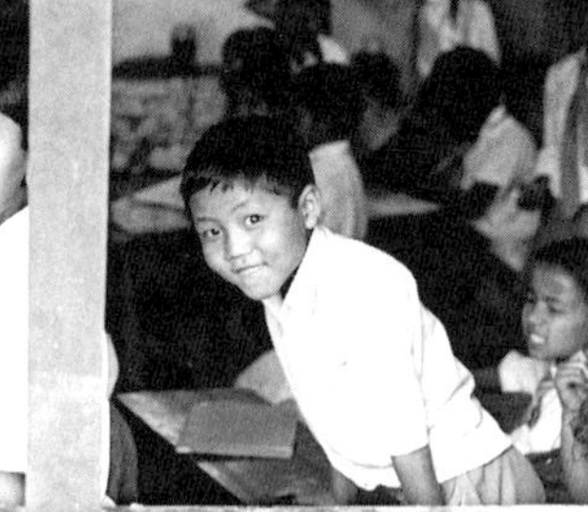

from Family Connection *by Kenny Bean*

Adamson in 1843) since 1876, when Alexander A. Inglis took over from the highly respected Archibald Burns. It remained there until it became necessary to move to larger premises in 1945 to allow the business to expand. Many of the photographs on display are prints made from these original negatives.

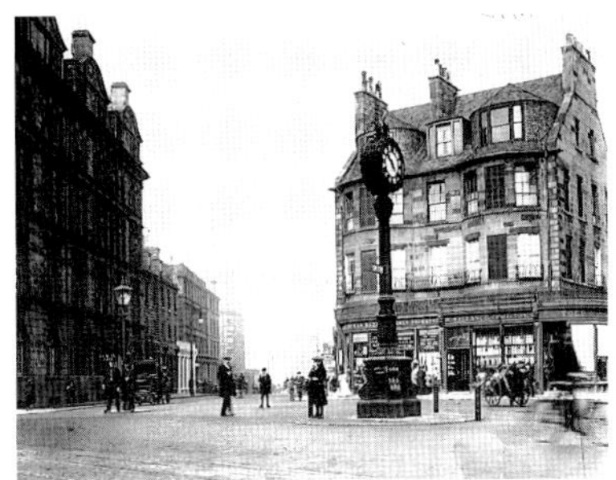

from The Inglis Era

At CRAIGMILLAR LIBRARY the results of a one-day photography workshop for children are on display. In this short space of time, and with little or no previous experience, the children began to come to grips with the processes of making a photographic image. Through this workshop, they took the first steps in understanding and taking control of the process of image production. But best of all, it was fun. As the organiser, Sandra George says, "The children in the project achieved a great sense of satisfaction whilst working as young photographers." Work by the Pefferbank Adult Training Centre Photography Group will also be shown at this venue.

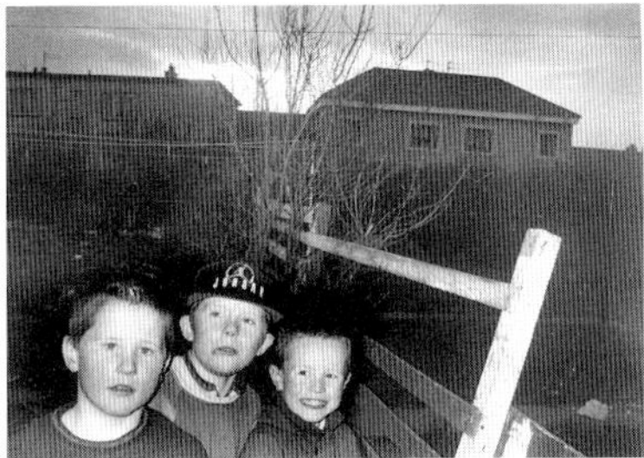

from the Folkal Point *project*

At FOUNTAINBRIDGE LIBRARY the Adult Learning Project is staging *Alive and Klicking*. This exhibition presents a broad and necessarily complex picture of the roles that older people play in our society, illustrating that age is not a barrier to pleasure or fulfilment. The exhibition does not ignore the problems which can arise as one gets older, but the humour, warmth and playfulness shine through.

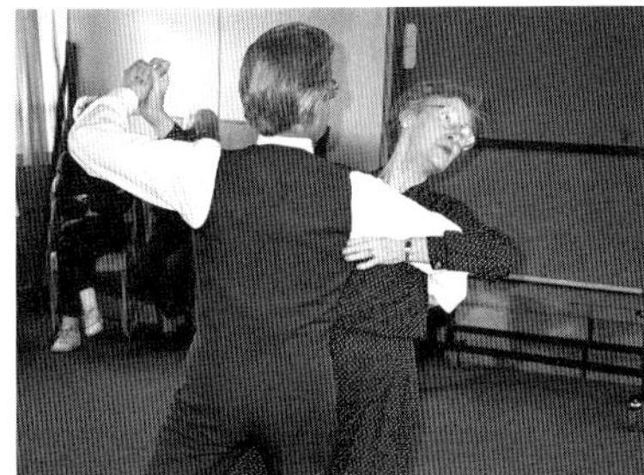

from Alive and Klicking

This exhibition is part of a larger project involving the communities of Gorgie and Dalry in Edinburgh. Spanning two years, the project began with two day-time photography courses of 40 hours per week which were run by the Adult Learning Project for a group of 12-14 local people of whom half were over 60 years of age and half were without full-time employment. When the course was over, the group resolved to continue their project, building an image library reflecting the lives of older people in the community.

An exhibition of work from the communities of Burdiehouse and Southhouse will be on show at GILMERTON LIBRARY. Stimulated and coordinated by the Folkal Point Photography Group the work has involved many people from this area: the young, the old, women's groups and the unemployed. Folkal Point follow a tried and tested 'rolling process' in their workshops. They bring together images and text which are then presented to the community groups as a stimulus – a starting point – from which ideas are identified and developed. This flexible approach results in a diversity of styles of presentation, from snaps to photo-murals.

Other exhibitions include work by members of the Edinburgh Photographic Society at the CENTRAL LENDING LIBRARY, and *Living Images* at MACDONALD ROAD LIBRARY.

Organised by Library Services
Department of Recreation

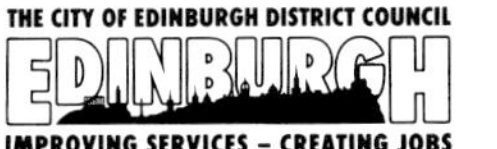

fotofeis

Photography Plus

ABERDEEN AND THE NORTH EAST

PHOTOGRAPHY PLUS

David Brittain

The story of the *avant-garde's* battle with traditional art is punctuated with skirmishes along the boundaries that separate disciplines. Even these days – when the existence of an artistic vanguard is vehemently disputed – the art establishment still views some forms of interdisciplinary art as 'experimental'.[1] Undoubtedly photography has been a major catalyst in the process of eroding distinctions between high art and popular culture, between science and art, artist and consumer. One need only quote the Surrealist Man Ray who stated that photography freed modern painters from the 'burden of representation'.

Recently, it has become common to find photography fully integrated into contemporary art. Sometimes it is exhibited in its own right in the form of fine art prints – but more usually it is omnipresent as part of multi-media work in the form of a poster, a screen print, a projection, a video installation and so on. Of course, one of the great properties of photography is its accessibility. Although generations of orthodox art photographers have regarded purity as their medium's greatest virtue, other artists like the fact that camera images are available in many forms – as snapshots, magazine illustrations, postcards. Also cameras are cheap, photography is fast and simple to use, highly adaptable to multiple applications, integral to many image-making processes and easily disseminated – especially recently in digitised form. Increasingly, artists are attracted to photography because it offers opportunities to intervene in a culture dominated by camera images.

During the 1960's, artistic collaboration between camera images and fine art reached an unprecedented pitch. The era of Pop Art, Happenings and Environments was really the apotheosis of a mixed media revolution that had been smouldering since 1916 when it was uproariously instigated by Dada. The American, Robert Rauschenberg is credited as the first to revive collage as a radical, iconoclastic medium. Rauschenberg's Pop collages of the 1950's combined splashy brush strokes with transfers of haphazard found images. On the one hand these were an ironic riposte to the dominant Abstract Expressionist school, on the other a serious visual response to the novel image environment of nascent information culture. In a similar interplay, this time between photography and text, novelist William Burroughs became interested in "how word and image get around on very, very complex association lines". At the same time as Rauschenberg, he began producing montages that juxtaposed his words and photographs torn from newspapers with the intention of exploring serendipitous connections between information, memory and first hand experience.

Collage and mixed media became sixties buzzwords. A typical work of the Pop period might combine painting, scavenged photographs, and *objets trouvé*. In fact the word 'image' was adopted as a better description for the heterogeneity of materials included within the picture frame. By appropriating artefacts of popular culture – as diverse as a complete sink or newspaper images of car crashes – these artists imitated Duchamp who had proved, with the 'readymade', that a banal object could become art if an artist said so. Not only were images imported wholesale into artworks, they were exported at a great rate from the artworks – indeed, thanks to photographs (mostly crude snaps), Pop and Fluxus happenings of the sixties and seventies still have an audience today. Some 'famous' performances and land artworks (think of Gilbert and George's much discussed 'Underneath the Arches', Robert Smithson's 'Spiral Jetty') still reside in the collective imagination solely as photographic icons.

As is well known, artists such as Warhol and Richard Hamilton co-opted commercial processes such as silkscreen to collapse the distinctions between high art and commercial art. In particular, Warhol's emphasis on applying photomechanical techniques can be read as another ironic attempt to distance himself from master painters of previous generations, and demystify what the theorist Walter Benjamin[2] once termed the art work's 'aura', as well as the myth of the demiurgic artist.

Afterwards, it became commonplace for artists to adopt photography self-consciously to stress their antipathy to the notion of the artist as author (the camera left no traces of artistic intervention). The first time photography had been invoked to efface the 'authorial' presence of the artist was in the photo-montages of the anti-artists (as they styled themselves) of Berlin Dada. Photomontage, like collage, involves combining preprocessed photographic fragments, out of context, with text or other media. Hannah Höch and Raoul Hausmann cut up popular magazines and postcards, and used assembly-line techniques to recombine them as absurd images which delighted in disrupting classical notions of perspective and space. They eschewed the word 'artist' for 'monteur' (or engineer/fitter). One of the group, the Marxist John Heartfield, went on to perfect photomontage into a powerful tool which, when published, made brilliant use of the public's susceptibility to the 'truth' of photographs.

The writer, Roger Shattuck, argues that, as early as 1911, Cubist painters pre-figured Dada by including fragments of everyday ephemera into their montages. They were aiming to breach the 'frame' separating art and life. Then around 1912, Russian artists adopted photomontage as a way of rejecting representational painting. Since then both collage and photomontage have been popular with successive generations of *avant-garde* artists. A variant of photomontage, the photogram, appears to have been 'discovered' almost simultaneously in Germany, Switzerland and France. The photogram and photomontage were adopted eagerly by the legendary boiler-suited polymath, Moholy-Nagy. He rechristened photomontage 'photoplastik' (literally photo-sculpture) and used it as the basis of the 'New Vision' while teaching at the Dessau Bauhaus. Interestingly, Moholy-Nagy used the photoplastik liberally to illustrate his many theories – even using it as a model of a revolutionary theatre of the future where the passive relations between spectator and performer would be dramatically transformed into something that sounds similar to a latterday 'rave'.

Photography, in the form of the photogram and the juxtaposed image, provided the Surrealists with what amounted to a visual analogue of 'automatism' – a writing technique believed to be the direct expression of the unconscious. The editors of Surrealist journals such as *La Révolution Surréaliste*, specialised in finding disorienting new contexts for scientific photographs and other documents. Formally, a photogram resembled a seamless photomontage comprising the outlines of any number of disparate objects. In fact, it was simply an updated version of Fox Talbot's 'photogenic drawings' of the 1830's which were made by interposing objects between sensitised paper and direct light. The photographer used these techniques which were coveted in Surrealist circles as examples of 'photographic automatism'. Man Ray also applied it to movie film that he cut together and projected at a celebrated screening which provoked the audience to riot. From our perspective in the nineties, rayograms still seem radical because they elevated chance to the level of an alternative 'order' opposed to the hated classicism and raised questions about the nature of an artist's subject matter that Pop Art would continue to pose.

The forces that eroded the distance between fine art and folk art in the sixties, conspired to isolate and 'ghetto-ise' art photography. According to the writer Kathleen McCarthy Gauss, the most significant development for photography and art in the sixties was the focus on photography rather than the photograph. "... for the photograph was fettered by tradition, while photography as a medium covered any kind of photographic imagery and could accommodate great latitude." [4]

Although these observations are accurate, it would be misleading to give the impression that photographers have been less adventurous than other artists in experimenting across media boundaries. Photography actually boasts its own tradition of 'synthetic practice' that draws on the same 'primitive' sources as Dada photomontage – including hand-decorated Victorian family albums, montage postcards, spirit photographs, narrative stereo cards and myriad anonymous documents. Some well known practitioners of this mode have been admitted into the canon of art photography; the American Joel-Peter Witkin, whose tableaux self-consciously reference nineteenth-century photographs, the sequence-maker Duane Michals, Les Krims, and Jerry Uelsmann who is a master of darkroom manipulation. Indeed, the concerns of Michals and Krims especially, coincide with some of the investigations of conceptual photography during the 1970's. For most of this century, however, orthodox purism disparaged most deviations from the path of realism and objectivity, prescribed as the 'essence of photography' by such founding fathers of modernism as Paul Strand, then echoed throughout the next 30 years by Edward Weston and Ansel Adams among others.

The constraining influence of 'purism' held sway until well into the 1980's, from the highest academic levels downwards. In these circles 'constructed' or 'post-visualised' photography (as such work would be categorised) was equated with 'low' variants such as fashion or table-top photography which were perceived to be both an embarrassment and a threat to art photography. As late as 1976, the critic A. D. Coleman used the pages of Artforum to launch an attack on 'a purist oriented photography establishment' for marginalising various forms of 'non-straight' photography that he included within the rubric, 'directorial photography'. During the sixties and seventies, fewer photographers than non-photographers – including Rauschenberg, Ed Ruscha and Lucas Samaras – made major contributions in the area between contemporary art and photography. As well as Michals and Krims, William Klein made films that extended the investigations of his still photography. The 1970's witnessed a short-lived renaissance of mixed media photography centred on America's West Coast. Photographers revived such printing processes as gum bichromate, once popular with turn-of-the-century Pictorialists, until they were proscribed by modernism. Although Pictorialism nominally challenged establishment notions of 'good photography', in reality it was a craft-based movement that broke no ground. Looking back at that era, from the vantage point of 1985, Lewis Baltz observed that "few photographers working in this vein were able to transcend their indebtedness to Robert Rauschenberg's late 1950's work ...". Towards the end of the seventies there was a retreat from the streets into the controlled environment of the studio that produced some lasting work – especially by women photographers including Judy Dater and Eileen Cowin.

By the late 1970's, at a time when the star of Conceptual

Art was fading, and the optimism of modernism was fast giving way to the anxieties of postmodernism, the institutions of art photography were emitting conflicting signals as they seemed to lose touch with the younger, informed part of their constituency. The 1978 exhibition, *Mirrors & Windows*, made a concession to contemporary taste by including a Warhol silkscreen, photographs by Ed Ruscha and Robert Cumming, and an offset litho by Rauschenberg within a survey of 'American photography since 1960'. But these images sat uncomfortably with the more familiar canonical works of art photography by the likes of Garry Winogrand, Robert Frank and Minor White. The critical tools necessary to make sense of Warhol or Ruscha were so alien to a modernist aesthetics grounded in formalism, that the essayist, John Szarkowski, neglected to even try. At this time the canon of art photography still precluded most artists who worked with photography (except Moholy-Nagy and Man Ray – who had, ironically, railed against purism in a famous manifesto). Those photographers who worked across boundaries – Michals, Klein and Krims, for example – were admitted because, whatever else they did, they were still craftsmen.

By the mid-1980's the legacy of art photography, with its internecine wrangles, had become a burden to younger photographers – certainly in Britain. In a critical climate influenced by the ideas of Sontag, Barthes and Burgin, the brightest of them associated with outmoded modernist concepts concerning authorship, truth to material and so on, and felt constrained by institutions which had become ghettos for purism. Distinctions between 'photographers' and 'artists using photography' polarised, but as photography galleries gradually accepted the new forms and methodologies, the old taboos began to melt. The eighties became a fruitful time for photo-based interdisciplinary work.

In 1989, the curators of the massive sesquicentennial exhibition, *The Art of Photography*, assembled a Who's Who of photography of the past 150 years. It accommodated Fox Talbot (the scientist inventor of modern photography and self-confessed amateur artist), Lee Friedlander (documentary exponent of the new art photography of the sixties), Andy Warhol (more famous for appropriating photographs than taking them), Cindy Sherman (whose pictures of herself in the role of fictional women helped to make a style of post-modern photography). Such an ambitious grouping demonstrated the overwhelming diversity of approaches – 'straight', 'manipulated', 'appropriated', 'staged' – which could be classed as 'art photography'. But, ultimately, the attempt exposed the folly of ever trying to homogenise them.

Photography Plus at Fotofeis explores some of the ways in which photography can operate with performance, installation, printmaking and so on. As more and more artists combine the camera with other creative tools the possibilities will be enhanced. An event such as this seems to indicate the way ahead.

David Brittain is Editor of *Creative Camera*, a freelance journalist, film-maker and broadcaster.

1 Nick Stewart interviewed in *Creative Camera* Feb/March 1993

2 Walter Benjamin's essay 'The Work of Art' in *The Age of Mechanical Reproduction*, Illuminations (Fontana)

3 *Photography and Art Interactions Since 1946* (Abbeville, 1987)

4 *American Images Photography 1945-1980* (Penguin, 1986)

TON ZWERVER *Netherlands*
Sculpture for the Moment

Aberdeen Art Gallery

SCHOOLHILL, ABERDEEN

UK PREMIERE

29 MAY – 26 JUNE

Subsidised by the
Scottish Arts Council

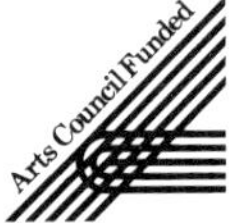

Exhibition courtesy of
TORCH Gallery, Amsterdam

Ton Zwerver has created a framework that allows him to combine sculpture and photography to great effect. The process is simple: the artist selects a space – a living room, an abandoned building – and, working over a period of days, constructs a sculpture from objects and materials he finds on site. This he photographs, and then disassembles. The photograph is the only trace that the occupants, or the public, see of the artist's activity.

The earliest incarnation of this work dates from when Zwerver found himself without a studio. He began to make what he called *Livingroom Sculpture*. Working in the homes of friends who were away during the day, Zwerver would construct a sculpture from the possessions he found there, photograph the work, return everything to its proper place, and be gone before the owner returned home.

The resulting photographs evoke a sense of fantasy, bringing to mind the childhood notion that during sleep, one's toys come to life. With the artist as mediator, inanimate objects are invested with intentions of their own. The *Livingroom Sculptures* were constructed from a few mundane, but crucially selected objects. They possess a striking formal presence that reveals Zwerver's rigorous aesthetic.

from a text by Janie Cohen

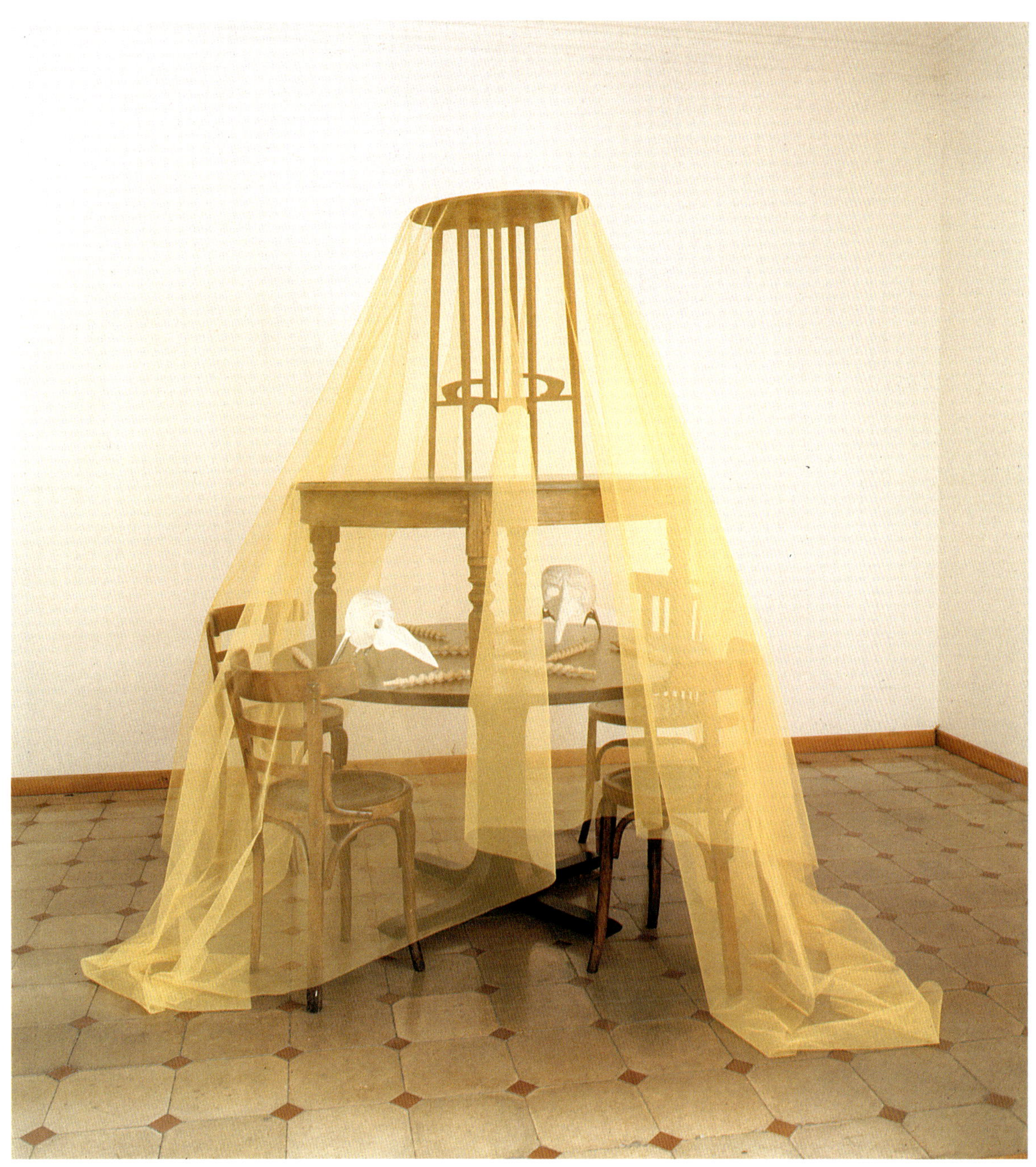

Ton Zwerver Livingroom Sculpture at C. Poy and C. Renau, Barcelona *mixed media*

BERNARD FAUCON *France*
Les Ecritures 1991-92

Aberdeen Art Gallery

SCHOOLHILL, ABERDEEN

UK PREMIERE

29 MAY – 3 JULY

Subsidised by the
Scottish Arts Council

Exhibition courtesy of
Rebecca Hossack Gallery, London

Taking excerpts from his hand-written manuscripts, Bernard Faucon makes enormous, carved, wooden transcriptions of phrases. Covered in a light-sensitive material, these have been installed in a variety of landscapes around the world: in Morocco, Vietnam, on the Isle of Elbe and Provence. At the moment of photographing these objects he illuminates them, transforming the structures into ribbons of white light.

Of the work Faucon says, these are "simple words, without a philosophy, without poetry, truisms that come slowly and painfully. Images once lived, filled with desires, in landscapes today without life where we find written, 'the prophesies of disenchantment'.

"As if the flow of timc had ceased to be a driving force, a true indicator. 'Life is a voluptuous tragedy'. If we dare to take away this voluptuousness, the tragedy pales; it becomes a flat desert where all is silent."

Bernard Faucon at work

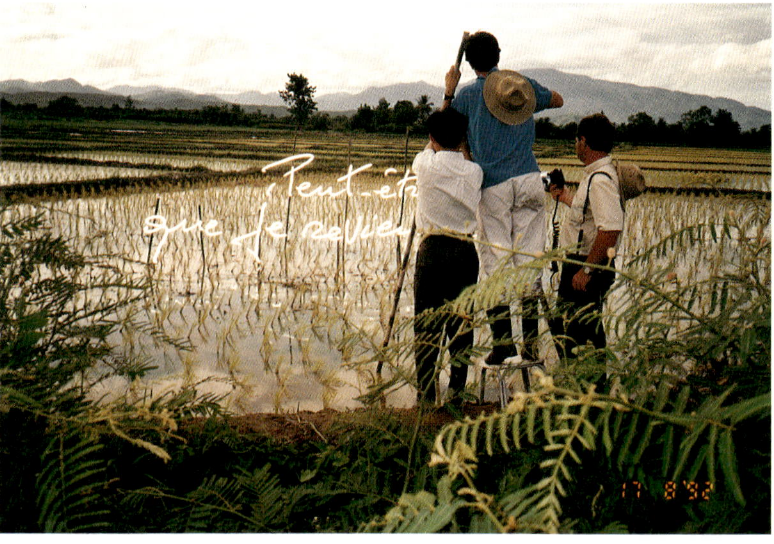

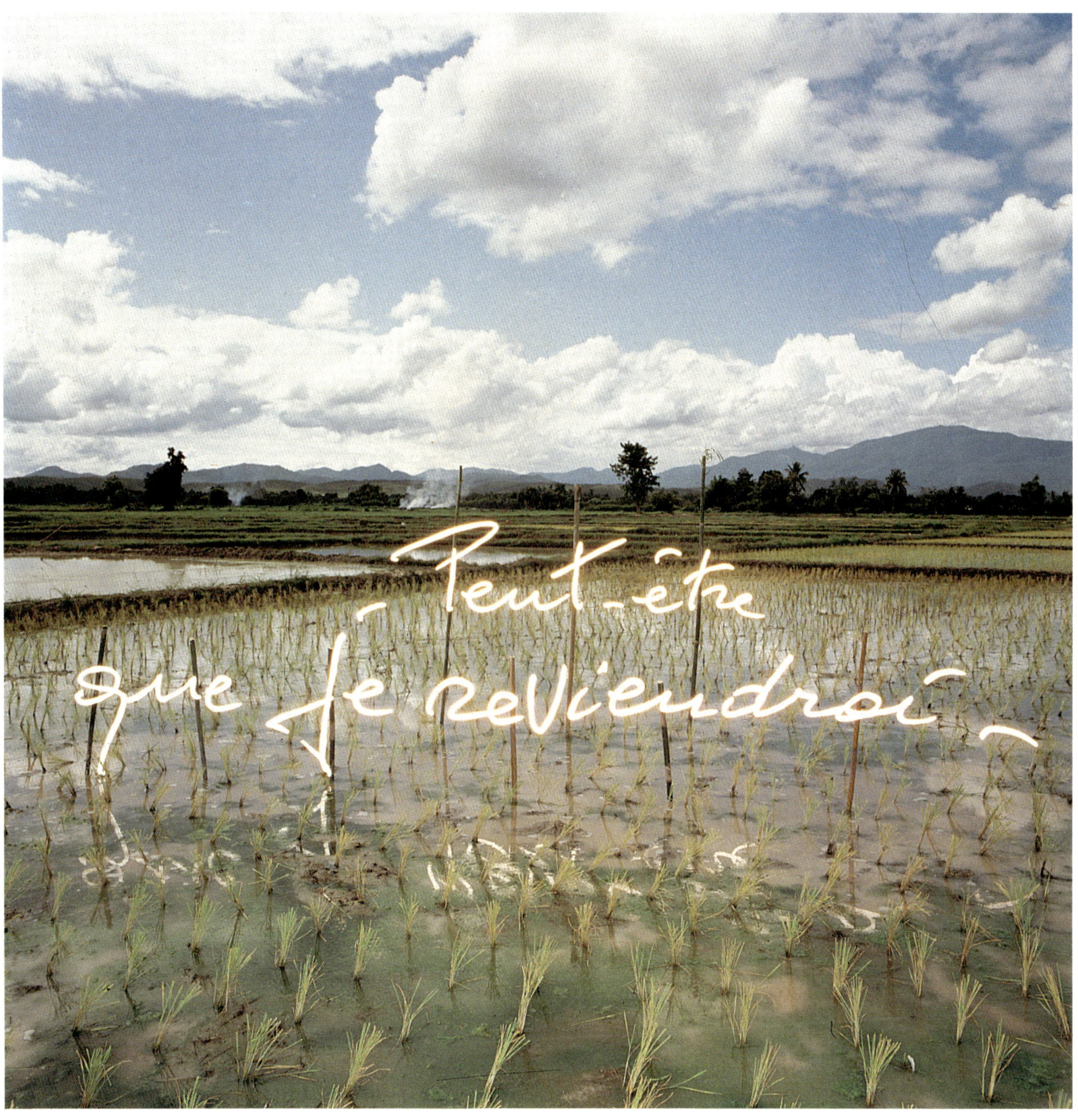

Bernard Faucon Peut-être que je reviendrai *colour print*

LENNART NILSSON *Sweden*

A Child is Born

Barrack Street Museum

BARRACK STREET, DUNDEE

UK PREMIERE

4 JUNE – 22 AUGUST

Subsidised by the
Scottish Arts Council

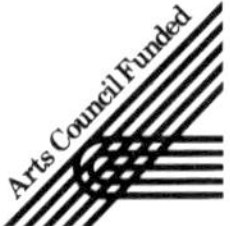

Exhibition organised by the Hasselblad Centre, Sweden. This showing in Dundee is supported by the Russell Trust.

Consult any of the standard anthologies of photography and you will find mention of Lennart Nilsson. His work covers half a century of Swedish photography. Born in 1922, Nilsson was a leading photojournalist long before he became famous as a scientific photographer. He remains a reporter with a camera, working, so to speak, in another dimension. Step by step he has closed in on the animal world and the human body. Special optics have been devised with 179 degree angle of view and extremely short focal lengths, (from 0.6mm to 4.0mm) that enable him to photograph the cavities of the human body with the necessary depth of field. Over the years, he has kept a balance between photographing the visible and researching the invisible. Using an advanced scanning electron microscope he has created enigmatically beautiful, yet frightening, photographs of the AIDS virus and the killer cells of the human body that do battle against these dangerous intruders. So far he has been able to photograph objects measuring as little as one millionth of a millimetre. Now, at the cutting edge of technology and using a new scanning tunnel microscope, he is studying 'the building blocks of life' – DNA molecules.

This exhibition is the story of human reproduction. Many people will remember Nilsson's image of the 'Star Child' floating above the earth at the end of Kubrick's film 2001. In a case of life imitating Art, in 1977, NASA's unmanned space craft Voyager I and Voyager II began their journeys towards Jupiter, Saturn and Uranus and on beyond our solar system into the infinity of space, carrying photographs from *A Child is Born*. A message from earth which may be read somewhere in space in a few million years...

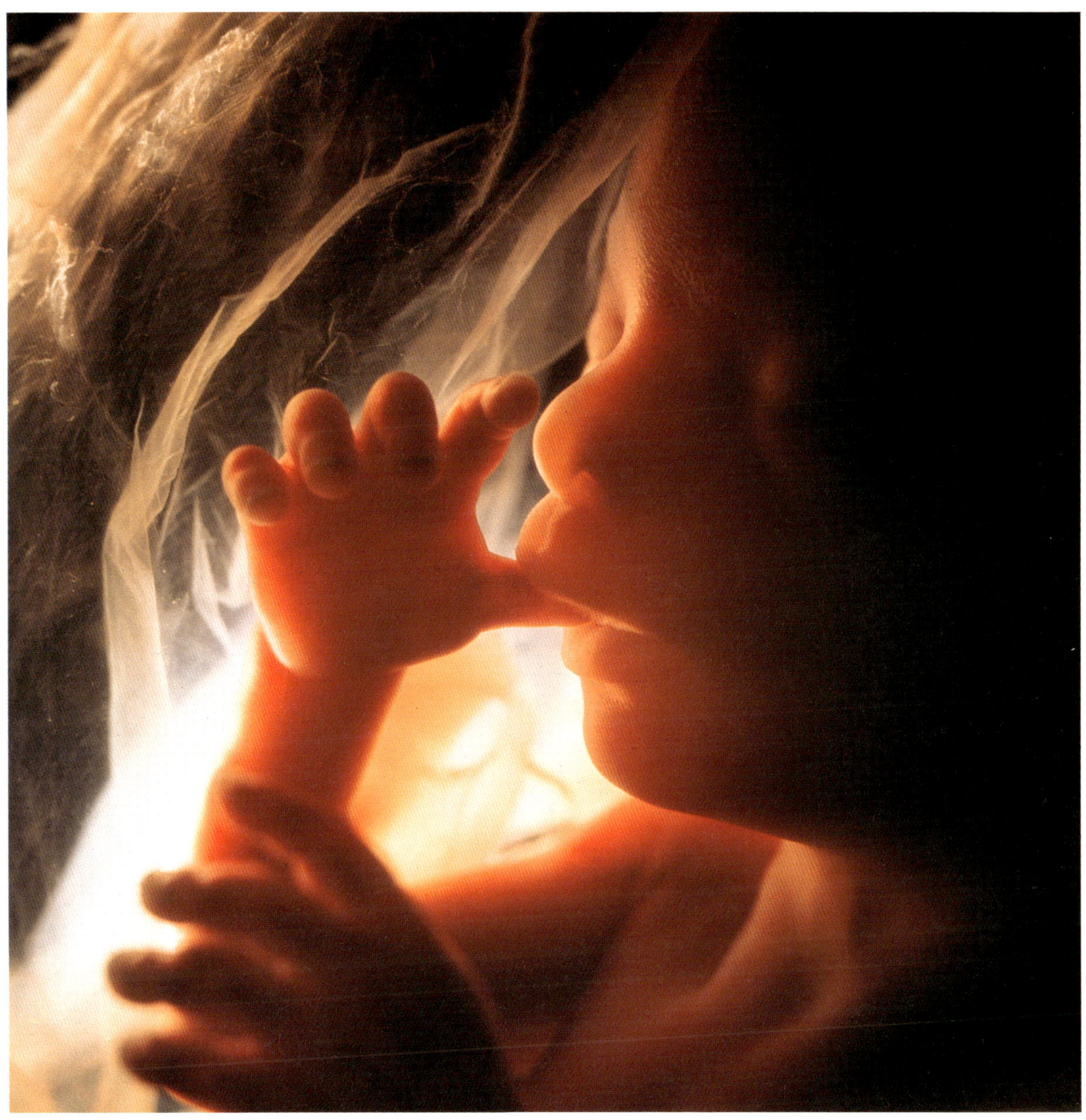

Lennart Nilsson A Child is Born: four and a half months *colour print*

KAIN KARAWAHN *Germany*

Fire Portraits

Peacock Artspace

21 CASTLE STREET
ABERDEEN

UK PREMIERE

4 JUNE – 4 JULY

"Surviving in a metropolis, day after day, means always setting yourself and others on fire. It means activating your physical and psychic energy-potential to the point of combustion. When I'm painting over my photographs with fire, I project these energies onto individual portraits. While I'm working, I consciously control the fire, its intensity, the direction of the flames, and for how long the image burns. What is left is a Fire Portrait."

For ten years, photographer, performance and video artist Kain Karawahn has been exploring the creative potential of that most elusive element – fire. His *Fire Portraits* hover tantalisingly between creative control and alchemical accident. Framed between glass and hanging in free space they are open to scrutiny. Their delicate filigree remains ambiguous – the meaning of the photographic image modified and partially obliterated by the precisely charred edges of the photographic paper. Emulsion bubbles, paper discolours and curls, before flaking away, black and insubstantial. They are imbued with all the enigmatic power of archaeological remains or forensic evidence – the remnant as artefact.

Subsidised by the
Scottish Arts Council

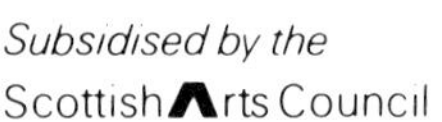

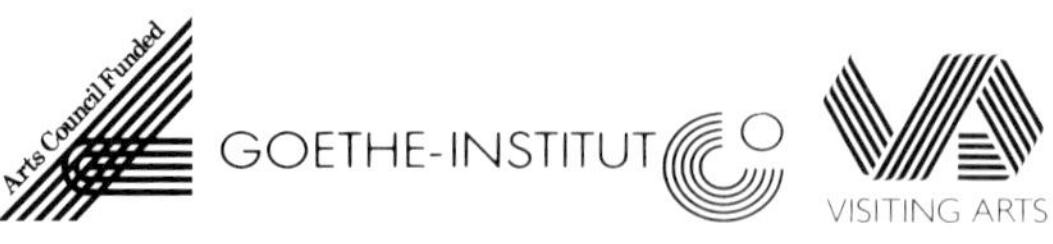

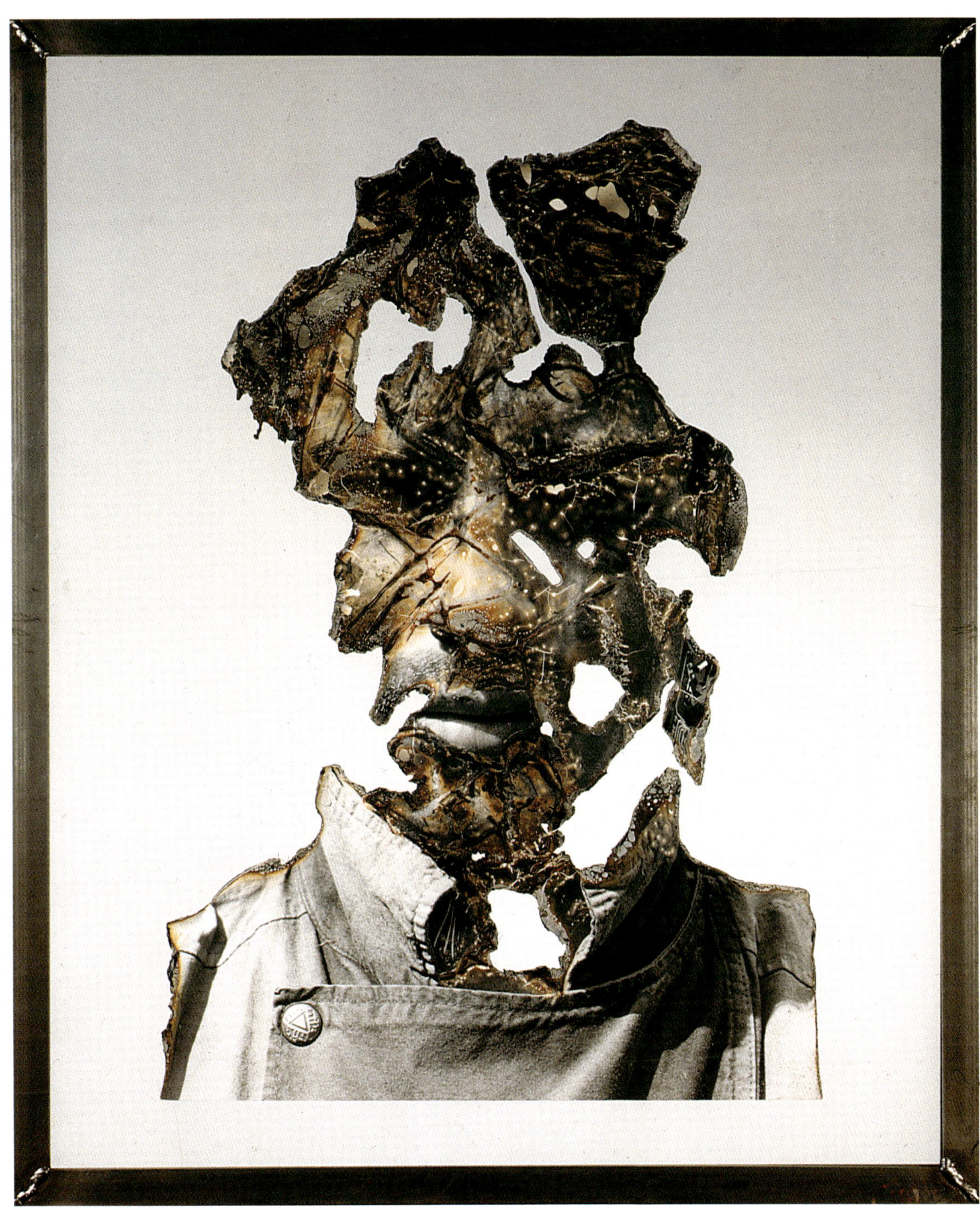

Kain Karawahn Fire Portrait *silver-gelatin print modified by flame*

STEWART WILSON UK
Burner

Peacock Artspace

21 CASTLE STREET
ABERDEEN

PREMIERE

4 JUNE – 4 JULY

Commissioned by Cambridge Darkroom and the Harris Museum and Art Gallery, Preston

Flicking TV channels we scan our world in flux. Images of war, satellite pictures of weather, minute insights into science and nature beamed simultaneously to receivers in millions of homes, each screen a fragment of world order.

Like the bricks of a furnace, 42 TVs stand in a concave pyramidal stack. Approaching the structure from behind we see the glow of flickering light in the mortar-like gaps between each set. The screens form a night sky – a technological culture dish where light and movement sustain a constant state of evolution.

Burner is a metaphor for political and ecological fragility. An automaton existing as a series of contradictions. Solid, monumental architecture displays ephemeral, mesmeric imagery itself embodying ambiguities of distance and proximity, gentleness and violence, growth and decay. Compiled and edited, phenomena refuse to conform to an overall picture.

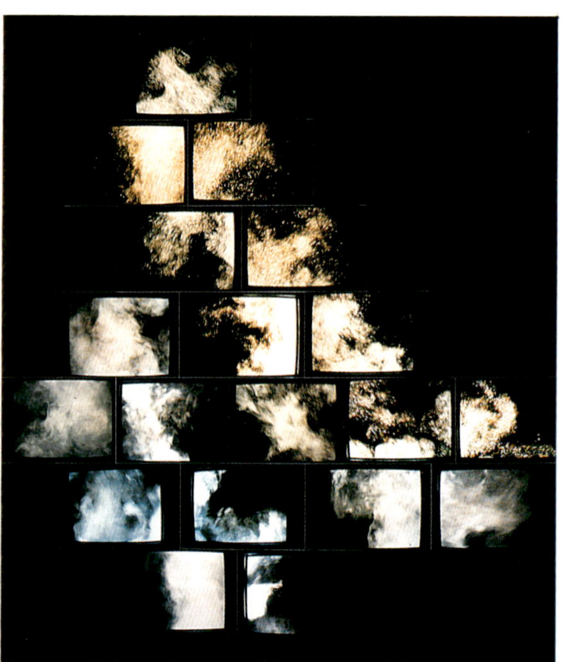

Subsidised by the
Scottish Arts Council

Stewart Wilson Burner *(detail) video installation*

JO BRUNENBERG *Netherlands*

Immagini Scoperte

Aberdeen Art Gallery

SCHOOLHILL, ABERDEEN

UK PREMIERE

29 MAY – 3 JULY

In these large photographic banners, Jo Brunenberg reaches back to the world of Leonardo da Vinci. Redrawn in light, Leonardo's scientific diagrams wrap themselves around the human body, at the same time augmenting and constraining its function and meaning. The drawings, both eloquent scientific notes and elegant artistic creations, give an apparent unity to the rational and the sensitive worlds. The body occupies a similarly ambiguous position, simultaneously a symbol of the generality of humankind and the specific site of sexual longing. Rational and emotional, cool and hot, freed and constraining – *Immagini Scoperte* (Discovered Images) presents a complex interplay of aspiration and desire.

Subsidised by the
Scottish Arts Council

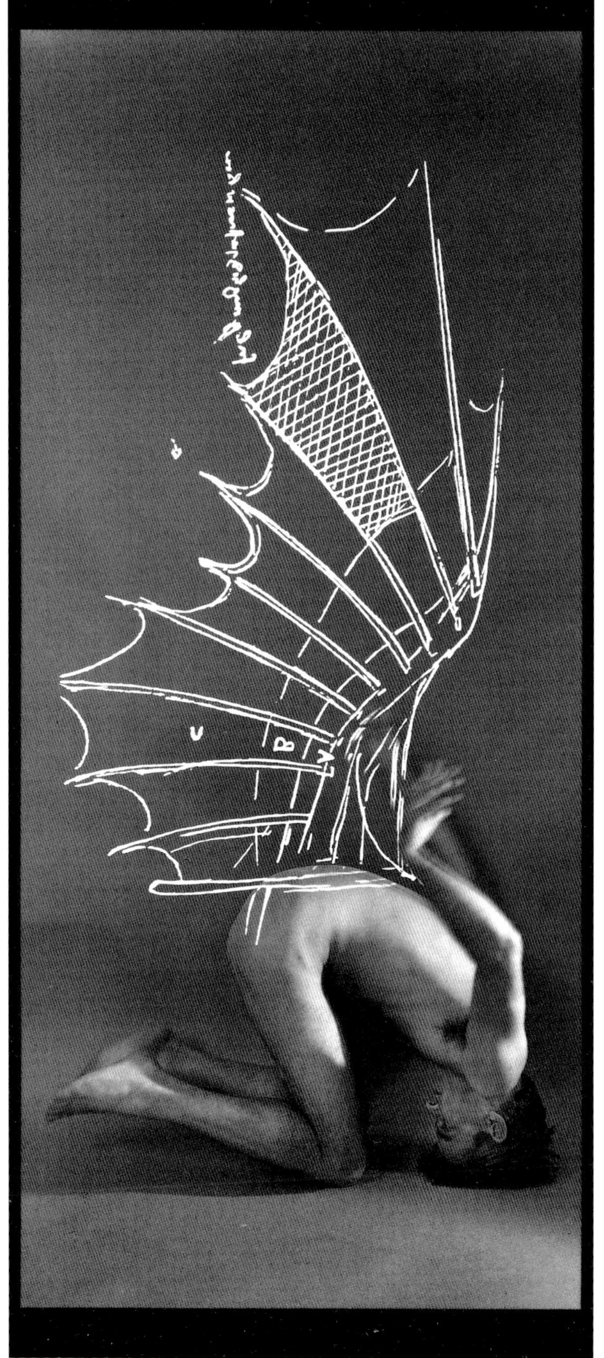

Jo Brunenberg Dell' ossatura di un' ala *ink on canvas*

JÜRGEN KLAUKE *Germany*

Sonntagsneurosen

Aberdeen Art Gallery

SCHOOLHILL, ABERDEEN

UK PREMIERE

29 MAY – 26 JUNE

For over a quarter of a century, Jürgen Klauke's oeuvre has been traversing and encompassing a bewilderingly wide-ranging repertoire of media – photography, video, performance-art, drawing and literature. Even so, his work continues to examine the same basic themes. At the centre of it all stands humankind, caught between life and death, lusts, desires and fears – longing for security yet also for isolation. In 1987, the fatalistic character of his work was summed up by the artist as follows: "Nowadays, looking out into the universe shows us that we are, more than ever, tiny arseholes incapable of enjoying a moment of self-recognition in the few seconds left to us."

The site at which his artistic activities crystallize has always been his own body. Despite this strict limitation to his own 'self', his precisely arranged configurations – dealing with androgynism and sexuality, depicting isolation, cruelty, and (unrequited) longing for fusion – are far removed from narcissism. The work steps outside the private domain through its provocative visual intensity and the formal precision with which it is executed.

The pictures themselves radiate coolness and detachment. The character in the works depicts his desperate moods and longings, his catastrophes and bouts of boredom with such clarity that the work appears to be that of a detached observer.

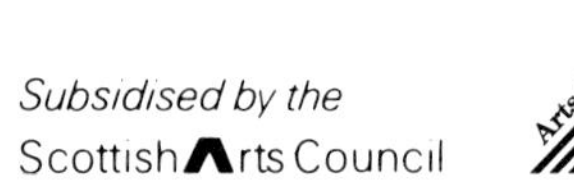

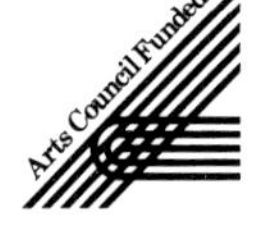

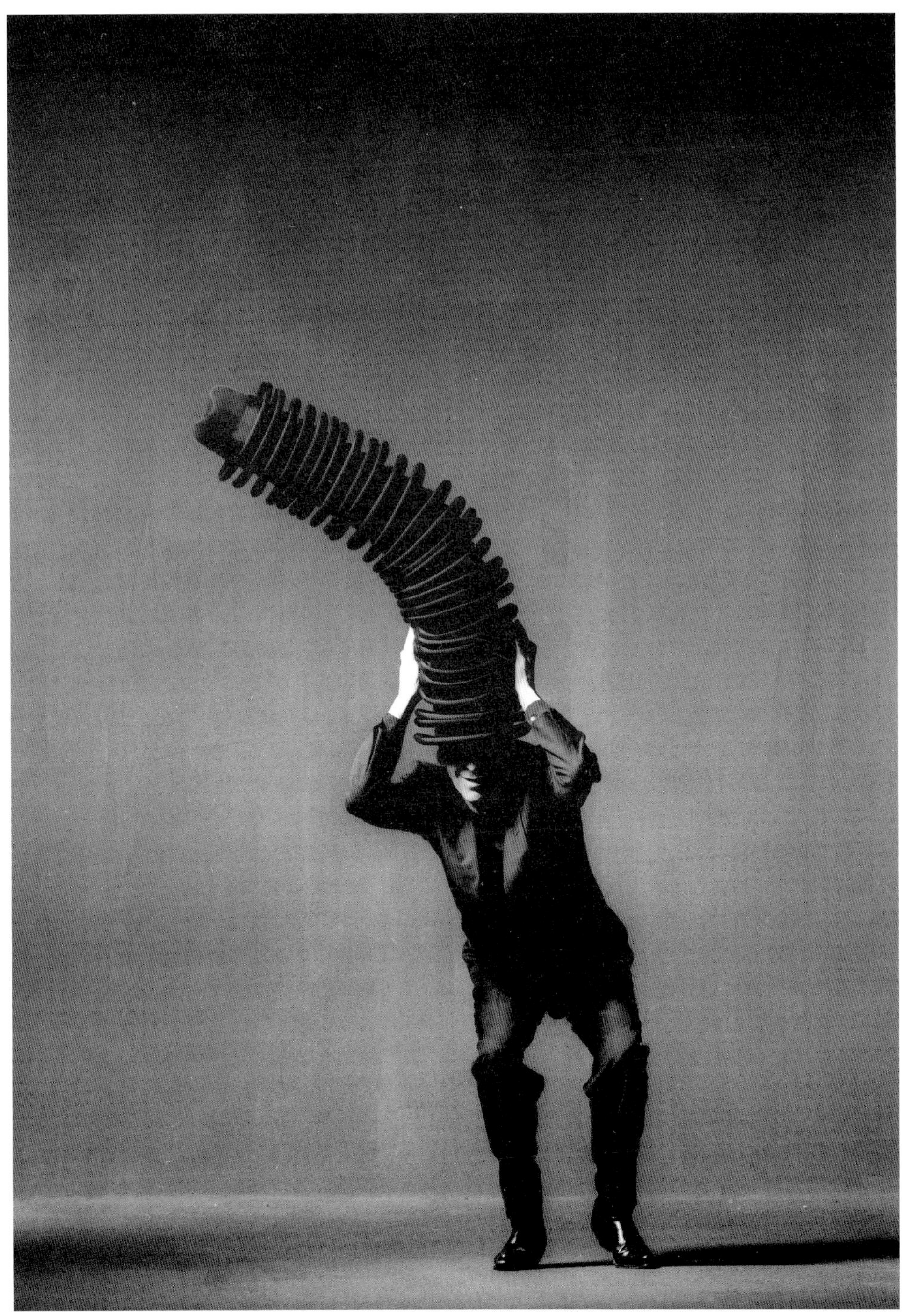

Jürgen Klauke Steigerungsphänomen *toned silver-gelatin print (original in blue)*

THIERRY GIRARD *France* and DELLA MATHESON UK

"X" – A Game of Words and Pictures

Aberdeen Art Gallery

SCHOOLHILL, ABERDEEN

PREMIERE

5 JUNE – 26 JUNE

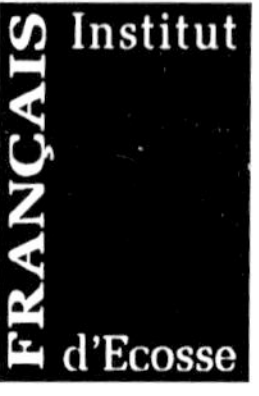

RULES OF THE GAME

The object of the game is to combine two modes of expression – photography and writing. Participants and viewers should be receptive to the spirit of game-playing and enigma.

The Game involves two photographers Della Matheson from Scotland and Thierry Girard from France, with eight writers: four from each country.

An exchange of one month's duration was organised for the two photographers, during which time they visited four writers in their working environment. The photographers' mission was to provide a 'file', or an ensemble of clues for each of the writers they met, without directly revealing their identities.

Each of the eight writers then received, at random, one of the files and was invited to write a short text, inspired by the photographs. Complete freedom has been left as to the form and content of the pieces.

At the heart of the Game is enigma. None of the writers knew beforehand the identity of the person s/he wrote about. The photographer is the Game Master, controlling just how much the writers should know and how much they must guess.

Finally, the eight portraits and texts have been gathered together to form this exhibition.

The show opens at the beginning of the Festival. For two weeks visitors will be invited to partake in the guessing game. At a special Fotofeis reception the identities of the writers will be revealed.

GAME ENDS

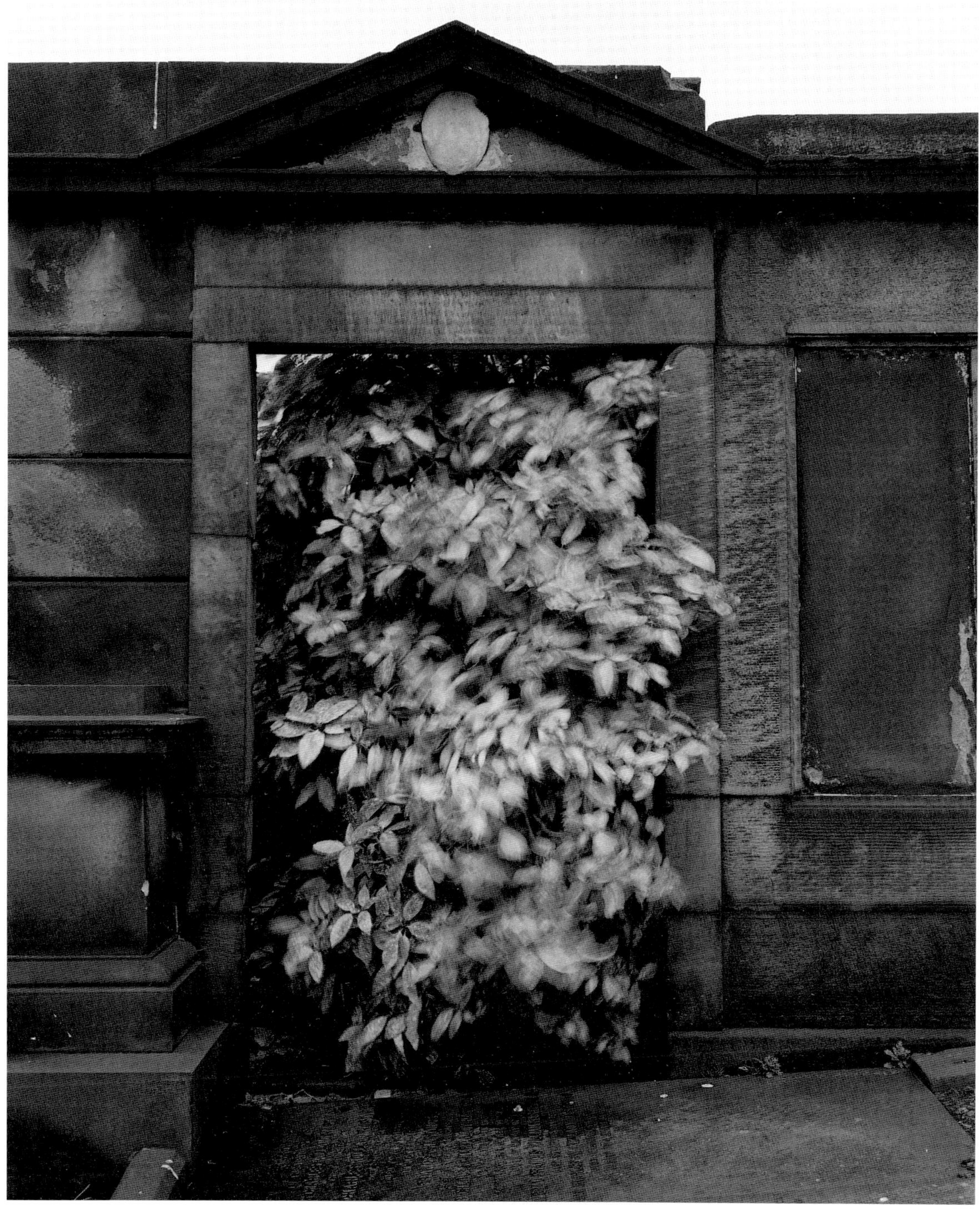

Thierry Girard *Untitled* *silver-gelatin print*

ULLA MARQUARDT *Germany*

Annäherung und Verlust (Approach and Loss)

Marischal Museum

MARISCHAL COLLEGE
BROAD STREET, ABERDEEN

UK PREMIERE

29 MAY – 3 JULY

I am more interested in undertaking a journey through the history of pictures and the representation of 'foreign parts' than in travelling to exotic lands and experiencing them as a tourist. The presentation of such visual material in our museums invites us to make such imaginary journeys. My work, *Approach and Loss*, is a critique of the representation of African cultures in European museums. It is a work on colonial depiction.

During my visits to museums of ethnography I photographed details found in showcases. Beneath all the exotic ballast in the thousands of photographs depicting African cultures, are often hidden a few, but very concise basic stereotypes: 'the destitute', 'the potent one' or 'the noble savage'. These form the outer panels of each triptych.

The middle panel examines what we have been influenced to think of as 'foreign'. Using a German actor, I staged scenes which have a resonance with the stereotypes found in ethnographic calibration. The human form is central in the triptychs, with the side panels showing only vague details in semi-darkness. The accompanying texts are fragments of contemporary African poetry.

Ulla Marquardt

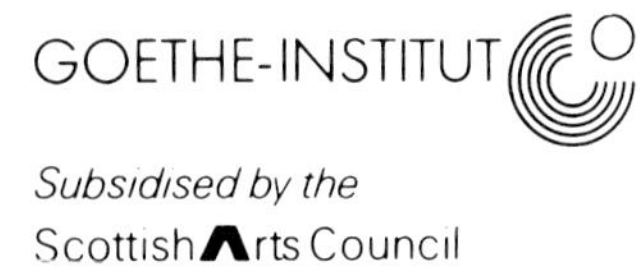

Subsidised by the
Scottish Arts Council

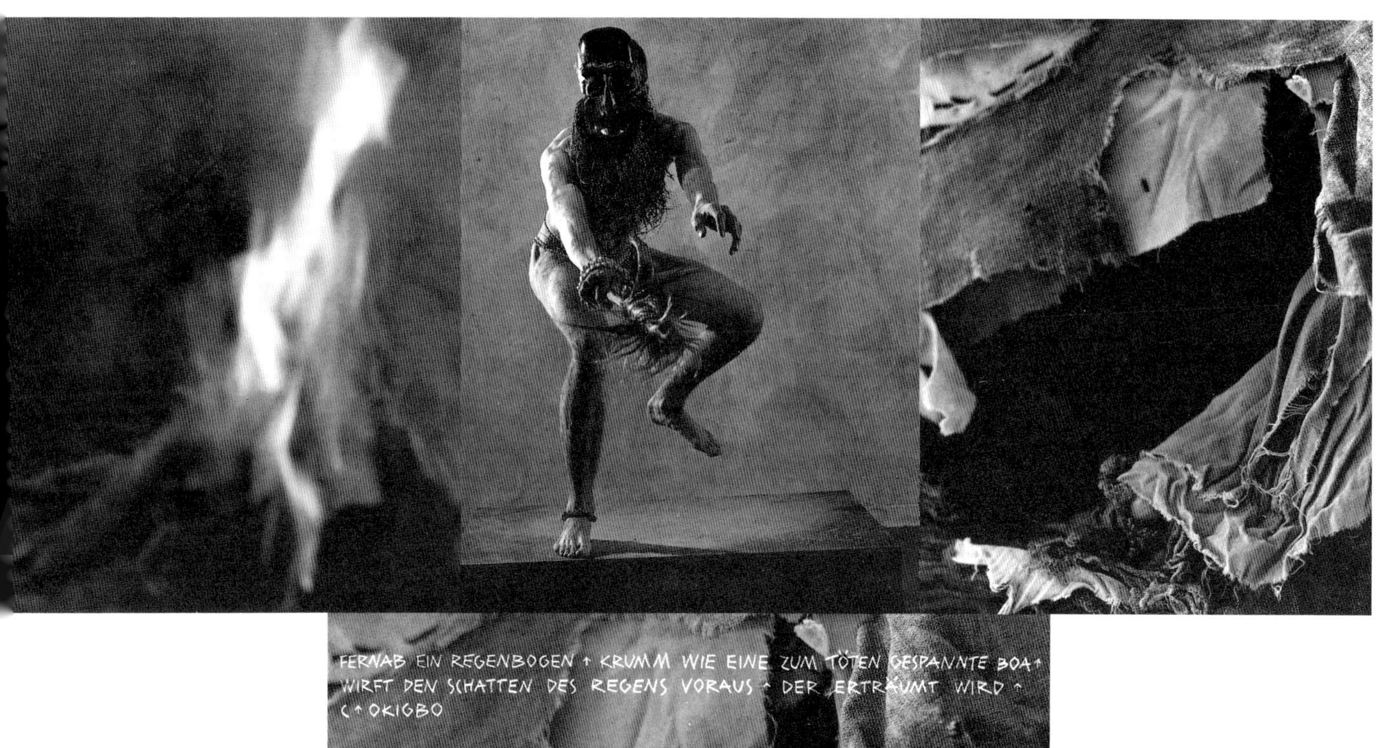

Ulla Marquardt Untitled *triptych silver-gelatin prints*

RALPH STEADMAN UK

Leaders: 'victims of fate'

Banners in Castle Street, Aberdeen

FOR WORK IN PROGRESS AT THE PEACOCK PRINTMAKERS GALLERY

JUNE – AUGUST

In this suite of screenprints I bow to the seemingly effortless colour wizardry of Arthur Watson, the Balzac of visual poetry, (in Scotland if not in Wales!), who has guided me towards a better version of what I might have had in mind. The series know as *Leaders* is the result of Polaroid inspired images I have collaged together to create a base from which to work, known to me and others of my acquaintance as *Paranoids* – a technique I developed and christened in the early eighties. They enable me to move quickly into a structured landscape where I can evoke a sense of the threat or power in colour and form. There is no other way I can produce them and the resulting screen prints achieve icons for which it seems the Polaroid camera was created. Assassins, Revolutionaries and Judges exercise a kind of power just as much as Kings, Queens, Presidents and Dictators and can therefore be regarded as Leaders. The only difference is how I choose to portray them, and that too is partly the result of the element of chance, covering my tracks behind me.
Ralph Steadman

These banners are part of an extensive printmaking project spanning ten months with Ralph Steadman. A major component in the project is an investigation of the fusion of photography and screenprinting and how both can be manipulated by the artist.

Initially the images are loosely collaged from a wide range of photographic source material, then photographed using Polaroid SX70. Whilst the emulsion is still soft it is distorted by the artist and drawing is thereby added. Half-plate line negatives are made in a wide range of exposures, and from them full size positives are enlarged. These positives are attacked with bleach, scraped away with blades and drawn on with ink before being exposed onto printing screens. The images are then proofed in mainly transparent colours. Ralph Steadman is closely involved with every stage of the process working in close collaboration with the printing team.
Arthur Watson, Director, Peacock Printmakers

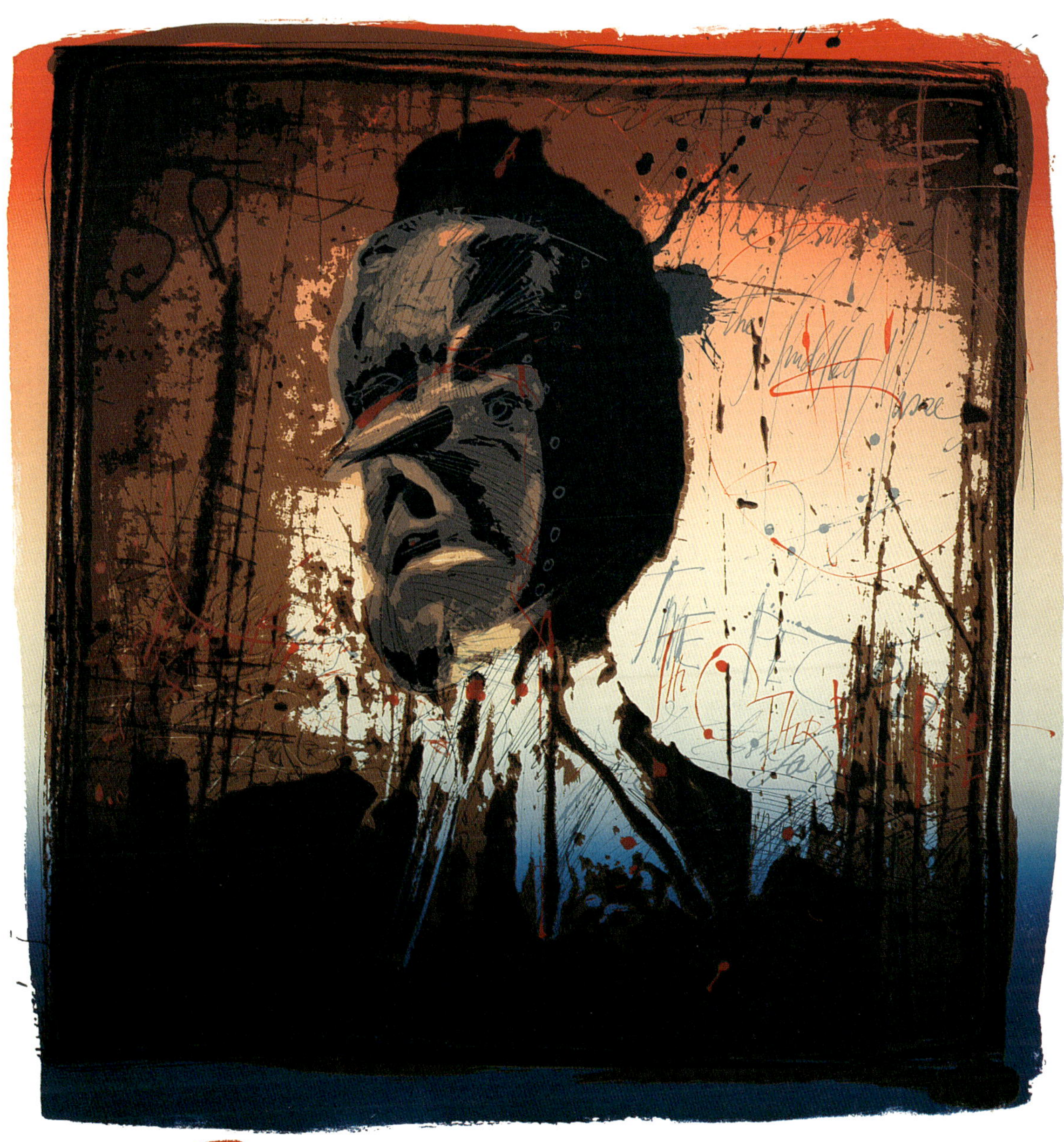

Ralph Steadman *President* 1993 *silkscreen print*

PIERRE RADISIC *Belgium*
Waldszene

Seagate Gallery

36–40 SEAGATE, DUNDEE

UK PREMIERE

29 MAY – 26 JUNE

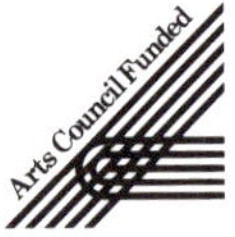

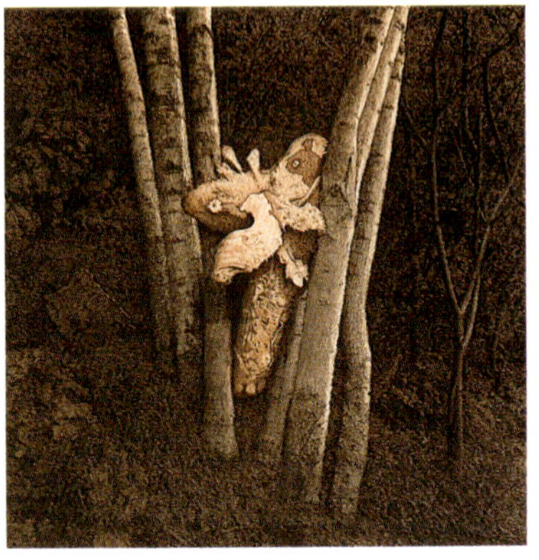

These pictures verge on the fantastic; they seem to emerge from the forest penumbra, from the darker side of nature, out of a sort of vegetational oblivion. This impression is strengthened by the curious atmospheric light and is marked by the total absence of shadow. The shapes, with their perfectly defined contours, produce double images so that, at times, the pictures seem to be collaged. The trees become totems, the roots monsters, and the vines are transformed into reptiles that coil about the trunks. Radisic's technical skill allows him to perform all the transformations of which only the final stage is revealed to our eyes:

"As for the picture, it is taken in the most unconventional way possible: through a translucent surface which splits the image optically... the paper is imprinted so that a very high density is obtained, almost black. Next [it] is chemically attenuated to the desired density and contrast. Then it is corroded in places, highlighting certain elements at the expense of others, which become muted to the point of merging with the organic matter."

Working from banal black and white photographs of the forest, like an alchemist, Radisic transforms reality by adding colour in the darkroom: Gold provides red and blue; Selenium produces mauve; Uranium brings out brick red; Antimony makes dark orange; Vanadium forms yellow. Sulphur causes brown to appear and other toners lighter blues.

Fascinatingly ambiguous though it is, Radisic's work remains eminently photographic. The alteration of the material on the photographic plate produces a modification in the perception of the image. Its connection with its source is disrupted in a controlled way whilst the actual structure of the picture remains unaltered. Radisic never adds anything, his purpose as a wizard of the black box is simply to reveal and develop.
from a text by Bernard Marcelis

Pierre Radisic Untitled *modified silver-gelatin print*

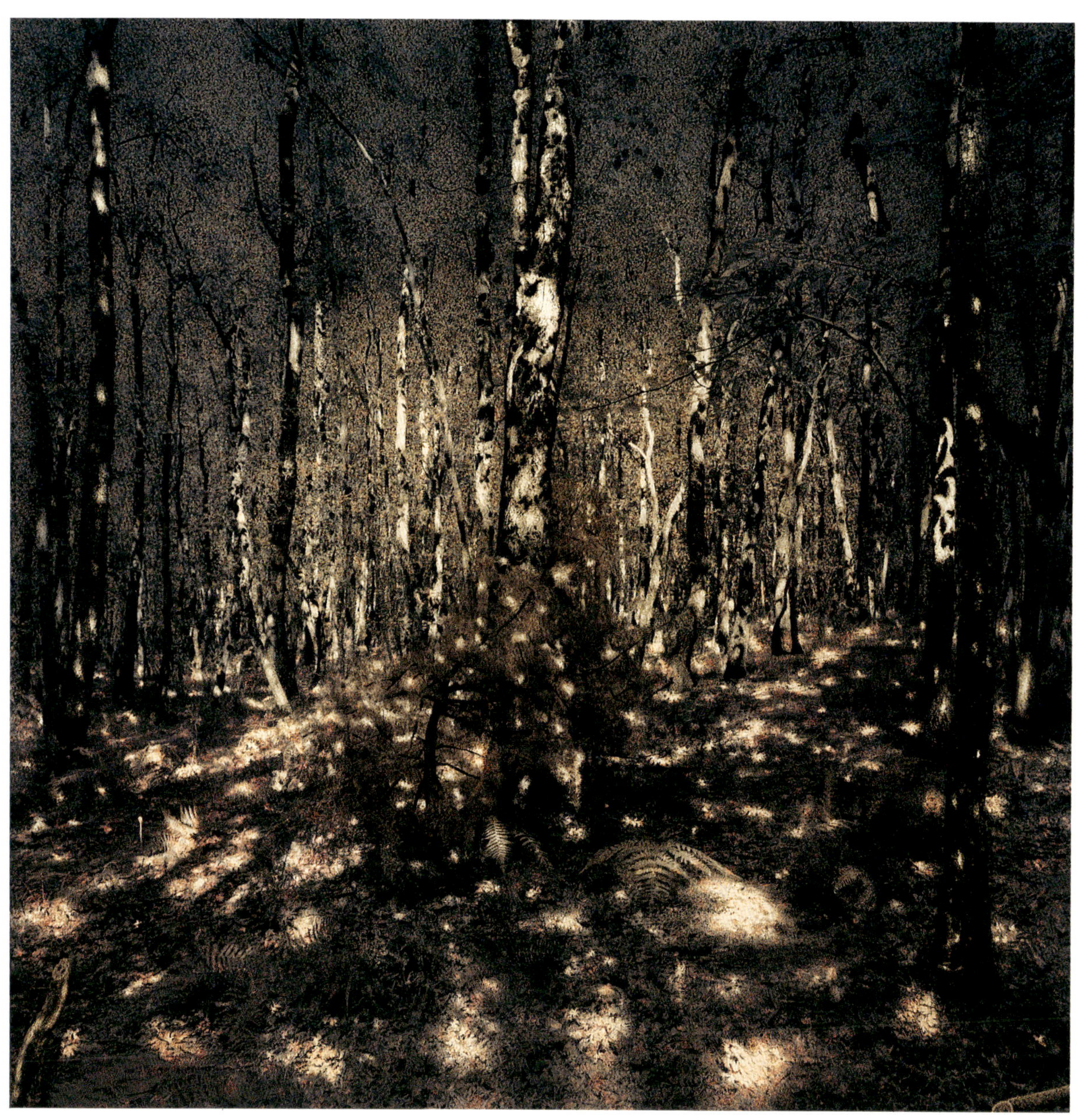

Pierre Radisic Untitled *modified silver-gelatin print*

WOJCIECH PRAZMOWSKI *Poland*

The War Machines

James Dun's House

SCHOOLHILL, ABERDEEN

UK PREMIERE

22 MAY – 24 JULY

Subsidised by the
Scottish Arts Council

The War Machines form part of the collection of The Centre Regional de la Photographie Nord Pas-de-Calais, France

It was in 1987 in Poland – the walls still existed – that I came across Wojciech Prazmowski. He showed me *Family Album*, an intriguing work that investigated the identity of the Polish nation and that of a Polish family through means which questioned what is specific to the photographic medium – the passage of time, the relationship to death.

When I showed these images in 1988, Prazmowski came to France for the exhibition. His visit inspired him to create new work and he became interested in the Monument to the Dead of World War I in Douchy. Having taken the photographs, the gestation of the project and elaboration of the final work took a long time – about three years. The Gulf War inspired an acceleration and focusing of the artist's thinking, and *The War Machines*, notable for their ambiguous playfulness, were born. The wheels of the works are a reference to the toys found in ancient tombs, yet inscribed on them is the martyrologue of war: the enormous lists of names squeezed into tight archive bundles. The pieces also evoke a leaden concentration camp universe. They were produced during a period when the media spoke much of 'clinical warfare' and images of war were replaced, on what Paul Virilio calls the Fourth Front, by video war games. *Pierre Devin*

GORDON STEWART UK

James Dun's House

SCHOOLHILL, ABERDEEN

22 MAY – 24 JULY

Subsidised by the
Scottish Arts Council

My current work is almost exclusively made in anodised aluminium. The brooches use old family photographs as source material. I started to look at these images after the death of my father in 1988. By transferring them from paper to metal they changed and took on a sombre quality. Related to 17th-century painted portraits, in a way, these pieces are contemporary mourning jewellery.
Gordon Stewart

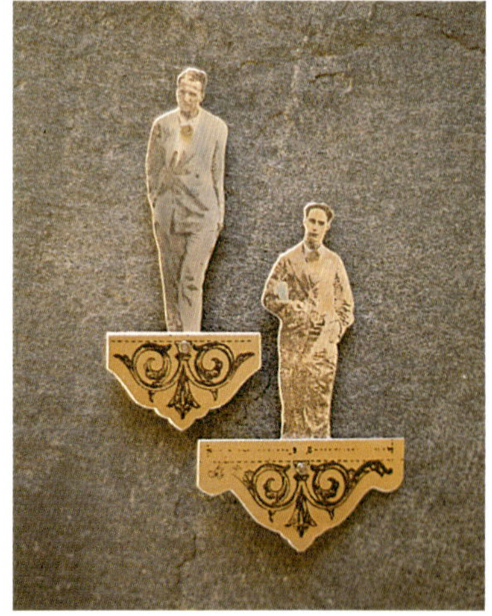

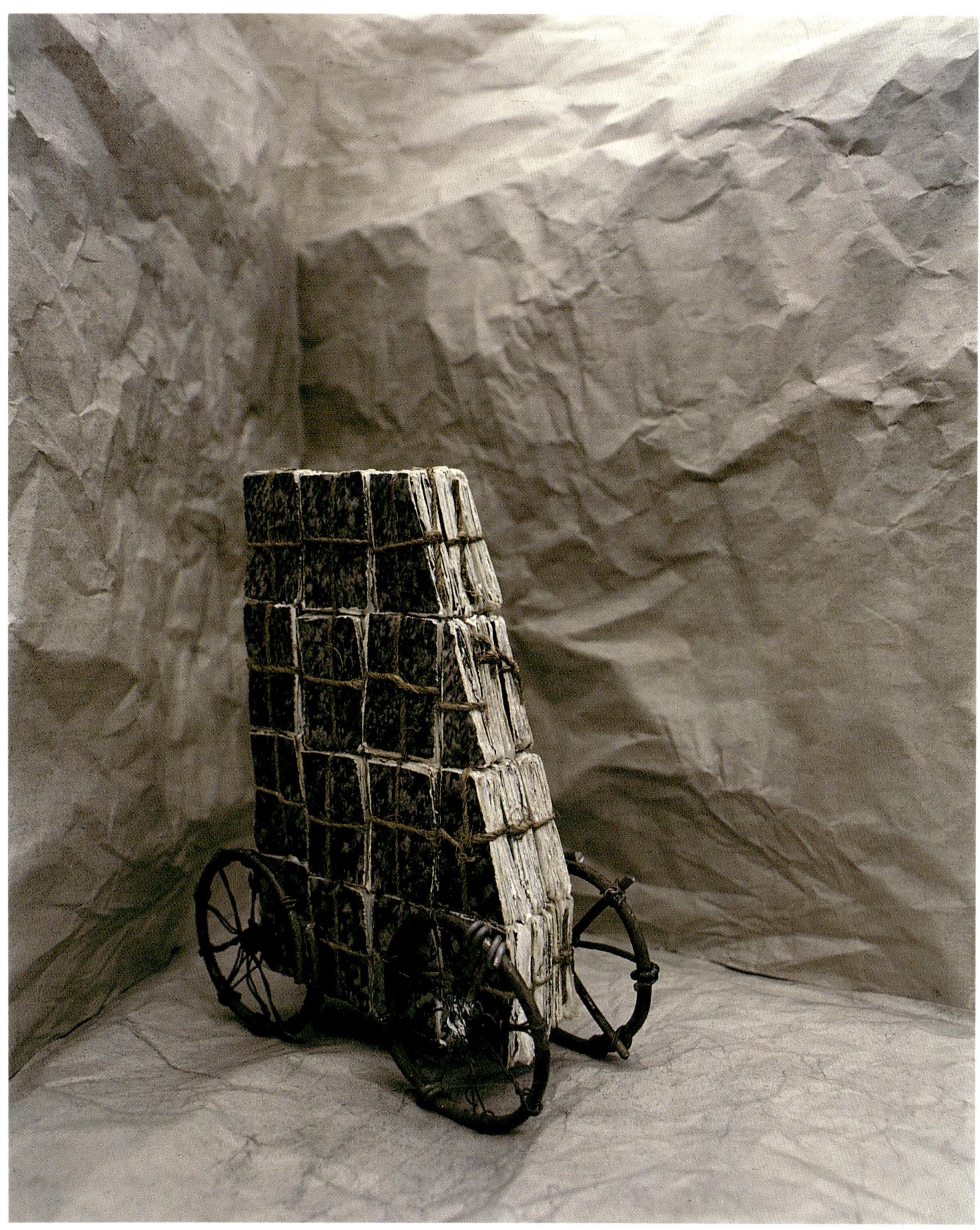

Wojciech Prazmowski Carriage of War *photo-sculpture*

KEN REYNOLDS UK
Secret Landscapes

McManus Galleries

ALBERT SQUARE, DUNDEE

29 MAY – 27 JUNE

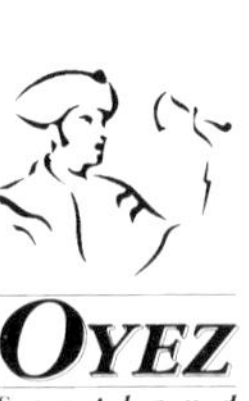

"From the beginning I was concerned with colour and texture. My work is a celebration of my wanderings over waste places searching for markings that result from elemental forces, for form and beauty where, at first sight, everything appears nondescript and desolate. It is the portrayal of secret landscapes, photographed as discovered, without manipulation either of the original material or of the photographic process. Between the eye of the photographer and the eye of the beholder an altered state occurs, the beholder being unaware of the original context. However, the photographs remain a precise record of what was found."

Ken Reynolds was born in Swansea, Wales in 1938. His early love of music, art and literature has been combined, through travel, with a fascination for the ever-changing nature of landscape, both urban and rural, and with those visual aspects that create a sense of time and place. His work is greatly influenced by where he has lived: the challenge of the ocean's moods during his childhood by the sea; the contrast between many hours of peaceful tranquillity in London's Richmond Park and the excitement, rush and debris of the city during his adolescent years; the variety of visual and psychological experience offered first by Glasgow and then Teheran. Now, coming full circle, he once more lives by the sea in North Queensferry, near Edinburgh, drawing on the richness of his experience to produce images of the everyday which transcend their own banality and take on the lush energy of abstract expressionist paintings.

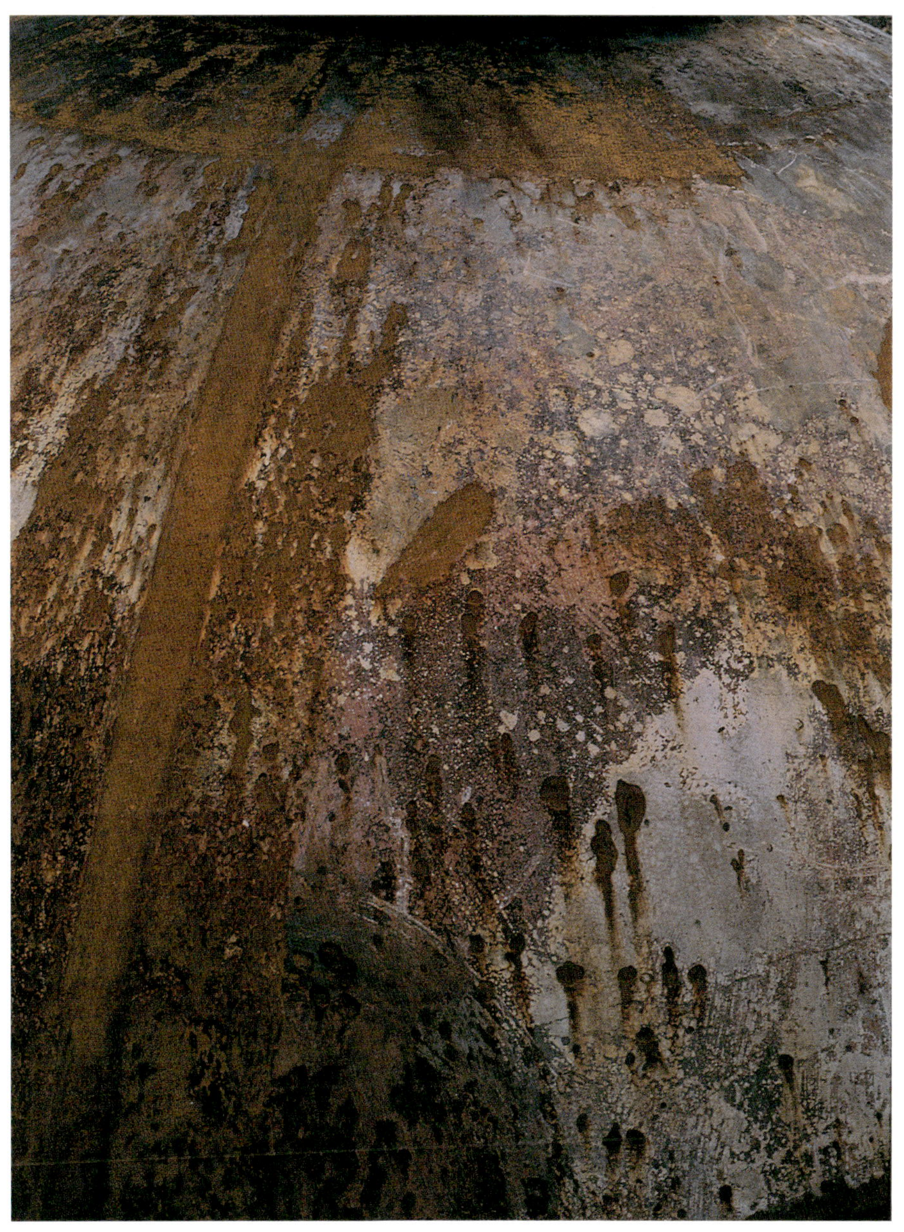

Ken Reynolds Secret Landscape XLVII: Inverkeithing, Scotland *cibachrome print*

IAN GREEN USA
Questions of Faith

Aberdeen Art Gallery

SCHOOLHILL, ABERDEEN

EUROPEAN PREMIERE

29 MAY – 3 JULY

The question of individual choice in contemporary society can be confusing and frustrating. The media tell us in no uncertain terms how to dress, what to eat and where to buy. Now, religious institutions are utilizing the same channels in order to boost their congregations.

The advent of religious advertising, with churches competing for market share, leaves those wishing to cultivate a more spiritual life in dismay. To complicate matters, many in today's society find it difficult to reconcile traditional religious practices with the demands of modern life.

My work addresses this dilemma. It questions traditional establishment religion in an attempt to discover where I fit in. What role do I play? And, at the second coming, 'What shall I wear?'.

Subsidised by the
Scottish Arts Council

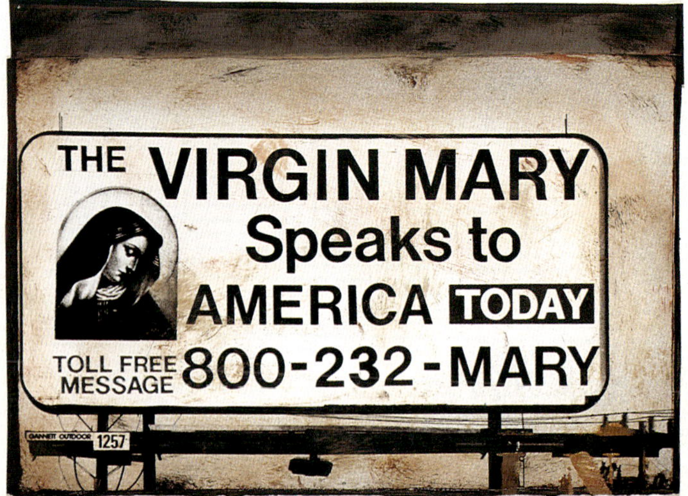

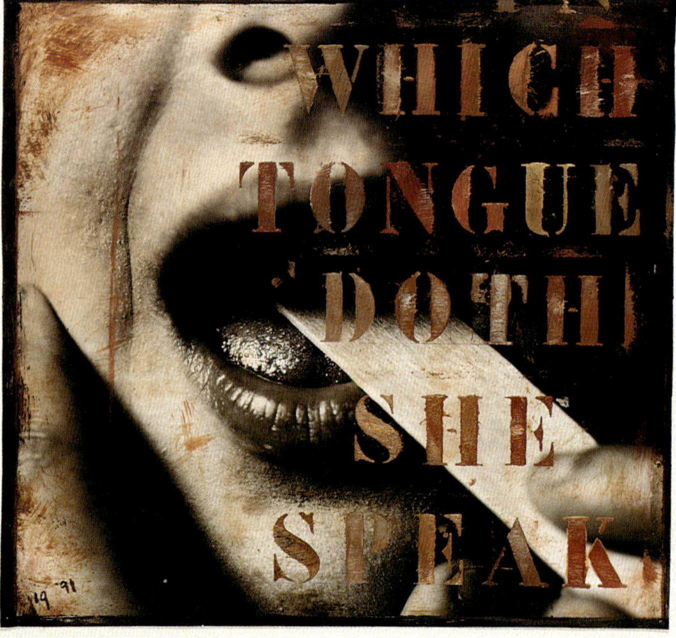

Ian Green In Which Tongue Doth She Speak? *colour photograph and paint*

ROY B. ROBERTSON UK

Productions

Dundee Rep Theatre

TAY SQUARE, DUNDEE

PREMIERE

8 JUNE – 26 JUNE

Productions explores the life of Dundee Repertory Theatre and the work of the Community Drama Department, the Community Dance Team and the Dundee Repertory Dance Company.

Presented within the theatre itself, this imaginatively staged exhibition examines the preparations which go into mounting a production and the work of the Dance and Drama teams with the wider community of Dundee.

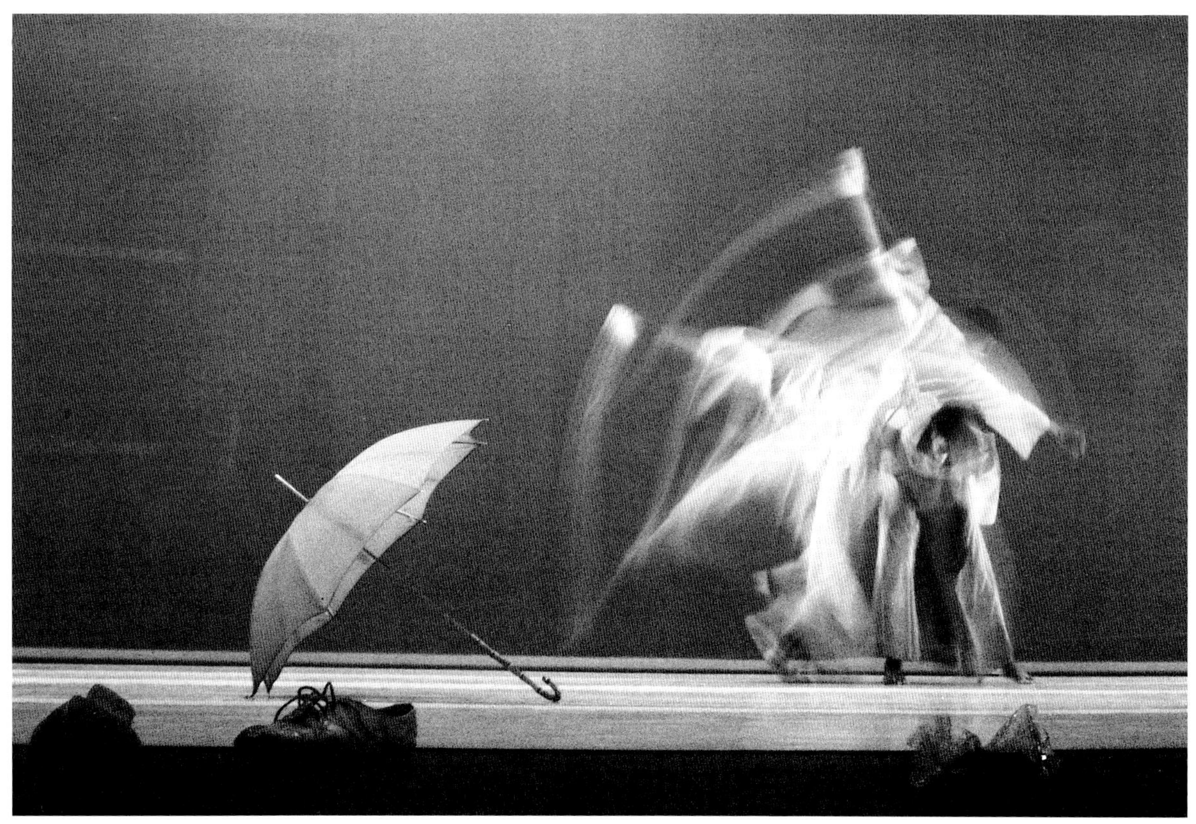

Roy B Robertson Untitled *silver-gelatin print*

SEBASTIAN HOLZHUBER *Austria*

Prophets

Aberdeen Art Gallery

SCHOOLHILL, ABERDEEN

UK PREMIERE

29 MAY – 3 JULY

Subsidised by the
Scottish Arts Council

The contrast of vulnerability and strength fascinates me. The space between them contains an energy that makes it possible to delve more deeply into the subtle layers of existence. The ambivalence of being touched – between the polarities of violence and lust – is a theme and undercurrent to my work. I am searching for rituals to overcome the numbness of society.

All human societies have seers and prophets. They are at the roots of cultures and many have had a profound influence on the course of history. Within the essence of humanity lies the potential for prophecy. Those with the sensitivity to hear the 'inner voice' are more receptive to such visions.

Prophets is a series of overpainted photographs made between 1990 and 1993. The men and women who participated in this project are friends of mine. Together, we developed a simple physical gesture which in some way connects to their 'inner path'. The works were named by Folie le Noble, a young Nigerian from the Joruba tribe, who recognized in these images archetypes from his own culture.

Sebastian Holzhuber

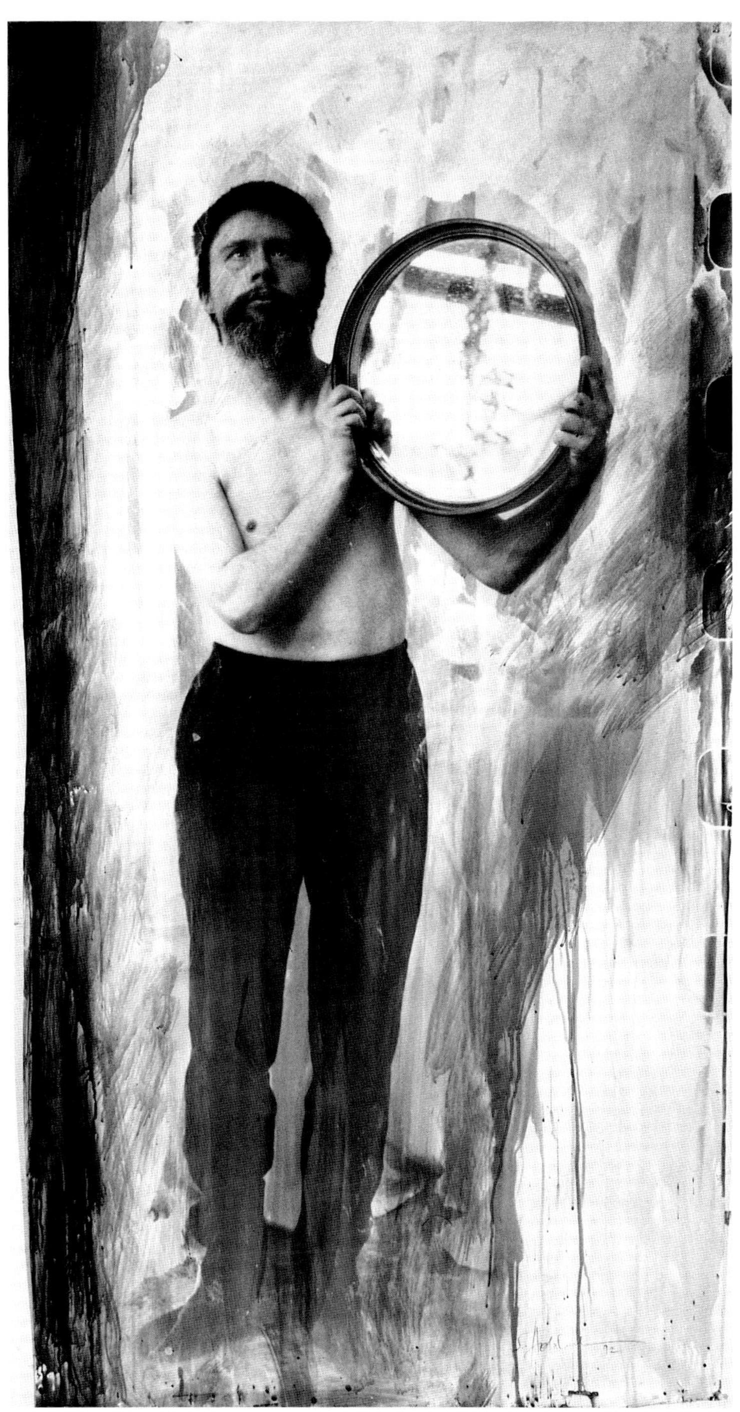

Sebastian Holzhuber Olorun Mimo *silver-gelatin print with overpainting*

DUNCAN HIGGINS UK
Leum-Uisge 1746-1993

Aberdeen Art Gallery

SCHOOLHILL, ABERDEEN

PREMIERE

5 JUNE – 3 JULY

Subsidised by the
Scottish Arts Council

The elements making up this exhibition are part of an on-going attempt to embrace a complex set of personal, cultural and historical ideas. To make visible these ideas, the pieces combine a wide range of pictorial methods, texts and materials, reflecting many layers of reality and experience.

The work involves specific locations in Scotland and uses the photograph as the record of a resemblance, as a tracing of light taken from the real. The application and understanding of the photograph in a cultural context in turn requires us to question our notions of reality and experience. Through the use of these layers of information, recording, re-inventing, translating, I seek not only to celebrate the unique features of the landscape but to address the question of our identity in relation to that landscape.

MARK JOHNSTON UK
Mother of Invention

Aberdeen Art Gallery

SCHOOLHILL, ABERDEEN AND ALFORD HERITAGE CENTRE, ALFORD

PREMIERE

5 JUNE – 3 JULY

Mark Johnston would like to acknowledge the generous support and advice of: The City of Aberdeen Arts and Recreation Division; The Gordon District Department of Leisure and Recreation; The Scottish Arts Council; The Gordon District Department of Planning and Economic Development; Grampian Initiative

The inspiration for this exhibition is the recumbent stone circles found almost exclusively in the area between the Grampian mountains in the west and the North Sea. Between eighty and one hundred examples still remain in various states of preservation.

In common with many other sites in the British Isles, these prehistoric circles remain enigmatic yet trapped in contemporary culture, laden with mystic and romantic clichés.

This project attempts to avoid the clichés, and provide a perspective and context for these monuments. Whilst stone circles or standing stones may well have a social, scientific or religious function, the strategy used here is to treat them as works of art. This then introduces the issue of representation. So much of the earliest art is enigmatic to us now that comparison with other ancient cultures is of interest.

The exhibition is split between two venues; Aberdeen Art Gallery, where the work is entirely visual and a rural site in Gordon District, an area rich in stone circles. Here the artworks are combined with contributions from researchers into subjects related to recumbent stone circles.

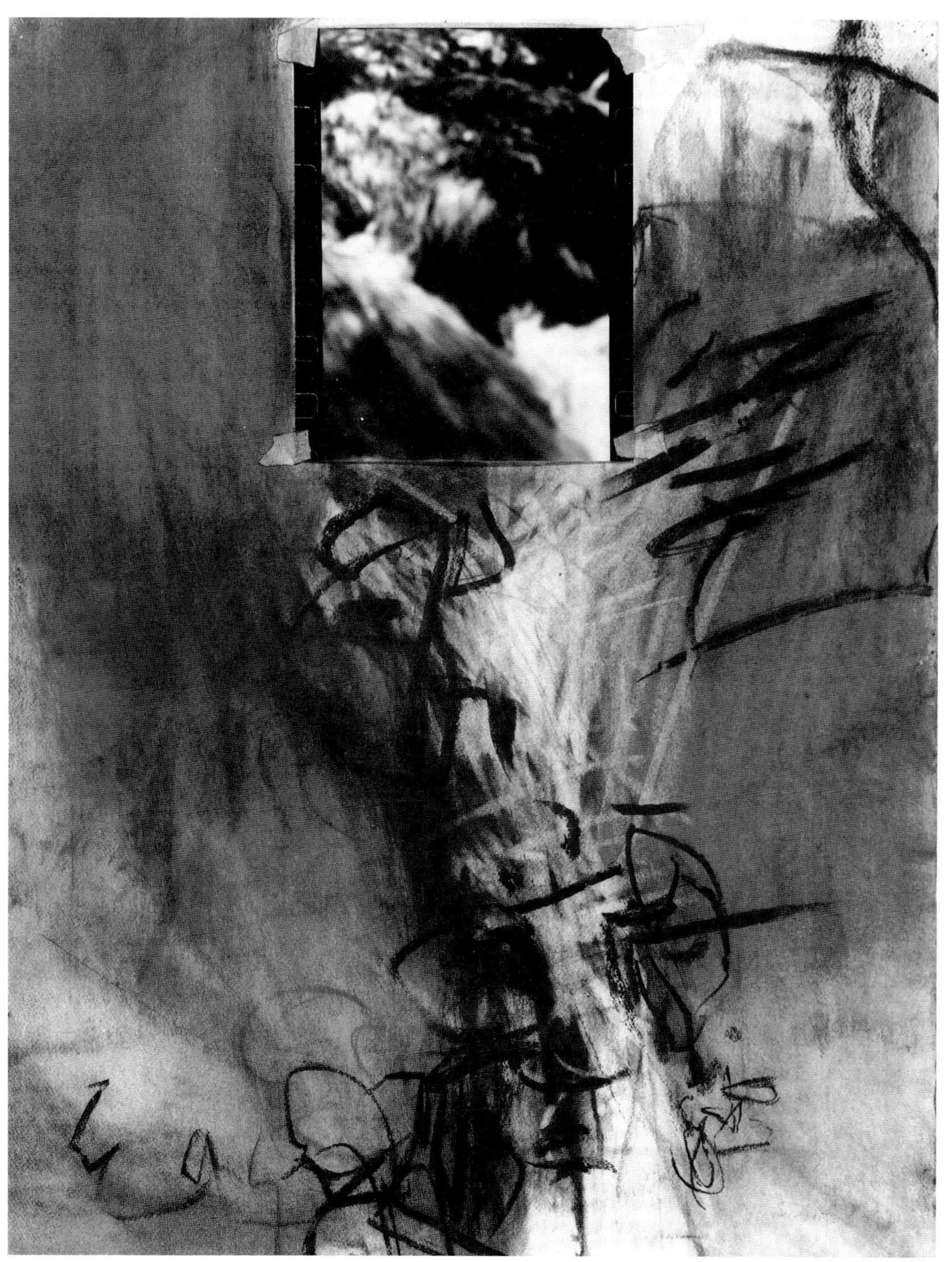

Duncan Higgins Leum-Uisge *photograph, charcoal, paper and text*

MIKE ROLES and DAVID MICHAEL CLARKE UK
Photo Sculptures

Aberdeen Art Gallery

SCHOOLHILL, ABERDEEN

PREMIERE

5 JUNE – 3 JULY

In the work of Mike Roles, the authority of the photographic image, the use of real objects and three dimensional construction are combined to explore the theme of male sexuality. The work has a strong narrative content. The viewer is placed in the active role of participant; there is both physical involvement and a requirement to consider the implied meaning of these life-sized, many faceted, photographic structures as, pace by pace, the viewer moves around the sculpture. Images are revealed or obscured, ambiguities manifested and relationships developed, building a cumulative story.

For David Michael Clarke the combination of photography and sculpture is the visual equivalent of a philosophical deconstruction with both mediums having similarly ambiguous relationships with representation:

"I have become fascinated by the fact that no matter what you do to a photograph, it still retains its 'trace' of reality. In that sense photography is similar to casting, but for some reason we trust it more."

The work Clarke is creating for Fotofeis is a specific response to Aberdeen, the Art Gallery, and what he has found there. The granite used for these new sculptures reflects the columns within the gallery and the subject matter refers to work from the art gallery's permanent collection.

Subsidised by the
Scottish Arts Council

David Michael Clarke wishes to acknowledge the help of David Cowling, The Scottish Sculpture Workshop and John Fyfe Ltd.

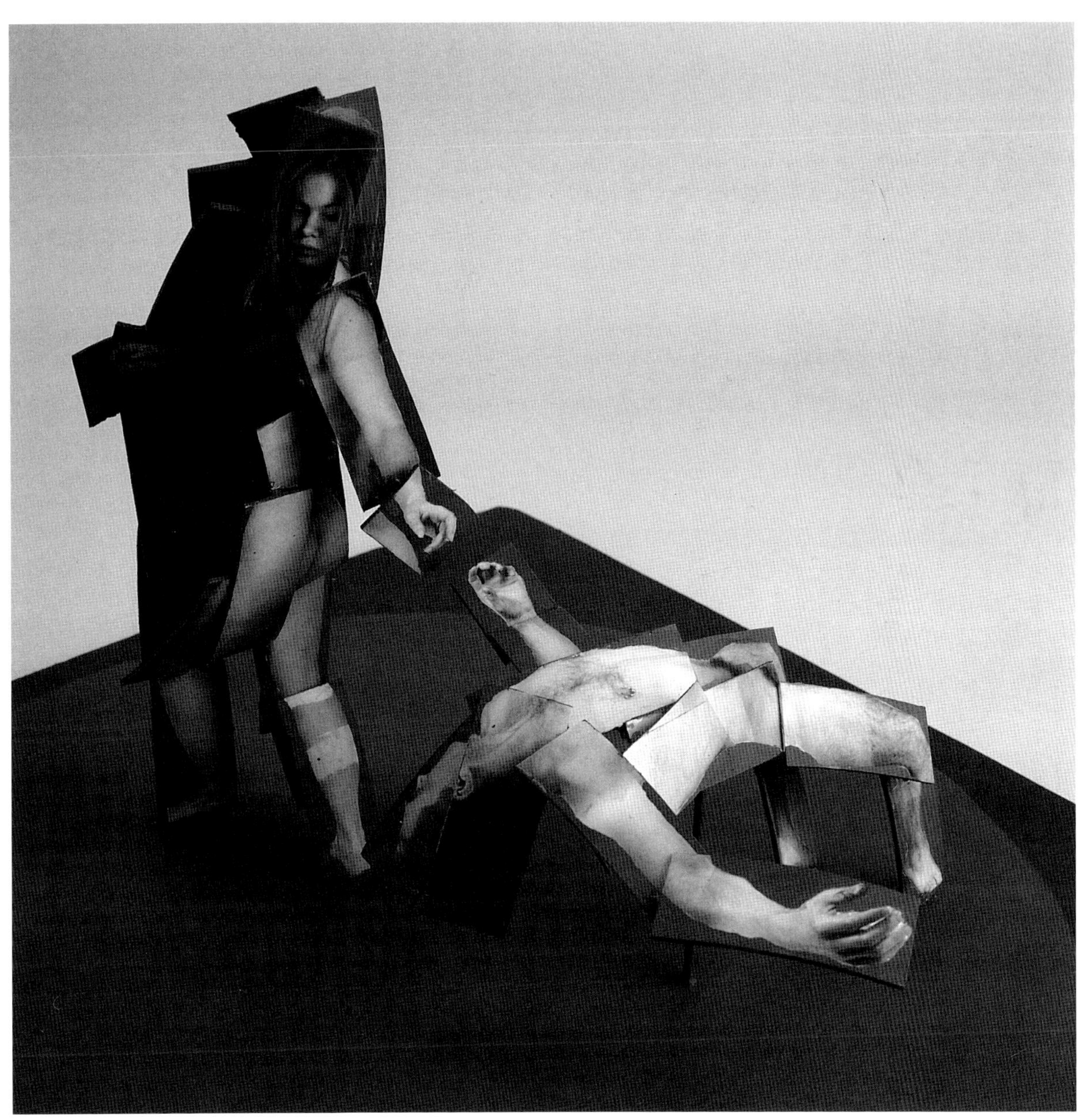

Mike Roles Maquette for Photo-sculpture

MOSES TAN *Australia*

Moments of Vision

Aberdeen Art Gallery

SCHOOLHILL, ABERDEEN

EUROPEAN PREMIERE

2 JUNE – 31 JULY

Subsidised by the
Scottish Arts Council

The real challenge for me is in the bringing together of two seemingly irreconcilable aesthetics. The Haiku, simple but eloquent, is like a mantra inviting meditation. The Australian landscape, on the other hand, is harsh and unyielding and lacks the vernal qualities of a more temperate climate which is so conducive to quiet poetic contemplation. I have not sought to illustrate the poems, but rather to photograph in the same spirit as that which inspired the haiku poets.
Moses Tan

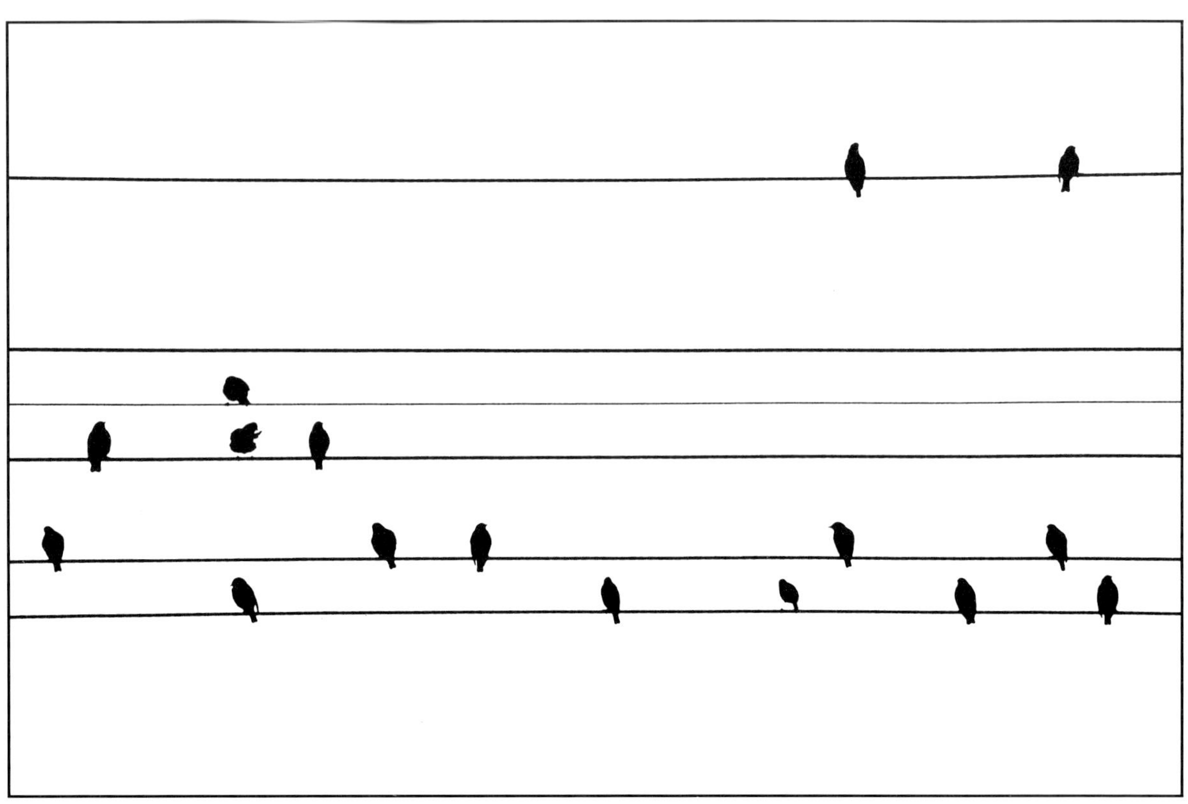

 Moses Tan Untitled *(original in colour)*

JOANNA REDMAN UK

In and Out the Windows

Arbuthnot Museum

ST. PETER STREET
PETERHEAD

PREMIERE

14 JUNE – 4 JULY

Sponsored by
Shell UK Exploration
and Production

This exhibition contains a wealth of playful ideas on photography. The framed colour photographs resemble film stills with characters seemingly captured at a dramatic point in a story. Colour, light and tone are exaggerated to heighten the sense of fiction.

A lightbox contains a series of photographs, which are animated by a sequenced light. The work refers to a children's rhyme, accompanied by a dance, and grew from the artist's leaving Shetland and returning again some time later to experience the island afresh.

A blue perspex book on a shelf, with the sign 'Do Not Touch' is displayed together with photographs of hands and parts of faces caught unexpectedly as people pick up the book. The work contains a hidden camera to document visitors touching the object. These photographs are then included in the work in the hope that viewers will return to see themselves.

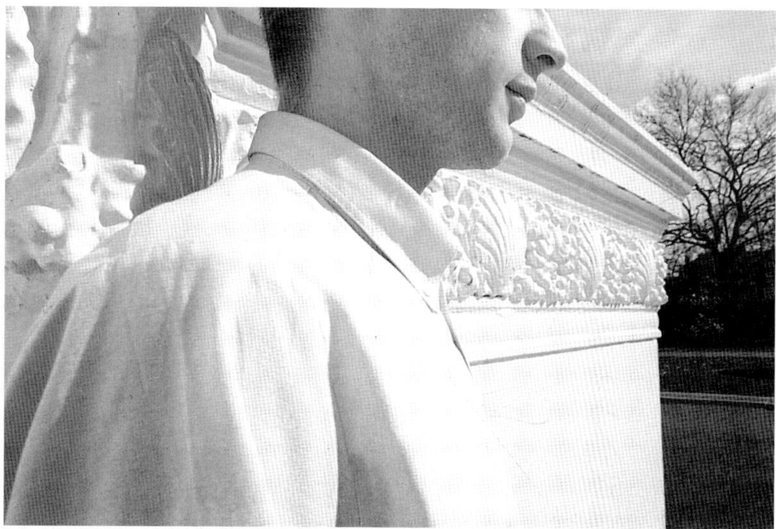

Joanna Redman Untitled *(original in colour)*

NEW IMAGING
is presented in collaboration with

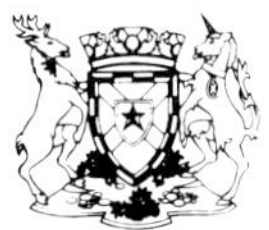

Highland Regional Council

Department of Libraries and
Leisure Services

fotofeis

New Imaging

INVERNESS AND THE HIGHLANDS

THE GREAT CONVERSATION

On the ethics of appropriating business media for inappropriate ends

Sean Cubitt

It is not exactly that we have no sense of truth, but that truth has a different status for us: it is always in the past. What was once possible to believe is no longer available to us, and perhaps even more than that – the very grounds on which belief could be based have shifted and dissolved. That is why it is so easy for us to judge the past, but so difficult to judge the propriety of cultural action in the present, especially once it moves outside the confines of the expected and comforting. Underpinning much of postmodern thought is the Heideggerian perception that, having lost any sense of oneness with the world, human knowledge has distanced itself progressively from the grounds of its own truth, first in the name of God, then in the names of science and technology.

We live in the age whose greatest intellectual achievement has been the self-overcoming of positivist science. I don't mean anything mystical by this, just that science, by its own logic, has gotten over the 19th century dependency of 'classical science' on observation and the construction of 'facts'. To a very large extent, 20th century media, including fine art, have lagged behind this cheerful freeing of speculative reason from dependency on the observable universe. We culturalists squabble over notions of truth – absolute, purposive – that are no longer in question for physics. We celebrate or condemn the death of Truth in terms that are simply out of date for a quantum mechanic.

The great contribution of idealist philosophy to the course of 20th century thought is the recognition that knowledge is not a question of the *subject* knowing its *object* – the definition, I suppose, of positivism – but the product of the imbrication of *knower* and *known* in an experience. To know is to partake in what you know, however limited that participation may be.

But what is it possible for us to know? To some extent, the world we inhabit is no longer natural. It is layered over by technology, the multiple technologies of the body and language, and crucially by the technologies that give us the metaphor for speaking of our physicality and our communication *as* technologies: the destiny of scientific reason as it comes, ineluctably, to control the world. Technology stands between us and nature, even when, in the guise of science, it seeks only to subordinate itself and us to the natural world. There is no return to some natural point of origin, at which we might imagine our forebears enmeshed and at one with their world. No less enmeshed, we are however condemned to meet the world only as it is mediated.

So we are embroiled in a world of others, those other people with whom we share our communications and therefore our experiences. At the same time, we have to recognise that the processes of mediation themselves give form to the world in which we must take our being. So we can abandon older metaphors – metaphors of management and control, of engineering, of conquest, of uncovering and penetration. There is no divine light for us behind the veil of Maya. If we are to see our culture as anything other than directionless, purposeless and defunct – the position implicit in many forms of postmodern thought (recently Kenneth Baker has been talking about his education policy as 'postmodern politics') – if we are to hang on to some hope of betterment, then we must recognise that the media of communication – language pre-eminently, but also all our other skills – are the material of which experience can be had, and of which experience is made.

There are no great thinkers any more. There is no need for them. The great bourgeois tradition in the West leads from Copernicus and Galileo, through Darwin and Freud, towards a diminished sense of the role of humanity in the universe. The only world in which or over which we can expect to find ourselves is the world of what Gadamer refers to as 'conversation'. No single statement or body of work can be the truth. No single statement or body of work is itself complete: the nature of the material of understanding is that it is always open to misunderstanding, to reinterpretation. We are all, every speaking creature, engaged in the great conversation, whose subject we are scarcely even aware of, save only that we know that we must keep on talking. Without knowing why, without trusting the materials which we use, without even the desire, we continue to communicate because that is our stake in the world. The oceanic play of dialogue, of words following and reinterpreting each other, is the human condition, the weight of history which, as Marx has it, weighs on the minds of the living like a nightmare. And yet this is also the raw material out of which we must make our own histories, albeit not under conditions of our own choosing. The great conversation of the human race is the grounds for hope.

I suppose, despite what faith still clings beneath the fingernails of the intelligentsia, that the West can no longer believe that its history has a preordained goal. When the critical theorist, Habermas, discusses the great conversation, he sees in its inherent rationality – for how else might we communicate if not rationally – the harbinger of that utopian moment at which its communicative rationality might become the basis for the whole of human society. The philosophers, tied still to the quest for wholeness and for permanence, understand this process as an ecology, a vast network of interweaving talk in which every moment, every thought, every word is simultaneously cause and effect of the whole, "for everywhere that communication happens, language not only is used but shaped as well"[†]. What we should steal from this philosophy in the interests of materialism – for which the point is not just to understand the world but to change it – is that the ecology of communications needs to be nurtured in such a way as to allow the greatest scope for its evolution. We may no longer be able to foresee or determine in which direction our history is moving: we have, however, an absolute duty to ensure that it does continue to move.

But what philosophers cannot see, because of the walls of their discipline, is that the world does not entirely fit their description of it. The innumerable murmurings of humanity are not so entirely democratic as the dream of rational discourse would have us believe. The world of speech, of discourse, of communication, is troubled by hierarchies both directly and indirectly. On the one hand, there is the direct impact of relationships between people, relationships which appear to us, as Marx again says, as relationships between things. Among those 'things' we seem to perceive (constraining and determining our actions) are possession and property, power and order, control over the means of discursive productions as well as all the other technologies with which we are surrounded. We feel as if, act as if, and our knowledge and hopes are shaped as though some social groups had a greater claim to the conversation than us. Not surprisingly, credited with such a position, such groups seize the moment, and actually take control of what has effectively been offered to them. The conversation is a sea, but one in which the major currents, the nodal points, are organised around dominant positions that form the whole process, marginalising and repressing some, taking up others and delivering them into the sunshine, restricting and channelling the flow of growth and change, and they themselves altering only as slowly as the coastlines or the ocean currents of the geographical world change.

More indirectly, the very nature of the conversation can be changed by altering the media which are available to it. The design of communications media is only ever partially conscious, but its effects are enormous. To the extent that it is conscious, the design processes involved in creating new media, through which the great conversation might take place, are rarely undertaken in the service of maximising variety and activity, of multiplying the sources and kinds of change to be hoped for. On the contrary, design is almost everywhere in the service of maintaining the status quo, of minimising change, variety and hope. Radio was introduced as an alternative to telephony, but was nipped in the bud as a two-way medium by the telephone monopolies, along with the military, who wanted to keep the wireless for themselves, and to keep the amateurs out for secrecy's sake – a secretive mode that still comes up in debates of late about overheard mobile phone calls. By the same token, the telephone is restricted to private conversations, not public ones, while the public media maintain the model of one-way communication. It is in this context that we need to begin to understand the powers of media designed at the interface of public and private, in the amateur and business arenas where the two sectors meet.

After all, the division of the world into public and private is itself a great historical shift, and one marked by huge rifts in the great conversation, what may or may not be spoken in which domain. The cultures of expertise emerge as brokers between the two worlds – cultures of medical and psychiatric professionalism, for example, policing and the law, sexuality and art. In the private world, you can say what you want: in public, the current flows against certain kinds of speech, certain kinds of speaker. These demarcations serve or are made to serve the interests of self-perpetuating streams or currents, themselves, I'd like to argue, determined by the continental formations we call capitalism. In any case, whatever their provenance, (and, to alter slightly the aqueous metaphor), they form dams, dykes and sluices to ensure the subordination of the flow and its variety to the irrigation of few selected fields.

This is the context, then, in which it is necessary to consider the ethics and aesthetics of the (mis)appropriation of business media for other ends. Running off fliers on the office photocopier, faxing Chinese government offices in support of the democracy movement, hacking into secret databases of the nuclear industry: these activities share only their illegality. It is important, however, to recognise that the laws under which we live are not the product of some great historical motion that brings them into being as expressions of some transhistorical Law. They are written by people, in the interests of themselves or others, in specific historical circumstances – they too are products of the great conversation, and more particularly formed in and forms of the steering of its course into channels favoured by the powerful. So there is no ethical imperative to obey them, as if in each abuse of power there lurked the majesty of a mythic Rule of Law.

Our ethics have to derive from somewhere else, and, since there is no divine watchdog, they will derive from pragmatic concerns – what can usefully and safely be achieved, or with what balance between sacrifice and gain – and ultimately from a sense of the aesthetic. It is in the aesthetic that we can perceive, if only for an instant and obliquely, the shape of a world other than our own. It is not the nature of that world that is in question – that would be the teleological fallacy, seeking to define in advance the route which evolution should take – but simply its difference from what we now have. Some sense of beauty, of justice even, informs us that a job's well done. Such beauty has to do with the great conversation, both because it facilitates it, and because the judgement you would make about a specific action is made with reference to the social, not the individual gain. There is no necessary charm to merely be subversive. What is needed is to whittle away at the irrigation system, so that as many flowers and crops as possible can bloom, as many as we can dream of, and beyond our dreams. This means of course, redesigning the conduits, for which not only art but scientific skills are needed. Our evolution can no longer afford to keep the 'two cultures' apart, just as it cannot afford to keep public and private separated. If this means laying yourself open, legally as well as morally, aesthetically and ultimately psychologically, then that is the cost we have to pay to end the curtailment of growth and change in the name of the End of History promised by our political and cultural masters. The aesthetic of the new media guerrillas must be founded in ethics: who is this work for?

Sean Cubitt is Reader in video and media studies at John Moores University, Liverpool. He is the author of *Timeshift: On Video Culture* (1991), *Videography: video media as art and culture* (forthcoming) and numerous articles on art, media and culture.

† Hans-Georg Gadamer. 'On the Philosophical Element in the Sciences and the Scientific Character of Philosophy' in *Reason in the Age of Science* translated by Frederick G Lawrence. MIT Press, Cambridge, Mass., 1990. p.4.

MANUAL USA, NAM JUNE PAIK *Korea*, GAVIN EVANS UK ALEX VERMEULEN *Netherlands* and AMY JENKINS USA

Virtual Interventions

Inverness Museum and Art Gallery

CASTLE WYND, INVERNESS

PREMIERE

4 JUNE – 4 JULY

Virtual Interventions brings together the work of six artists from around the world in an exhibition which explores the often ambiguous juxtaposition of two forms – the 'real' world of photography and the 'virtual' universe of the computer.

The Texan team of Manual (Suzanne Bloom and Ed Hill) set computer generated imagery, suggesting a simulated Nature, amid archive photographs depicting 19th century timber felling and production. An artificial future meets a materialist past, throwing up questions of how we manage and preserve our natural environment, and what will replace it if it is lost forever.

Widely respected as an artist, composer and performer, Nam June Paik has become increasingly obsessed with the medium of television. Converting TV monitors into whimsical, functionless objects which display on their screens computer generated video loops, Paik challenges the omniscient and omnipresent nature of television. "TV," he says, "has attacked us all in our lives; now we're hitting back."

The images in 'dis' a collaborative project by Gavin Evans, have been produced using technology which allows undetectable manipulation. These are shown alongside prose, one of the oldest and purest forms of communication. Ten writers collaborated with Evans, including Arthur Miller, Eda Čufer and Nobel prize-winner Wole Soyinka. The bold imagery and complex text challenge us to consider how presentation itself can be used to manipulate and distort information.

Alex Vermeulen believes that "Only wonder puts you in the frame of mind to judge situations properly". Staged like stills from a film, his images seamlessly blend computer-generated 'contraptions' with narrative photographs. The photographs reconstruct a story that was not there before; or rather, a story that has not yet come to pass.

Amy Jenkins' work sets out to capture the tension and potential harmony between elements existing in differing visual states. Her arrangements of objects stand before a video screen which itself displays an array of articles which are, in reality, no more than specks of light on the phosphor. But illusion and reality become intertwined in the lush colour of her prints, and the boundaries between actual and virtual, seen and imagined, dissolve, only to be re-invented.

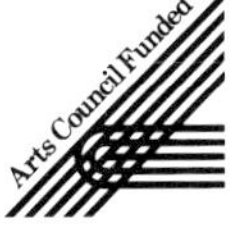

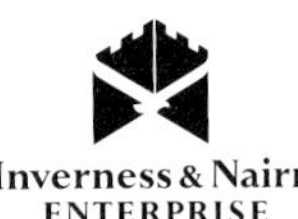

Manual appear courtesy of Jayne Baum Gallery, New York
Nam June Paik appears courtesy of The Mayor Gallery, London
Alex Vermeulen appears courtesy of TORCH Gallery, Amsterdam

Gavin Evans is sponsored by QUAD 1·2·3·D Computer Graphics, Tapestry Scanning services, Superchrome Image printing services, Ilfochrome Photographic paper

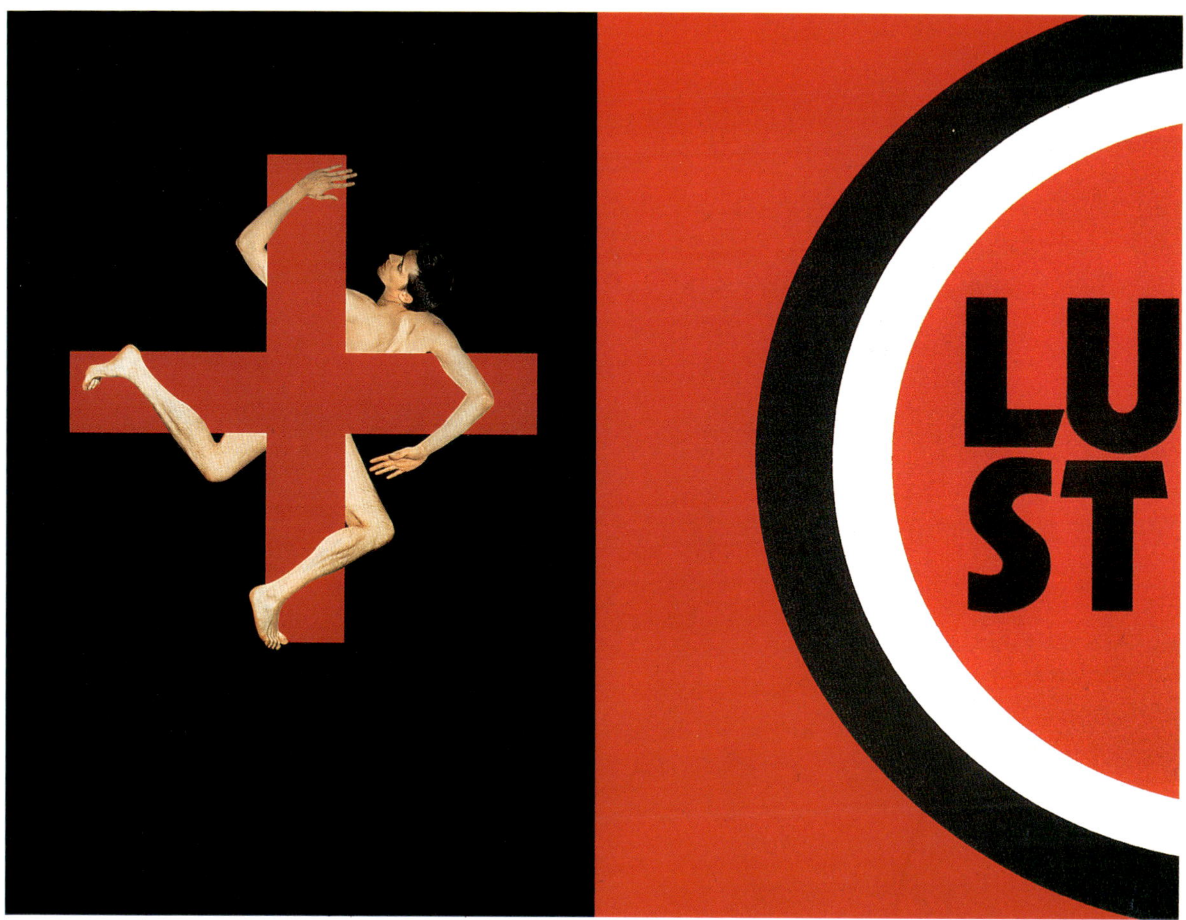

The *sense* – producing human machine works on the basis of a very simple law:

**We cannot see all the phenomena we can think of,
and we cannot think about certain images we can see.**

**The power of the *sense*, which cannot be reproduced in words or images,
belongs to the world of human feelings, as inner side of every image or word.**

**The *sense* we live in – the *sense* behind the one we believe in – is a vehicle which can be
used for our journey or abused for the journey of someone else.**

Eda Čufer

Gavin Evans Untitled *colour print and text*

MANUAL USA
Woodland Installation

Craig Phadrig Forest

INVERNESS

SPECIAL COMMISSION

OPENS 21 JUNE

Suzanne Bloom and Ed Hill are two artists from Texas who work under the collaborative name of MANUAL. Widely exhibited internationally, their work explores environmental issues and involves the integration of computer generated imagery with both their own and archival photographs of forestry practices. (An example of their work is shown opposite.) In this innovative Fotofeis commission the artists are asked to take the process one step further and to place their images directly into the woodland environment itself.

Arranged in association with Forest Enterprise, a branch of the Forestry Commission, MANUAL will create a series of images for installation on interpretation boards within Craig Phadrig Forest, Inverness.

"At a time when we seem to be collectively focused on the state of health of the world's forests there is an additional insidious threat to the whole of Nature through the development of what is popularly known as virtual reality. It may be regarded as a threat in the sense that it distracts us from the increasing loss of nature by creating self-contained designer worlds. These worlds are totally artificial but also totally seduce their audiences with the promise of a perfect hyper-reality." MANUAL

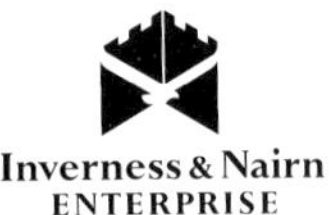

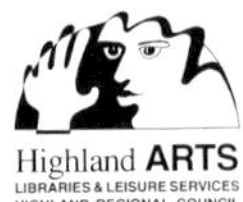

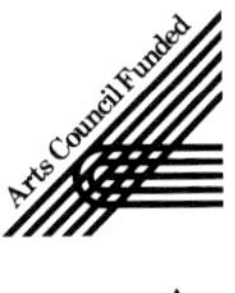

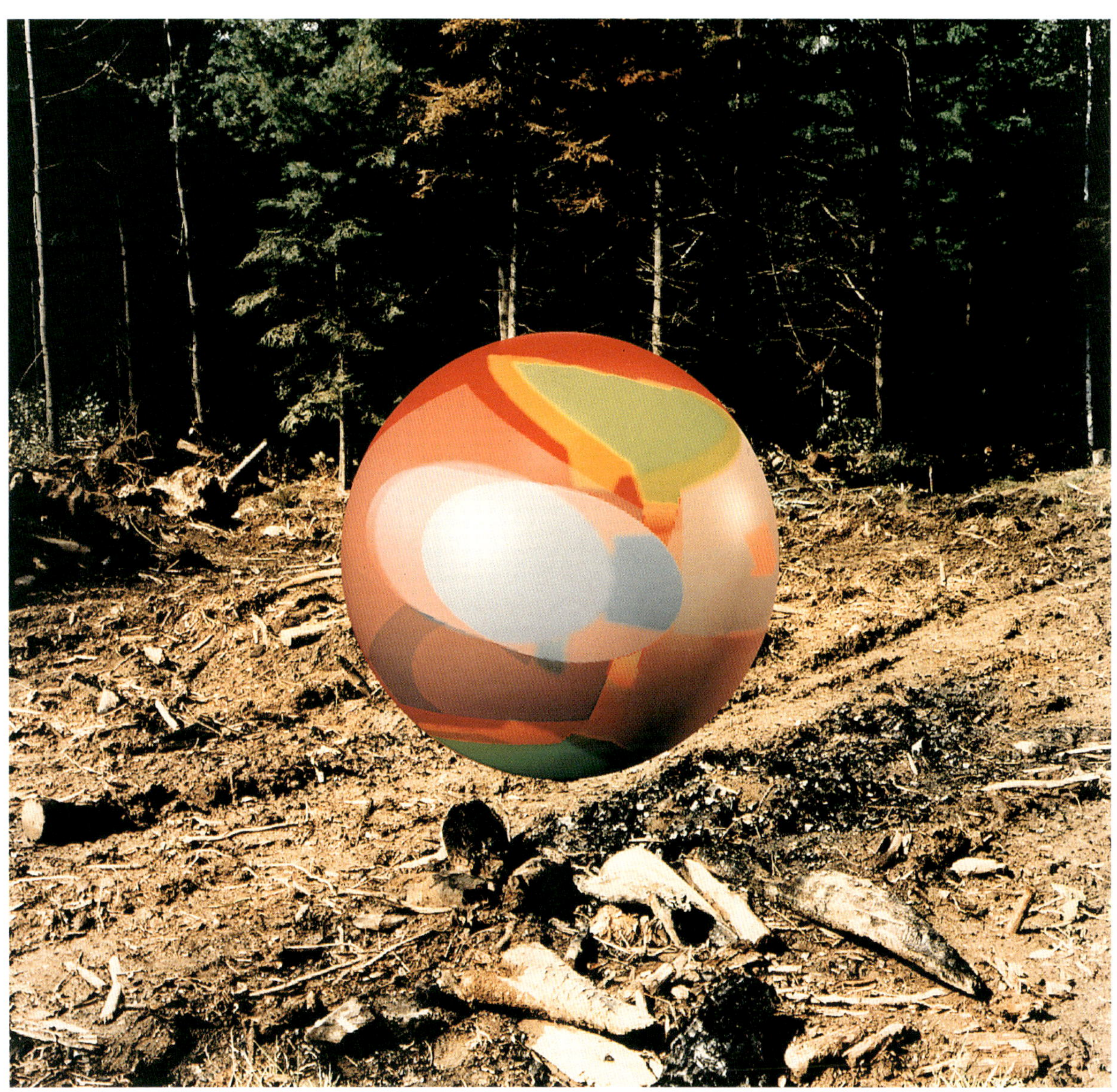

Manual Worldmaker *C-type print*

NAT FINKELSTEIN USA / *Netherlands*

Two Installations: Merry Monsters *and* Elena: a story

The Spectrum Centre

FARRALINE PARK
1 MARGARET STREET
INVERNESS

UK PREMIERE

21 JUNE – 4 JULY

"I have been assigned the task of describing my installation, *Merry Monsters*, but I find this impossible to do. After all, the images are on the wall, screen, monitors: they are in the air, eyes and ears under assault. The switches have been pulled, impulses transmitted... are you there? The medium is not the message, merely the messenger. Pixels, fractals, bytes and lines are the sinews, tendons, muscles and guts of this slice of living that we, me, us artists have placed before you.

"'Isn't it electricity and artificial?' one might ask. 'Aren't we all,' one might answer. So come on now, do not ask what it is. Let us go and make our visit."
Nat Finkelstein

Nat Finkelstein first came to prominence through his documenting of Andy Warhol's 'Factory'. More recently, he has established a reputation for his video-based installations which draw on 'rave' culture and present images excised from video and enlarged on a bubblejet printer. His work has been shown at a number of key European museums and galleries including The Fodor Museum, Amsterdam, The New Museum of Modern Art, Istanbul and the Ludwig Museum, Cologne.

Nat Finkelstein's work is made using Canon BJA through the kind cooperation of the Canon Corporation

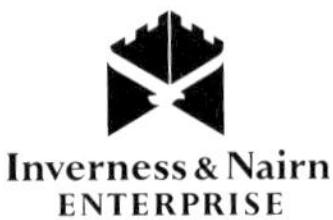

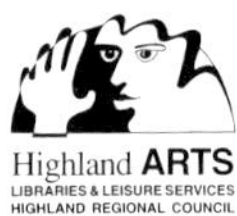

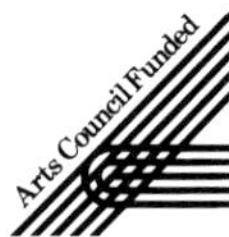

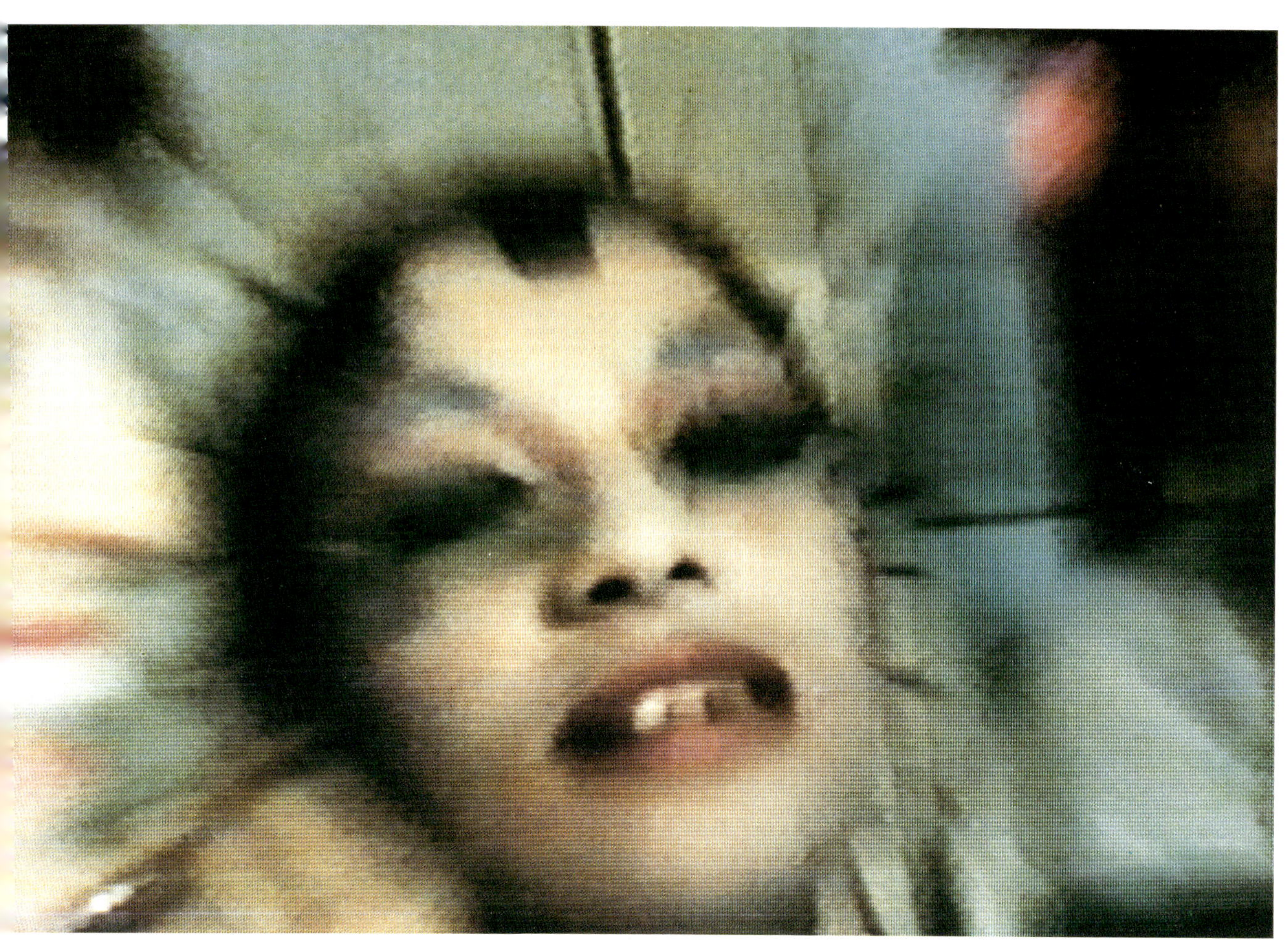

at Finkelstein Crazy Face *bubblejet print*

CAROL FLAX USA

Banners

Inverness Railway Station

STATION SQUARE
INVERNESS
SPECIAL COMMISSION
UNVEILING 26 JUNE

Recent Work

Highland Printmakers Workshop & Gallery

20 BANK STREET
INVERNESS
UK PREMIERE
5 JUNE – 29 JUNE

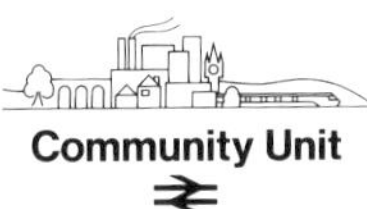

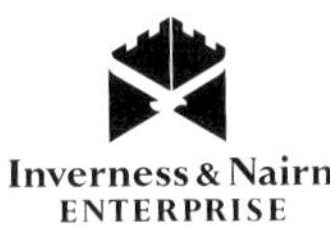

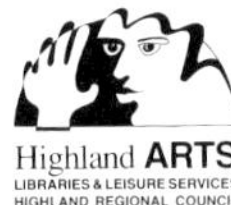

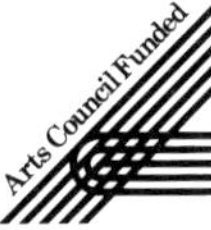

The Inverness station banner project involved an unusual three-way collaboration between the celebrated American computer artist, Carol Flax, the Highland Printmakers Workshop and people from in and around Inverness. During her six week residency, the artist worked closely with community groups, school children and local archivists to draw together a diverse array of imagery from the area.

Carol Flax then spent two weeks as the guest of Duncan of Jordanstone College of Art, Dundee, in their sophisticated computer imaging laboratory, integrating the many pictures she had found or taken herself, into composite images reflecting such themes as communications, mythology and the experience of young people in the Highlands. Returning to Inverness she worked with the artist Evelyn Pottie who is a technician at the Highland Printmakers Workshop to create limited edition silkscreen banners from these computer manipulated images. The banners will hang as a semi-permanent fixture in the main concourse of Inverness railway station as part of an environmental partnership scheme under the British Rail Community Fund. Created as a special Fotofeis project, these banners will be unveiled to the public on 26 June.

Carol Flax would like to thank the following for their generous help during the production of the banners: Nigel Johnson of Duncan of Jordanstone College of Art, Mike Lothian at the Whyte Photographic Archive, Hugh Webster at the Scottish Highland Photo Library, Katie MacGregor at Comunn na Gàidhlig, Bob Steward at the Highland Regional Archives, Catherine Niven at the Inverness Museum and Art Gallery, Anita Elliot at the Highland Museum of Childhood and Elizabeth Sutherland at the Groat House Museum.

An exhibition of some of Carol Flax's most recent personal work will be on show at the Highland Printmakers Gallery during the festival. Ranging in its subject matter from family issues to the Gulf War and the control of information, this exhibition offers an interesting insight into the artist's oeuvre. "Woven throughout my examination of family and society in this work," she states, "is the everpresent knowledge that these new technologies have an awesome potential to change the way we communicate and the way we understand the world. I try to maintain an awareness of their power, never simply thinking of them as painting tools, but always as communications devices."

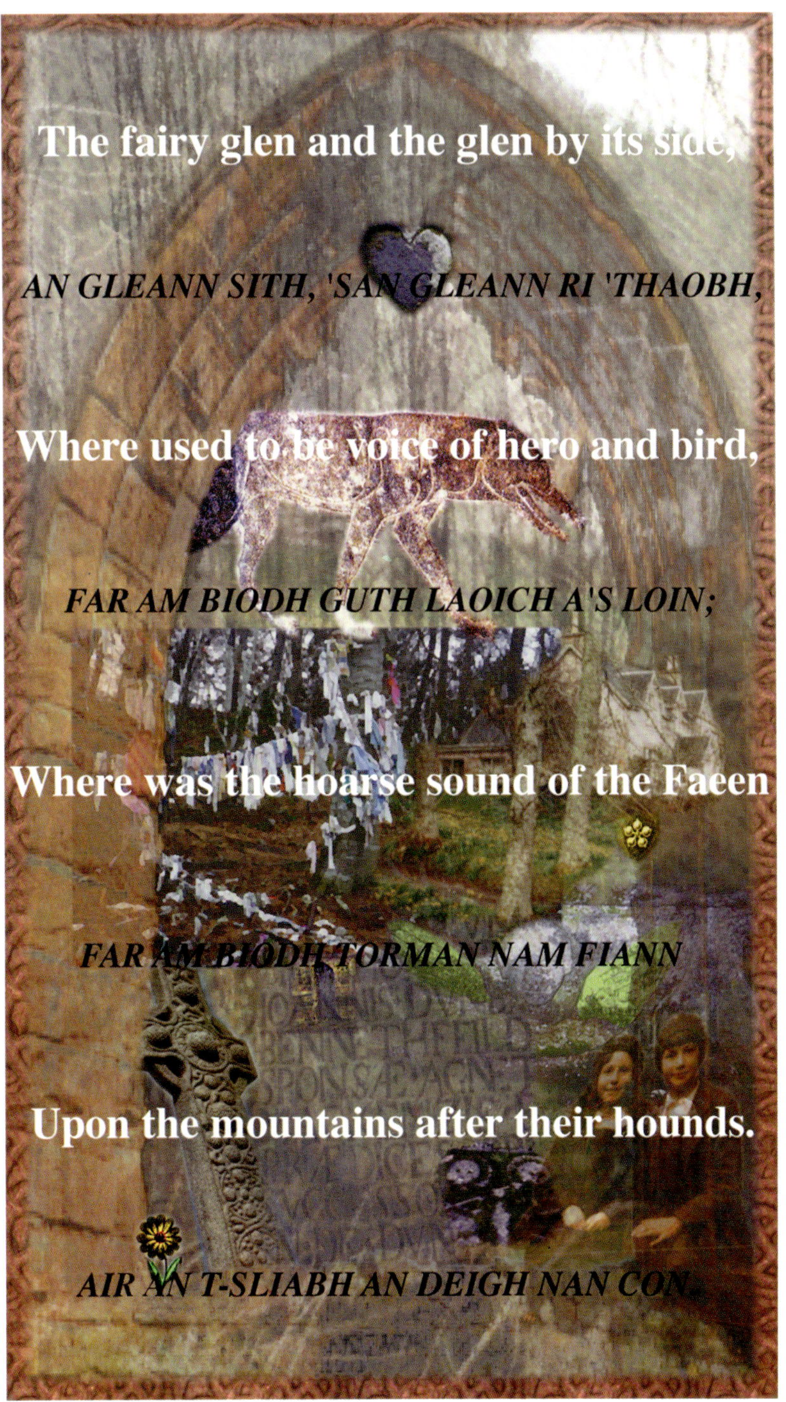

Carol Flax Untitled *silkscreen*

JOSEPH DeLAPPE USA and KEITH PIPER UK

New Dimensions in New Imaging

St. Fergus Gallery

SINCLAIR TERRACE, WICK

PREMIERE

21 MAY – 12 JUNE

Swanson Gallery

DAVIDSON'S LANE, THURSO

18 JUNE – 10 JULY

Iona Gallery

DUKE STREET, KINGUSSIE

17 JULY – 7 AUGUST

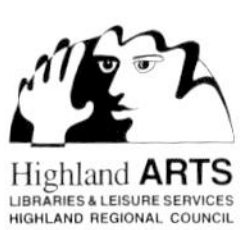

"Much of what has been considered cutting edge use of technology and art in the past 20 years has demonstrated high levels of technical proficiency but, all too often, lacked much artistic merit. As the technology of computing becomes further accessible, less novel and easier to use, we are seeing more artists employing these systems to create art that moves beyond technical mastery to critical, aesthetic, and conceptual concerns." *Joseph DeLappe.*

Drawing on the work of Joseph DeLappe and Keith Piper the exhibition demonstrates this new dimension in a technological art extending beyond mere technical virtuosity. Both artists explore the body as a form of social, cultural or moral currency. DeLappe's *Modern Man and Woman* is a contemporary interpretation of the Adam and Eve myth. The figures are assembled from individual colour prints photographed from the screen in sections. Before the two figures stands a TV monitor on which is displayed a golden sphere which suggests an impossibly perfect world. "The piece questions ... the state of the world we have nearly destroyed in our continuing search for answers," DeLappe explains.

Keith Piper's installation, *Trade Winds*, consists of four rough wooden crates in the form of a cross in which video screens display constantly changing images of the head, hands and feet of the black protagonist. Here, the body is contained in a receptacle of trade – suggesting not simply a dependence on the movement of goods, but the trade in human beings themselves – slavery.

The critic Sean Cubitt has observed that in this work "Piper makes technology work doubly. Here are the new surveillance technologies ... an apparatus of racist representation built upon the missionary and anthropological images of empire. But Piper also works on the transitions from frame to frame so that the spurious naturalness of the imagery is interrupted to expose manipulation. At any point in these cyclical histories, what television's smooth flow proposes as destiny is revealed as an engineered oppression."

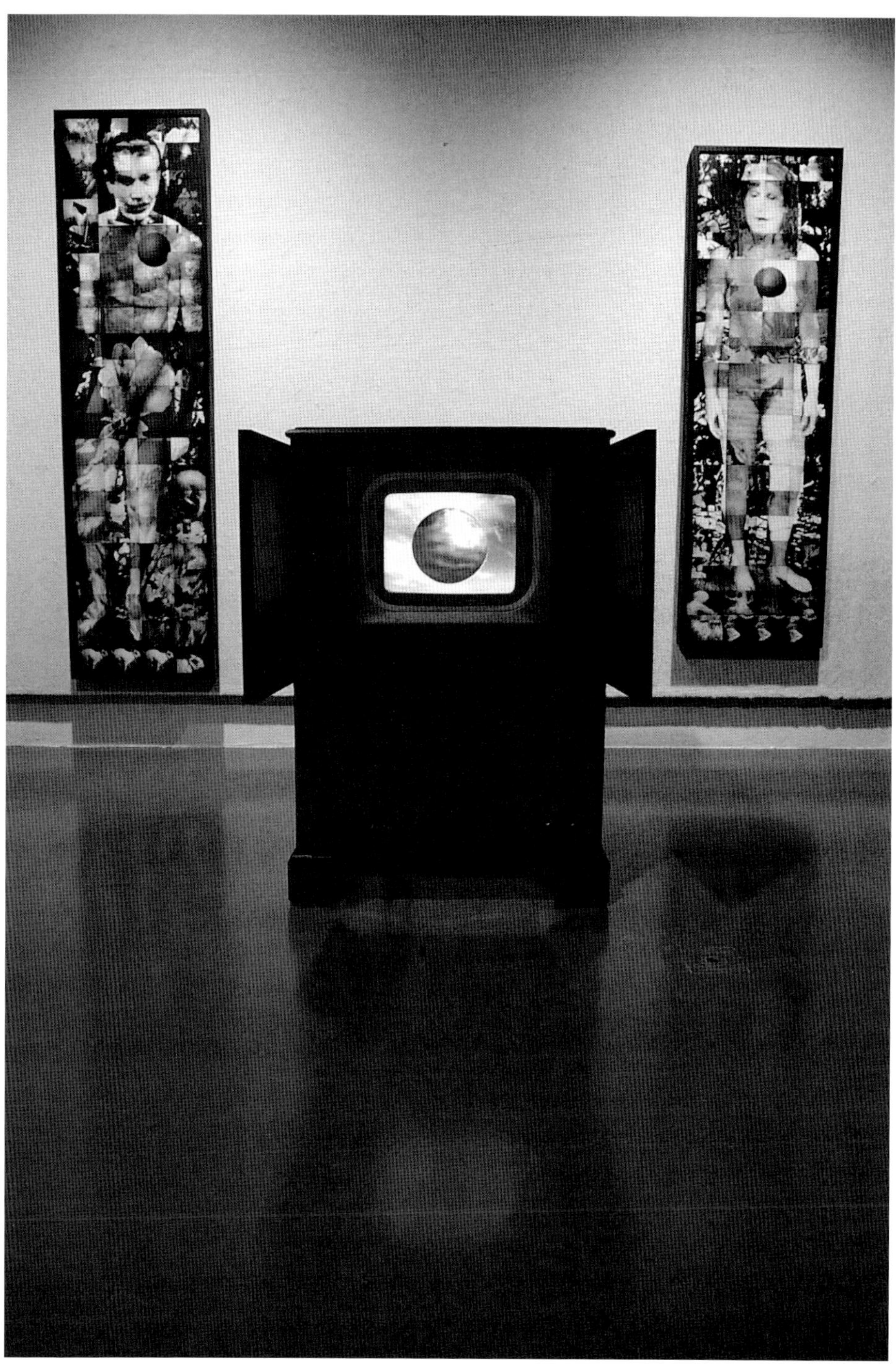

Joseph DeLappe Modern Man and Woman *computer generated images and video*

MUSEO INTERNACIONAL DE ELECTROGRAFIA *Spain*

The Photocopy Show

Eden Court Theatre

BISHOP'S ROAD, INVERNESS

UK PREMIERE

4 JUNE – 3 JULY

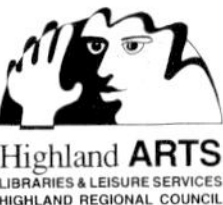

"The importance of the image in our environment goes hand in hand with that of the media which make it possible and which permeate all aspects of our daily life. Without losing sight of what is real, or abandoning the creative motivation of the artist, these technologically processed images open up new possibilities for the user. They answer a technical and creative need, stimulating a dialogue which is, however, more complex than 'correct'."

Fernando Ñ Canales, Director of MIDE

The Museo Internacional de Electrografia (MIDE), was established by the University of Castilla-La Mancha in 1990 as a research centre and archive. It exists as a response to the increasing number of artworks based on electrographic imaging which has seen spectacular advances in recent years thanks to developments in optics, chemistry and electronics. Linked to developments in computer software and data transmission, such technological processes are having a tremendous impact on the whole course of image production.

For Fotofeis, the curators of MIDE have selected an exciting and diverse array of works by artists from around the world who have developed their creative activity around electrographic imaging and reprographics. They include: Arianne Thezé, Georg Muhleck, Sarah Jackson (Canada); Heta Norros (Finland); Joseph Kadar, James Durand, Sophie Boursat, Miguel Chevalier (France); Klaus Urbons, R. Henss-Dewald (Germany); Arno Arts (Netherlands); Francesca Mazzola, Vittore Baroni (Italy); Takasure Nakayama, Hirotaka Maruyama, Fumiko Shinkai (Japan); Ibírico, Jesus Pastor, Angeles Pascual, Daniel Monzó, Paco Rangel, Alcalacanales, Ruben Tortosa, Montserrat Vallés, Mercedes Romero, Gemma Araque, Cristina Barrera (Spain); Daniel Faora (UK); Buzz Blur and Mary Marsh (USA).

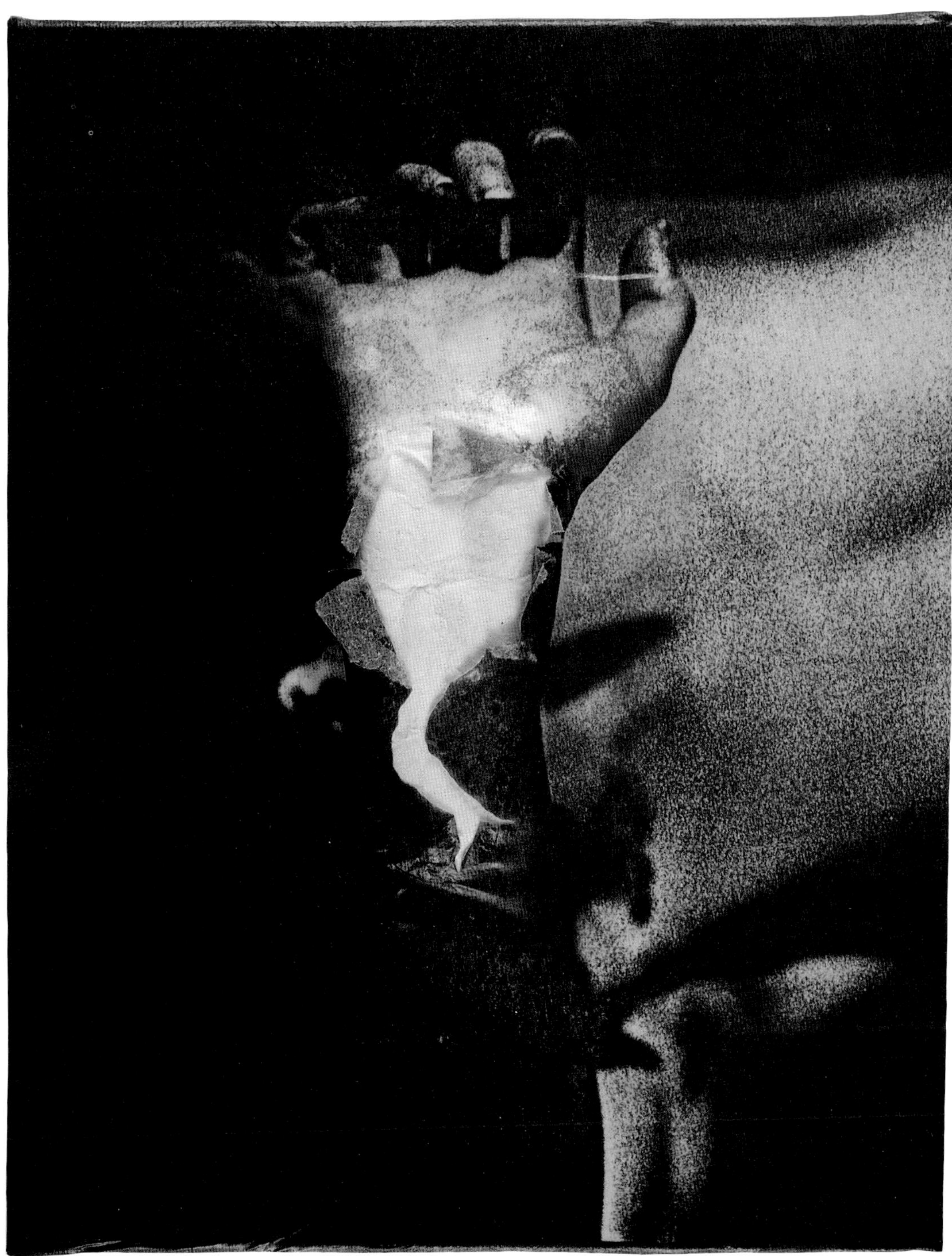

Ariann Thezé Perception No.11 *photocopy*

Four Exhibitions at An Lanntair

TOWN HALL, SOUTH BEACH
STORNOWAY, ISLE OF LEWIS

5 JUNE – 3 JULY

CHILDREN FROM LEWIS AND LONDON
Looking in reaching out

A joint project with the Photographers' Gallery in London, splicing together and contrasting, through technology, images from the lives of two groups of children from apparent extremes: a rural isle in Scotland and the metropolis of London. Working with an artist/educator in both locations, the children have looked at the development of technology in their own areas and the impact it has on their lives.

Central to the project is cultural exchange. The results of the project are showing simultaneously at An Lanntair and The Photographers' Gallery during Fotofeis.

The project is funded with assistance from the Calouste Gulbenkian Foundation.

PREMIERE

CALUM ANGUS MACKAY UK
Satellite / X-Ray Triptych

The initial concept for this piece arose out of the human obsession with climate.

At the NERC satellite station in Dundee University, I came across beautiful black and white images of Europe showing no obvious sea or land boundaries. They had an intimacy which gave the impression of being internal. From that point, I developed the idea of using X-rays / radiography, a process with a similar function to that of a satellite – to forecast human dilemma and to generate a response.

The black and white triptych is created to human scale in relation to the X-rays, i.e. head, finger, spine.

Calum Angus Mackay

PREMIERE

DANIEL REEVES *USA / UK*

The Sleepers

The Sleepers: Passing, Gazing, Bending, Stooping is an electronic triptych evoking the transformative power of remembrance. Using old family photographs and working with computers, I have created metamorphic passages of computer-animated and / or hand-coloured images which create a resonance of mystery and emotive power.

Extracts from *The Sleepers* by Walt Whitman, a vibrant metaphor for the process of looking deeply, are woven into the textual elements of the installation along with sections of my own writing. They serve to articulate the shadowy areas of family history, both real and imagined, and attempt to shed light on the phenomena of remembrance and introspection.

Daniel Reeves

PREMIERE

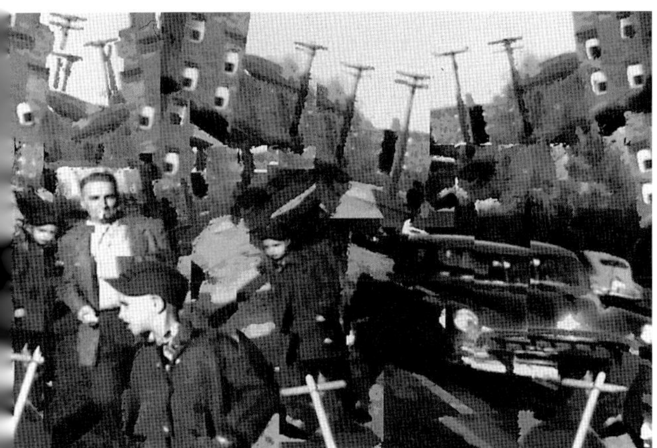

Daniel Reeves February '57 *computer processed collage*

GIJS VAN GENT *Netherlands*

Pictures in Pictures

The result of a five year project which took Gijs Van Gent throughout Europe and ultimately to the Hebrides. In each country, he photographs individuals or groups and returns a year later to retake them holding the original photo. This may be repeated annually several times.

In other instances, people with similar occupations from different countries are pictured holding photos of their counterparts in other countries. In this way, he documents the changes, differences and similarities in cultures and workplaces throughout the new Europe.

"In the framework of Europe post 1992 and on the way to a multicultural society, I hope, with my pictures, to contribute to better understanding, solidarity and respect for each other."

Gijs Van Gent

UK PREMIERE

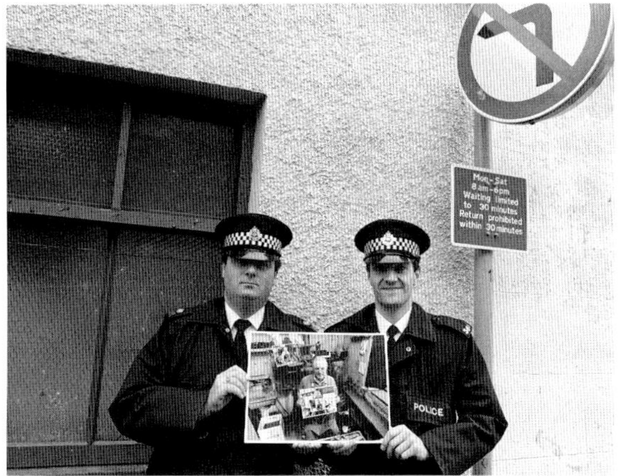

Gijs Van Gent Two Stornoway Policemen ... *silver-gelatin print*

THE MAGNUS BUS
The New Technology Touring Show

Touring throughout the Highlands

PREMIERE

4 JUNE – 16 JULY

The New Technology Touring Show is moving throughout the Highlands, bringing innovative artwork in electronic imaging to communities already conversant with a global telecommunications network through 'telecrofting'. This in itself challenges an assumption that 'rural' means craft based artisan culture, and that cutting edge exploration in the visual arts is the preserve of the urban communities. The sophistication of the telecommunications network in the Highlands debunks this myth.

However, distances between these isolated communities can be very large. The audience for this travelling show is diverse. It is visiting high schools, villages, and tourist hot-spots. The show is intended to build a broad picture and provide an insight into the many strands being pursued by artists.

Patrick Boyd's witty and fascinating sculptures use the inherent nature of holography to show apparent movement within the image. Unlike many early arid examples of the medium, Boyd's work exploits this potential with complex overlaid narratives. Hannah MacPherson's *Apollo* series, was produced entirely on computer. Using visual material from the real world, which is then manipulated to produce fantastic environments, frequently including text, they have a soothing, contemplative quality. Examples of work made by artists using digital technology are also included in slide and video form.

To put this work into context, the exhibition includes background reading material and interpretation panels which help to show how the world of silver-halide photography relates to the world of electronic imaging.

The tour begins in Sutherland and continues south through Ross-shire, Kyle of Lochalsh, Nairnshire, Ross and Cromarty to Badenoch and Strathspey.

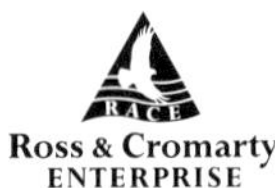

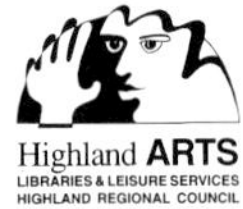

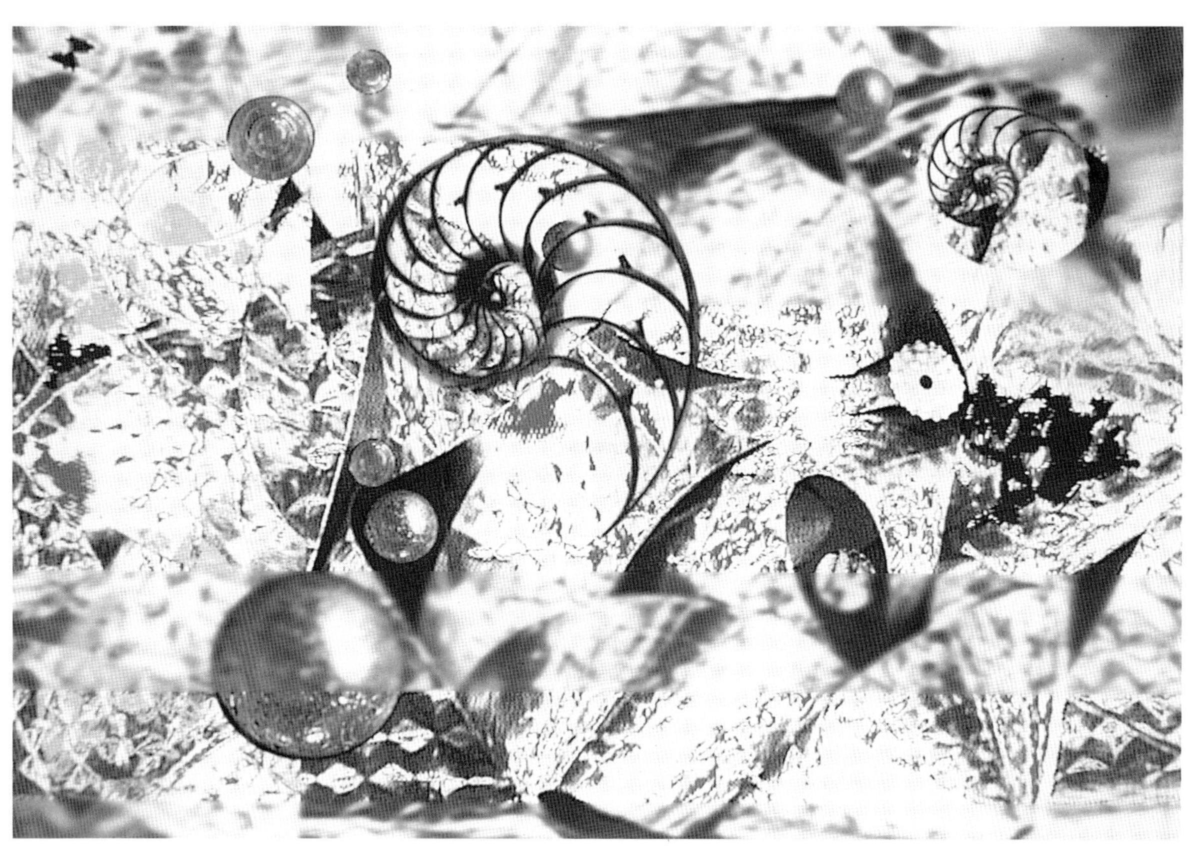

Hannah MacPherson The Secret Place *electronic image*

The Six Continent Fax Performance

Old Renthouse, Foulis Ferry

EVANTON, ROSS-SHIRE

PREMIERE

24 JUNE 1993

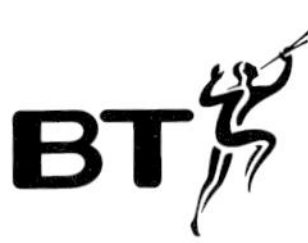

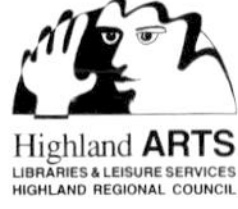

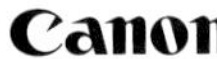

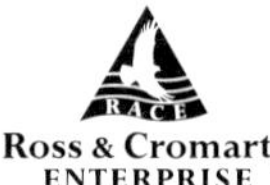

So, now it is official: the fax machine was invented by a Highlander. Today, the Highlands remains a leader in the field of telecommunications with a recently completed network which is the best rural system anywhere in Europe. In order to exploit this innovation and to demonstrate that, through the appropriation of business machines and networks, artists can initiate cultural dialogues on an international scale, Fotofeis is undertaking two projects: *The Six Continent Fax Performance* and a short summer school in electronic imaging: *Digital Landscapes*.

The *Fax Performance* will be staged within an 18th century renthouse at Foulis Ferry on the Cromarty Firth. This barn, originally built to hold grain (paid as rent) prior to export, will now be the site for an international commerce in imagery, as photo-based artworks are received from around the world by fax and computer modem during the evening of 24 June. The exchange will be completed with the return transmission of a specially commissioned new work by a Scottish artist to all the international artists involved in the performance.

Coordinated by the artist Stephen Hurrell with technical support from Albanet .
The Old Renthouse has kindly been made available by Hector Munroe.

Digital Landscapes

Sabhal Mor Ostaig

SLEAT, ISLE OF SKYE

27 JUNE – 2 JULY

"Digital photography provides us with new ways of seeing. This technology releases certain skills of creativity and perception normally locked out by traditional photography". *Colin Macleod*

Digital Landscapes is a special summer school for up to eight photographers who are already experienced in landscape photography using traditional silver-halide processes. Organised by Colin Macleod of Napier University (the man who first coined the term 'electronic imaging' and Scotland's leading authority on the subject) and staged at Sabhal Mor Ostaig, the Gaelic College on the Isle of Skye, it is, in effect, an intensive course in the use of the Canon Ion camera. There is however, a twist. Within the seven day span of the course, the group must not only master the new medium, but create between them a small exhibition of electronic landscape work. This will then be transmitted at a pre-arranged time to Canada for exhibition at The Works, a festival of the visual arts in Edmonton, Alberta.

Canon

Digital Landscapes is made possible through the kind cooperation of Sabhal Mor Ostaig.

TIM HUNKIN

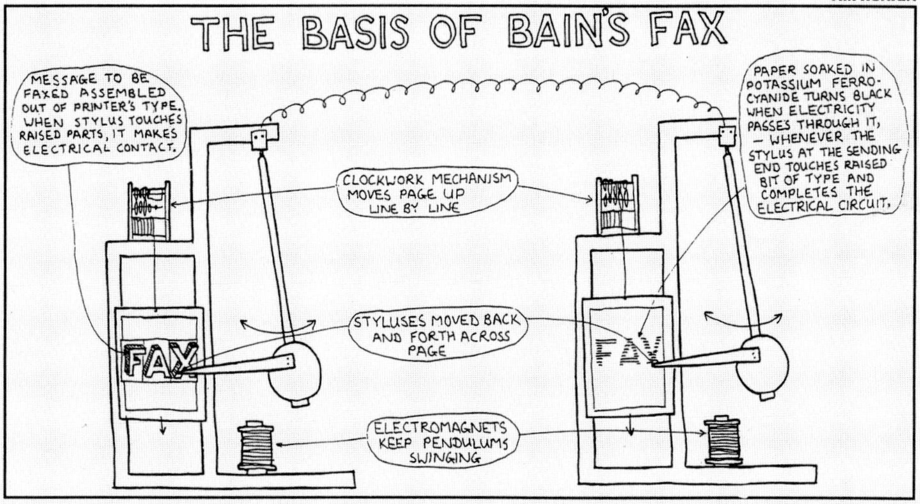

Scottish crofter's son invented the fax machine 150 years ago

By Steve Connor
Science Correspondent

THE FAX machine, which is supposed to let you run a business as easily in a remote Scottish croft as in the centre of a city, was invented 150 years ago ... in a remote Scottish croft. The inventor used heather as springs and cattle jawbones for hinges.

A little-known patent was filed in 1843 by Alexander Bain, a crofter's son. But it took nearly a century and a half to become the favoured medium of communication in the global village.

Bain's invention came more than 30 years before another Scotsman, Alexander Graham Bell, invented the telephone. The French built 7ft high versions of his fax machine to operate between Paris and Lyon for a few years in the 1860s, but the experiment failed, largely because the pace of life was fairly slow.

Bain's fax relied on pulses of electric currents transmitted over telegraph lines to send images. Britain's failure to capitalise on it may have had something to do with the title he gave it: "Certain Improvements in Producing and Regulating Electric Currents, and Improvements in Electric Time-Pieces, and in Electric Printing and Signal Telegraphs."

Next week, however, Bain's contribution will finally attract the recognition it deserves. A working model of the French fax will go on display at the Science Museum in London. It will also be celebrated in a Channel 4 programme on 18 February presented by Tim Hunkin, a cartoonist and engineer who re-discovered the 1843 patent.

Mr Hunkin, who built the replica machine for the museum, said Bain's invention is "one of those little known things that occur in the footnotes of scientific books".

It works by swinging two pendulums in synchrony. The sender's makes electrical contact with a raised image, and the receiver's swings over heat-sensitive paper that turns black when an electric current flows (see drawing).

Bain, who also invented the electric clock, first began experimenting with electromagnetic pendulums in his father's Caithness croft, where he used anything he could find to build prototypes, including heather and animal bones.

Bain himself soon lost interest in the fax machine and spent much of his later life wrangling with more famous inventors over alleged infringments of patents on his other inventions. He died penniless in a home for incurables, Mr Hunkin said. "He developed a complex that everyone was against him."

Leading article, page 24

reprinted courtesy of The Independent on Sunday *7 February 1993* *illustration by* Tim Hunkin

TONY COOPER UK

S/i: Work from a Residency

Highland Regional Council Headquarters

GLENURQUART ROAD
INVERNESS

PREMIERE

4 JUNE – 4 JULY

Exhibition and residency organised by Highland Regional Council's Department of Libraries and Leisure Services in association with the Council's Information Technology Department.

Tony Cooper's work investigates the creative potential offered by electronic business machinery. His images form the component elements of larger installations. This involves reconstituting both original and appropriated imagery in the fax, photocopier and computer software package. Working intuitively, he subverts the intent, meaning and implication of the original through digital distortion. Concentrating on a single motif – the reconstitution of the human form – Cooper's images have evolved around four themes: The Monolithic, The Phallocentric, The Industrial, and The Technical.

The work on show during Fotofeis was produced during a ten week residency at the Information Technology Department of Highland Regional Council. The residency allowed the artist access to machines normally used for routine business work such as the designing of council forms, and demonstrates the creative possibilities of machines originally designed and installed for administrative purposes.

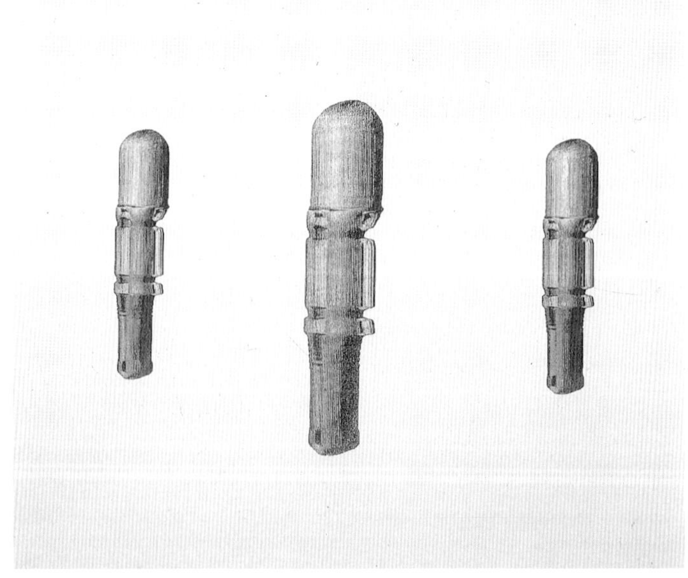

Tony Cooper Trio *plan copies of manipulated fax images*

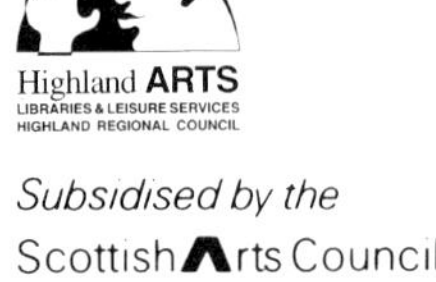

Subsidised by the
Scottish Arts Council

PETER CLARKE UK

Wicked Perversions

The Corridor Gallery

INVERNESS LIBRARY, INVERNESS

PREMIERE

1 JUNE – 1 JULY

With no formal art education and having failed 'O' level art, Peter Clarke went on to be Fleet Street's youngest ever political cartoonist. He has since worked on many national Dailies and is currently staff cartoonist on *The Guardian*. He was recently named 'Cartoonist of the Year', an honour bestowed only ten times in its 36 year history.

Clarke first began making photographic caricatures in 1974, but abandoned the process as too laborious. Now, with the aid of sophisticated photocopiers and computer techniques, he can rapidly breakdown, selectively enlarge and reassemble a physiognomy to create what one art critic has described as "wicked perversions" of his victims' faces. This exhibition brings together some of the more wickedly perverse of his caricatures from *The Guardian* 'Monday Profile'. Also showing at the exhibition is a ten minute film by BBC 2's *The Late Show* in which he demonstrates his unique technique.

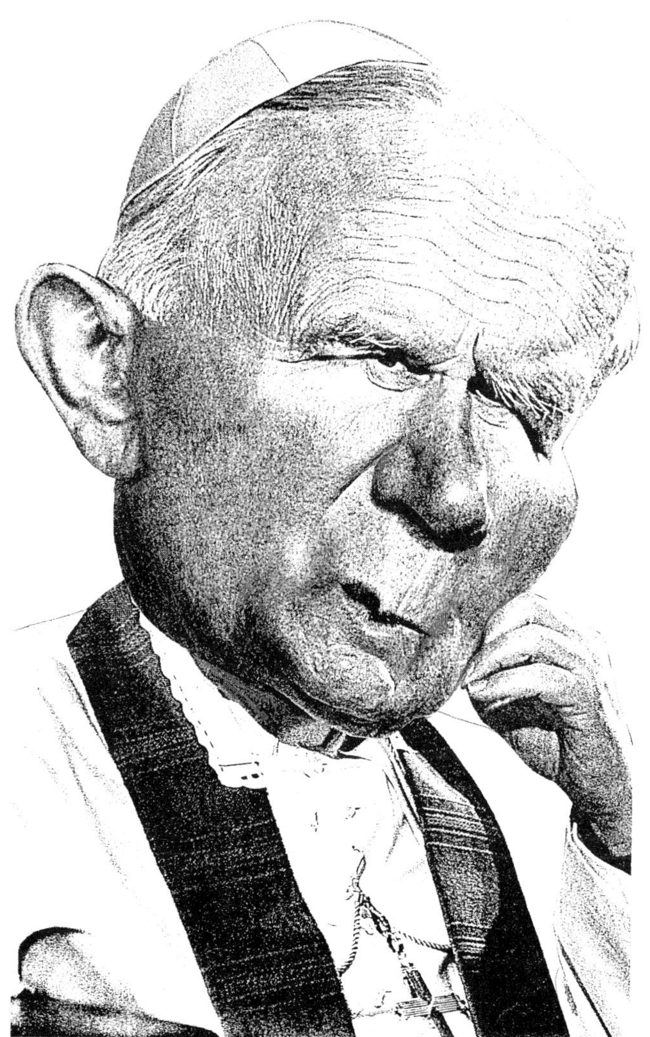

Peter Clarke Pope John Paul II *collaged photocopy*

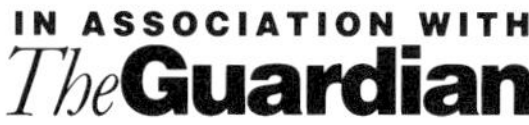

Views from the Edge

GLASGOW AND THE SOUTH WEST

REVIEWING THE EDGE: Thoughts on margins, marginalization and photography

Jan-Erik Lundström

No nation but the imagination Derek Walcott

We fantasize, hope, and know that art, photography, cultural practices, may work like acupuncture – that one peripheral intervention will make the larger system change its course, that one tiny disturbance at the edge will summon the centre to redress its ways and make it evolve in another direction. Perhaps this is not contrary to that other knowledge, concerning cultural and artistic work, that an ocean, no matter how vast, is made up of a finite number of drops.

In order to have a viewpoint, as the word itself implies, one must be at a specific place, a locale, a concrete site, from where the viewing is to be done. But, just as no word is autonomous but defined by its place within the system of language, so no viewpoint is simply defined by or of itself. Only when a viewpoint is related to other possible viewpoints and other places, can it be said to be viewing something, or indeed carrying on a dialogue. The view from the edge is dependent on the location of the centre. The centre is only a centre in terms of the edge. The margin exists only in relation to a mainstream, be it real or imaginary.

Photography has, historically and traditionally, been drawn to edges, indeed, been involved in the very process of marginalization. Perpetually, photography has been aimed at the Other – the exotic, the disenfranchised, the dispossessed, the exiled, the homeless, the disfigured, the stigmatized (further stigmatizing them through the photograph). From the American Civil War to AIDS, from Indian famine in the 1860's to Somalia, photographers have produced an immense encyclopedia, cataloguing and indexing the victims and the calamities of the world. It is as if the camera by its very nature had to be directed downward at spectacle or misery. This phenomenon involves the historically evolved photographic practices which constitute the genre of documentary. Its predisposition towards decay and desolation, its tendency to preserve and extend marginalization, rather than question it, have begun to be addressed in recent years. Criticism has proposed a number of philosophical as well as practical solutions. Scepticism towards classical realist modes has proliferated, and alternative practices – staged photography, image/text combinations, assemblages of photographs with other media, meta-photographic works, etc – have developed.

But why does marginalized photography or marginalization in photography exist today? Marginalization may occur within many spheres – the economic, the social, cultural, or the geographic. By way of class as well as by way of gender, race, sexual preference, or ethnic background. It is not just a question of another author or audience, but of content. Certain themes or topics may be ignored, suppressed or censured (remember that the most common kind of censorship is self-censorship). It could be the Irish conflict or homelessness, or, in particular, questions of the apparent causes of social ills. Modernism ignored or aesthetized more politically charged subject matter. Social or political ills were not welcomed in abstract expressionism. Similarly, certain topics are considered taboo in particular contexts – defined as obscene, anti-patriotic, vulgar, difficult, 'not art'. Nor can one simply single out subject matter when some practices or styles may be beyond the pale as well. Just as modernism outlawed narrative, contemporary art institutions tend to proscribe certain variants of classical documentary. We must be particularly wary of such developments today. For example, are we creating new blind spots in the prevalent anti-realist position towards independent photography? It would be absurd if the conclusion of the post-structuralist discourse on photography were to dismiss documentary as a reactionary discourse in and of itself.

Access is perhaps the most central issue when examining marginalization. Who is doing the photographing? Who has access to the finished work? Groups – geographically, economically, culturally, socially – are marginalized in terms of their access to art/culture, as producers and as consumers. With a cultural system dominated by Western privilege and WASP standards, groups such as Third and Fourth-worlders, ethnic minorities, women, gays, people with special needs, must struggle for access to mainstream venues.

The first step in this struggle is the call for the right to one's own image. In revising documentary (parallel to revisions in anthropology and ethnography) it became clear that the constituencies in question (female, poor, ethnic minorities, etc.) were seldom in control of their own representation. The centre photographed the margin, not the other way around. Nor did the margin photograph itself. As a consequence however, we saw, during the 1980's, a number of important works produced on this basis: people taking control of their own representation. It is a radical shift, from being object to being subject. People, previously and traditionally only passive objects of representation, began to participate in producing the images of themselves. Black photography, for example, strived to promote positive imagery of black people, produced by black people, as alternatives to the images of passivity, victimization and otherness, which were the norm. If the 'other' is always represented in the position of lack, then we know that the representation will not go far towards any alternative. These new approaches do not simply articulate self-identity in terms of opposition and otherness, but as growing out of one's own experiences, building one's own language.

In addition to the work coming directly from specific constituencies, other independent photographers developed a variety of collaborative, multivocal and dialogic strategies, for example – Wendy Ewald's photography with children from Appalachia and later Latin America. Rhonda Wilson's poster series *A Sense of Place*, blending theatrical and photojournalistic genres, was produced with the help of many women's groups addressing the questions of homelessness and poverty among women in Thatcher's England. Similarly, Stephen Willats explored a variety of collaborative methods while working with people living in housing projects on the outskirts of London. Martha Rosler's project, *If you Lived Here*, addressed the situation facing homeless people in New York with a multi-dimensional and multi-strategic approach. Beyond these specific examples, many community projects are based on collective and collaborative means.

In a different way, Jorma Puranen's *Imaginary Homecoming* an exhibition at Gracefield Studios during Fotofeis is a series where 19th century photographs of the Lapps, taken by French explorers and found by Puranen at the Musée de l'Homme in Paris, are returned to their place of origin and reinstated in the contemporary Lapp landscape of northern Scandinavia, bringing the representations back to where they were taken. A reclamation, a homecoming, but also a dialogue between cultures and between two historical moments.

The work of criticism and practice in addressing the wishes and demands of the marginalized, aimed at empowering the margin to represent itself, has met with some success. New issues are on the agenda, awareness has been raised. It will surely continue, but there is no ultimate method or strategy which dissolves these problems for ever. The ground gained is always under pressure from the forces of incorporation and assimilation. Dynamic and independent cultures of economically or socially subordinate groups are constantly plundered by the mainstream for new images, new ideas, in its continuing quest for stylistic refreshment and expansion.

Clearly, redefining, re-evaluating and revising artistic strategies and practices is not enough. Nor are theoretical insights. To accomplish real political ends, efforts need to be made to redefine the meaning of art, the way it is interpreted, the spaces and venues in which it can be found, and the audiences to which it speaks. Responses to such revision may be very local and very specific, having little to do with the 'international' art world.

In the midst of an unstable present, the concept of the margin, both economically and culturally, is hard to define. In our diverse and challenging age, with its continuously changing cultural and ethnic landscape, borders are constantly redrawn and margins redefined. We live with daily demographic turmoil. The nation-state is being transformed from inside out and from outside in. Waves of humanity ebb and flow in and out across borders in a global and unremitting process of negotiation between languages, cultures and traditions. It is a mark of our time. Identities are articulated across borders, in dialogue, in polylogue. Peoples are made refugee, exiled, migrant, diasporic. Europe is becoming more like Latin America, with its syncretic, energetic, disjointed fusion of European, American-Indian, and Afro-Caribbean culture.

We are not only living in a global village in terms of communication, but as witnesses and participants in an ever-increasing traffic in people. Yet this global communication and movement of individuals across borders is not simple or easy to analyse. In Europe, immigration laws are becoming more restrictive, racism is on the rise, trade barriers are being re-erected between Europe and the rest of the world. The chasm between the haves and the have-nots is widening. In the western nations, as in Scandinavia, this is seen in a particular kind of exiled community – non-sited, atopic. The refugee camps where people wait, sometimes for years in hope and in despair, for a response to their application for political asylum, are wounds in the cultural landscape, reminding the privileged West of its Others.

The process of global change is complex – simultaneously homogenising and heterogenizing. Coca-Cola and Hollywood everywhere, yet they are always being reinterpreted, re-articulated locally. There are as many Dallases as there are viewers of it. It is not the same Dallas in Kautokeino in the Lapp country of northern Norway as in Kuala Lumpur, Malaysia or as in Manila, Nicaragua.

Cultural theorists have given the name *deterritorialization* to this complex process of exchange which characterises late capitalism – a steady loosening of the links between peoples, money and territory, immersing us in fluidity. A flux of individual and of collective identities. We can no longer depend on firm ground as we discover and re-invent ourselves.

Thanks to skilled footwork by a variety of advocates, awareness of exclusion and marginalization is more acute. A catchword of recent coinage is *multiculturalism*, aimed at developing equity between cultures, etc. We can see concrete instances of 'multiculturalism' in contemporary (marginal) art: the work of Border Art Workshop in the USA – bilingual performances and installations addressing the culture of the Mexican-Californian border. Much of Chicano art is a similar hybrid or synthesis. Two 'languages' similarly meet in some British photography – Black and British in Ingrid Pollard, Asian and British in Sunil Gupta or Sutipa Bashawas – to take only two examples.

And just as the discourses on gender and race have moved out of early essentialisms (the 'True Woman' or the 'Real Black'), so work addressing marginalization in general has come to the conclusion that there is no right view, no single ultimate perspective. All imagery from the margin is provisional, contingent, in flux. 'It ain't where you're from, it's where you're at.'

Similarly, our institutions of art and culture are not unassailable. Parameters may be redrawn. Paradigms may be thrown overboard. The magazine, the daily press, the TV channel, the radio station, the gallery, the museum, the art hall – all are historical phenomena, under constant revision supervised by the forces of the present.

Marginal discourse has two purposes. First, to make the marginalized visible, to articulate its identity and its desires. Second, to make power itself visible. To give gestalt to the centre. As cultures connect, collide, collude, and as marginalized cultures contend the centre, power will be made visible. It is when power is contested that it has to make itself manifest.

Despite the ground gained in the discourses on multiculturalism and the increased awareness of marginalization, reactionary politics are in the ascendent – social ills are treated by trickle-down or 'crumbs from the table' theories. Strategies, not aimed at a cure but at temporary relief; not aimed at changing a system, but at masking its flaws.

Dream then of a social practice of multiplicity that is neither assimilative nor separative, but relational. And know that the centre can only consolidate itself and struggle to maintain the status quo. If achieved, it can only deteriorate, collapsing under its own weight. It falls prey to its own self-righteousness. The margins grow, returning the paper to its original state, usurping the page, erasing the established texts. The margin is the unwritten, the not yet formulated, the not yet spoken, the unsaid. The margin is the future.

Jan-Erik Lundström is a curator, critic, writer, lecturer and teacher. He has worked with many Scandinavian museums and is currently Director of Fotografiska Museet in Stockholm.

JANE EVELYN ATWOOD USA / *France*

Two Stories – Prostitutes: a Photographic Essay
Jean Louis: Living with AIDS

Art Gallery & Museum

KELVINGROVE, GLASGOW

PREMIERE

24 JUNE – 22 AUGUST

The people that Jane Evelyn Atwood has photographed are often thought of as belonging in the margins of society: the blind, the elderly, women in prisons. An American who has lived in Paris for twenty years, she begins as something of an outsider herself, but has gained the trust of her subjects through working with them over a long period of time. She has described this process of familiarisation in her *Prostitutes* series (1976-77):

"At first, the women were suspicious of me; that was normal. I had a camera, and furthermore, I was an outsider ... They gradually became very maternal towards me, very protective ... finally, the crucial difference between us was that they went up with the clients and I did not."

Her more recent series, *Jean Louis*, taken between 16 July and 27 November 1987, involved a different kind of intimacy.

"Throughout the course of our work, even during his most difficult moments, Jean Louis never asked me to stop photographing him. It was his unique personality, his intelligence, the deep friendship that developed between us from the very beginning, and his extraordinary dignity that made this work possible. His own words best express our purpose in doing this story: 'I want these photos to be everywhere, in every living room on every coffee table, so that the world's youth can see them because the danger is there. Young people have to know. They are the future of our planet, and the AIDS virus is threatening the world. It is a form of war. We have to fight it, and to do so we must be united. Let's fight it, let's fight it together.'"

Atwood's photographs bring these people from the margins into the centre of our vision.

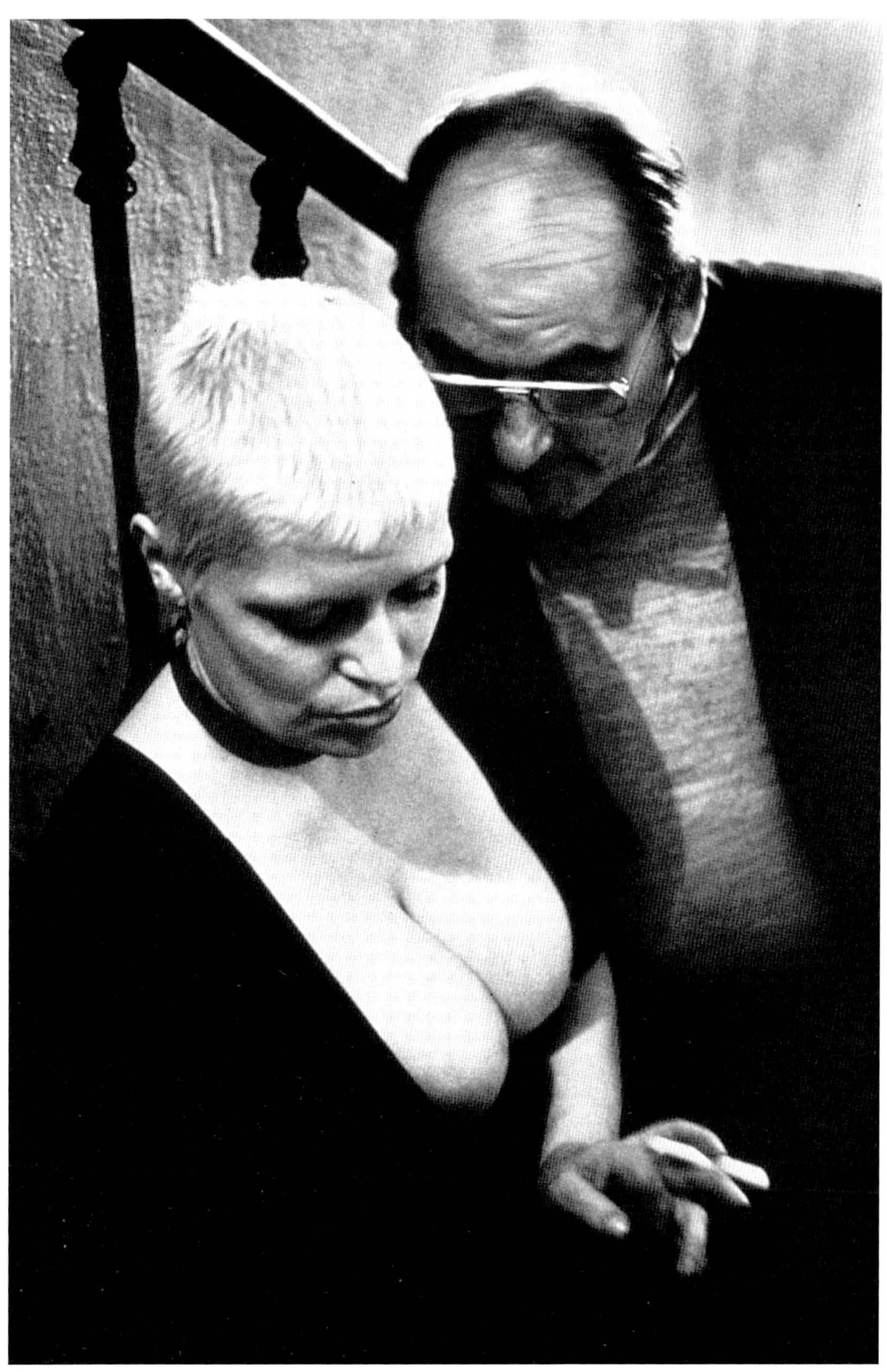

Jane Evelyn Atwood from the series 'Prostitutes' *silver-gelatin print*

JOHN McQUEENIE *Australia*
Details from Amnesia

Lillie Art Gallery

STATION ROAD, MILNGAVIE
GLASGOW

EUROPEAN PREMIERE

29 JUNE – 29 JULY

John McQueenie lives and works in Hobart where he is tutor in the Photography Department of the University of Tasmania Centre for the Arts. He was born in Milngavie, Scotland and lived there until the age of twelve.

This exhibition began three years ago with the discovery, at his mother's house in Milngavie, of a drawer containing exposed rolls of 126 (Box Brownie) film which had lain undeveloped for almost 25 years. They were taken to a local laboratory which processed the film but refused to make prints as the emulsion had deteriorated badly, the negatives were fogged, the images practically worthless. However, when Mrs McQueenie subsequently visited her son in Tasmania, she took the 'useless' negatives with her believing he would have sufficient patience to produce a set of prints.

In the darkroom, John McQueenie had the uncanny experience of recognising many of the images as photographs he himself had taken as a child. The decay of the emulsion and its erosion of the image suggesting to him the perfect metaphor for fading memory, with all the pathos and poignancy that attends temporal and geographical dislocation.

Printed very large, the images in the exhibition resonate as both banal and poetic, their ubiquity as snapshots tempered by the sense of loss in the cracked emulsion. The work was acclaimed when first exhibited at the Adelaide Festival. This showing in Milngavie (the first outside Australia) brings the project full circle.

Supported by The Australia Council

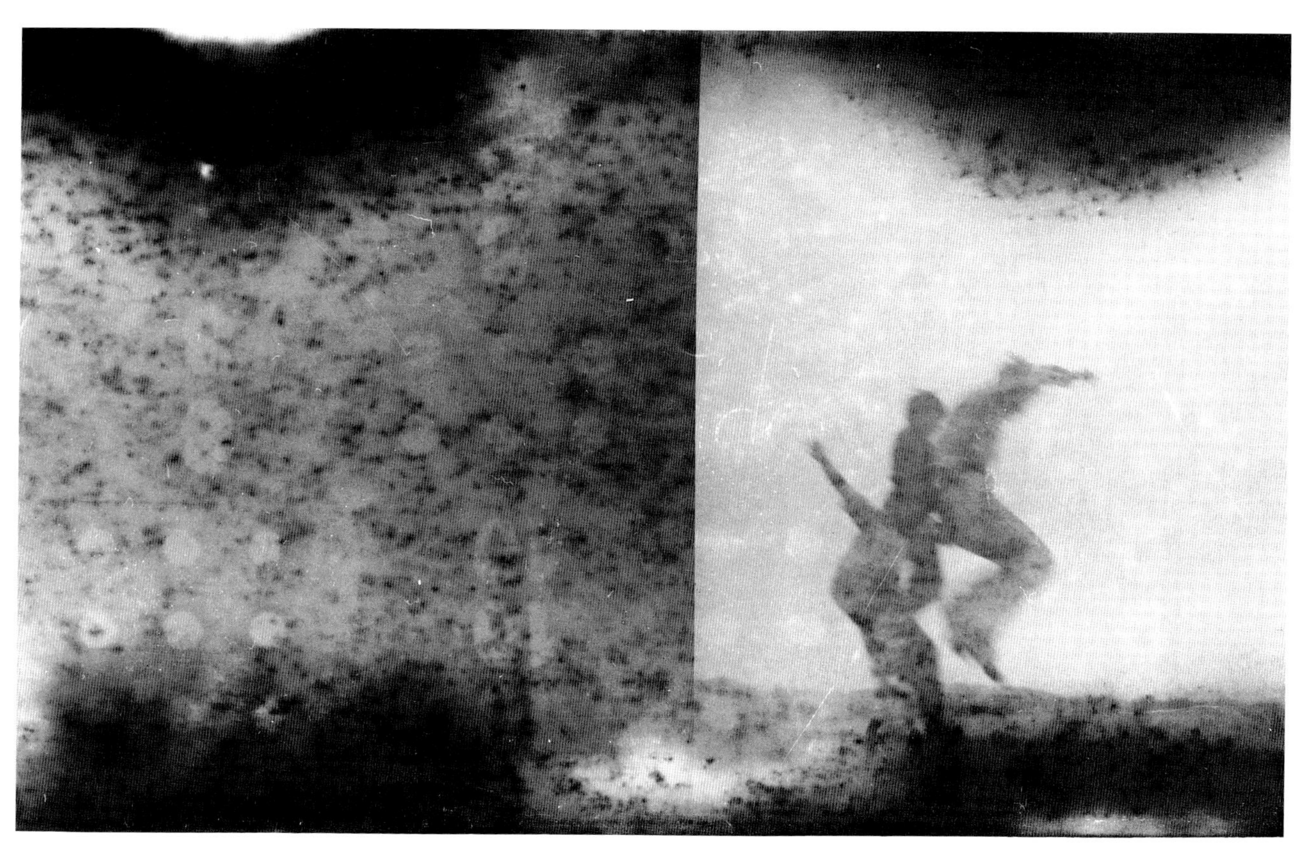

John McQueenie Untitled Diptych (detail) *silver-gelatin print*

CZECH PHOTOGRAPHY OF THE 1990'S

Maclaurin Art Gallery

ROZELLE PARK, AYR

PREMIERE

11 JUNE – 25 JULY

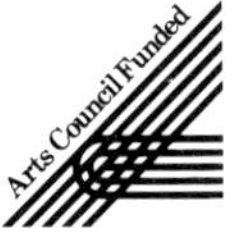

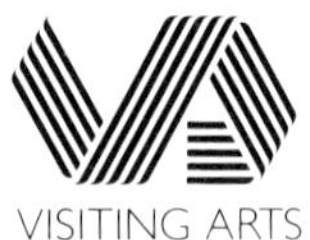

Curated by Vladimír Birgus and Miroslav Vojtěchovský

Presented in conjunction with The Ministry of Foreign Affairs of the Czech Republic and The Association of Photographers (Czech Republic)

The situation in the Czech Republic since 1989, following the collapse of forty years of totalitarian rule, has been reflected in the fracturing of the ideological straitjacket imposed on art and an end to strict censorship. The country has opened itself to the outside world, but these positive processes have been accompanied by the demise of many state-subsidised cultural institutions and ever growing pressure from the art market which has not yet been sufficiently offset by a new system of public or private subsidy. Surprisingly, as far as photography is concerned, these radical changes have not yet manifested themselves in daily life to any great extent.

Although photojournalism enjoyed a brief renaissance during the dramatic 'velvet revolution' in Czechoslovakia, it has since all but returned to the documentation of daily life. Exceptions to this are Jindřich Štreit and Viktor Kolář, whose exciting photographic work gives evidence of the country's recent agitation. They have been joined since November 1989 by Josef Koudelka who is working with increased frequency in his native land.

While it no longer holds the dominant position it did in the 1980's, *mise en scene* photography is still a major area in Czech practice, its most celebrated practitioner being Jan Saudek. The same is true of multimedia work which oscillates between photography, painting, graphic art, sculpture and conceptual art, represented by Aleš Kuneš, Jiří Korecký, Robert Portel and Jiřé David. Recent years have seen a re-emergence of existential themes and expressive forms in staged and interdisciplinary photography, as illustrated in this exhibition by the work of Michal Macků and Ivan Pinkava. A traditionally prominent position has always been occupied by classic art photography. Often inspired by the memory of the *avant-garde* movement of the thirties, such artists include Jaroslav Rajzík and František Chrástek.

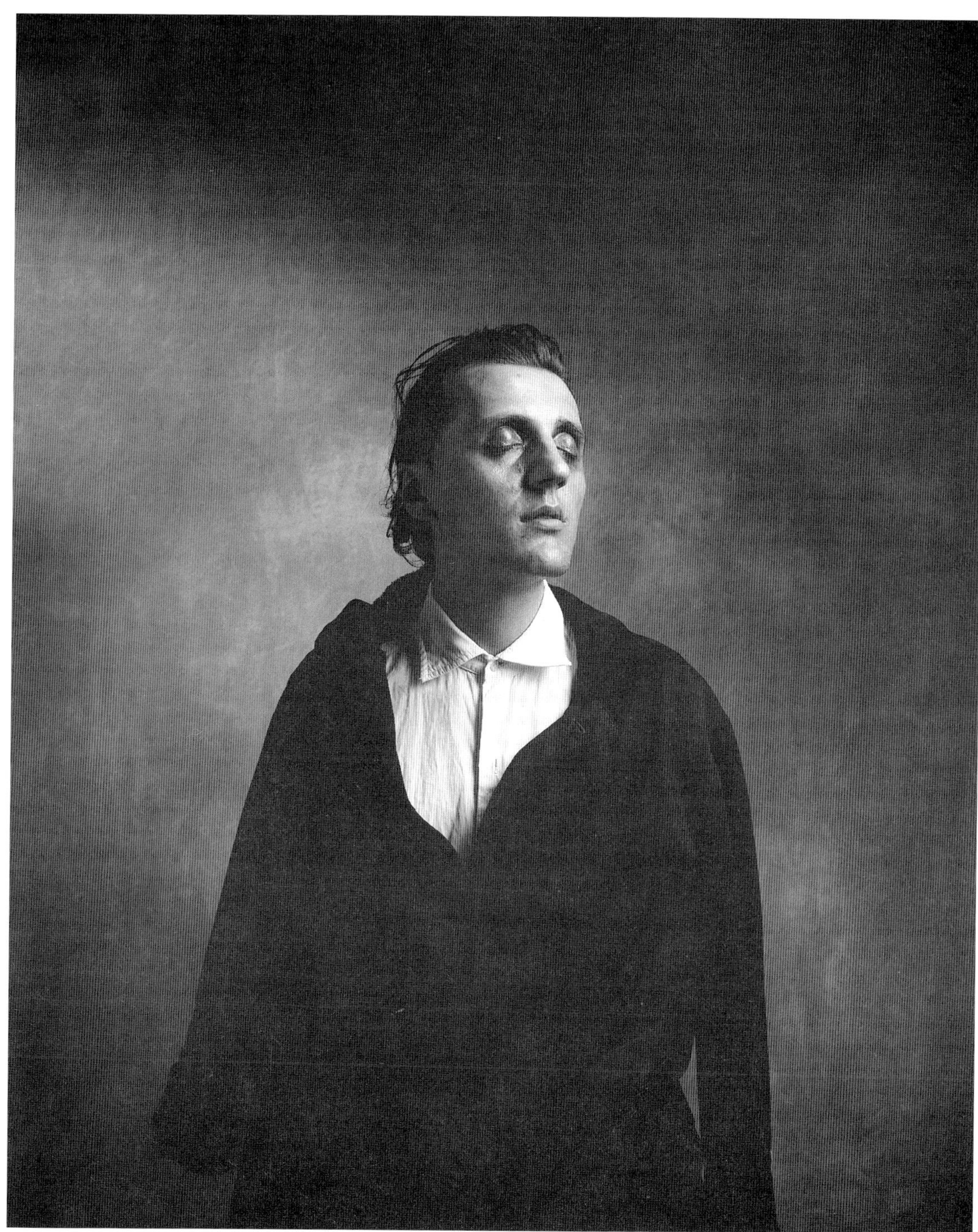

Ivan Pinkava Dynasty No.10 *silver-gelatin print*

RUTH STIRLING, WENDY McMURDO, JANE BRETTLE and SALLY RICE UK

Locate: Public Bodies – Private States

Collins Gallery

UNIVERSITY OF STRATHCLYDE
22 RICHMOND STREET
GLASGOW

PREMIERE

12 JUNE – 15 JULY

Locate is a unique collaborative project between four artist/photographers who, through different approaches, examine the concept of the body as a cultural construct across the authoritative practices of the Arts, Architecture, Social Science, Medicine, Theology and the Law. Leading academics, scholars, practitioners and other artists, who are all women working in an interdisciplinary way, have been invited to collaborate in an investigation of the different levels at which this affects us all.

Consisting of an exhibition, siteworks, a publication, and a conference with practical workshops, the project accesses debate and ideas, broadening the parameters of art practice in its consideration of the highly theorised and privatized fields which constitute Western society. It specifically examines the way dominant institutions affect our understanding and experience of the world mediated through our bodies, in both the public and private spheres.

Recognising the temporal, spatial and representational qualities inherent in the medium of photography, and using mixed media, computer imagery and sound, exhibition work by the four artists incorporates large scale photographic installation and sound works. The artists consider aspects of experience which include the encoding of gender in Western culture; the place of fantasy and desire; the relationship of the body to the law; the body as site in ecclesiastical architecture. Further siteworks extend into the city in the form of banners and leaflets.

A publication, *Public Bodies – Private States* (Manchester University Press), considers the issues raised by the artists' work in conjunction with essays by six prominent academics and practitioners. The contents form a matrix in which interconnections and differences between practice and lived experience are recognised – where the body becomes the point of convergence.

A conference takes the interdisciplinary approach further. Practitioners in the areas considered by the project, but working outside the arts, are invited to debate the issues with a broad audience.

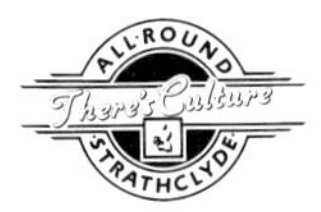

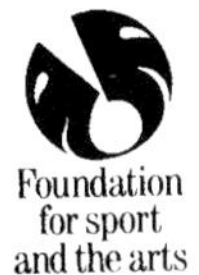

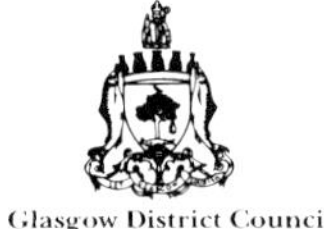

Subsidised by the
Scottish Arts Council

The Gulbenkian Foundation
Glasgow Development Agency
The Russell Trust
The Hope Scott Trust

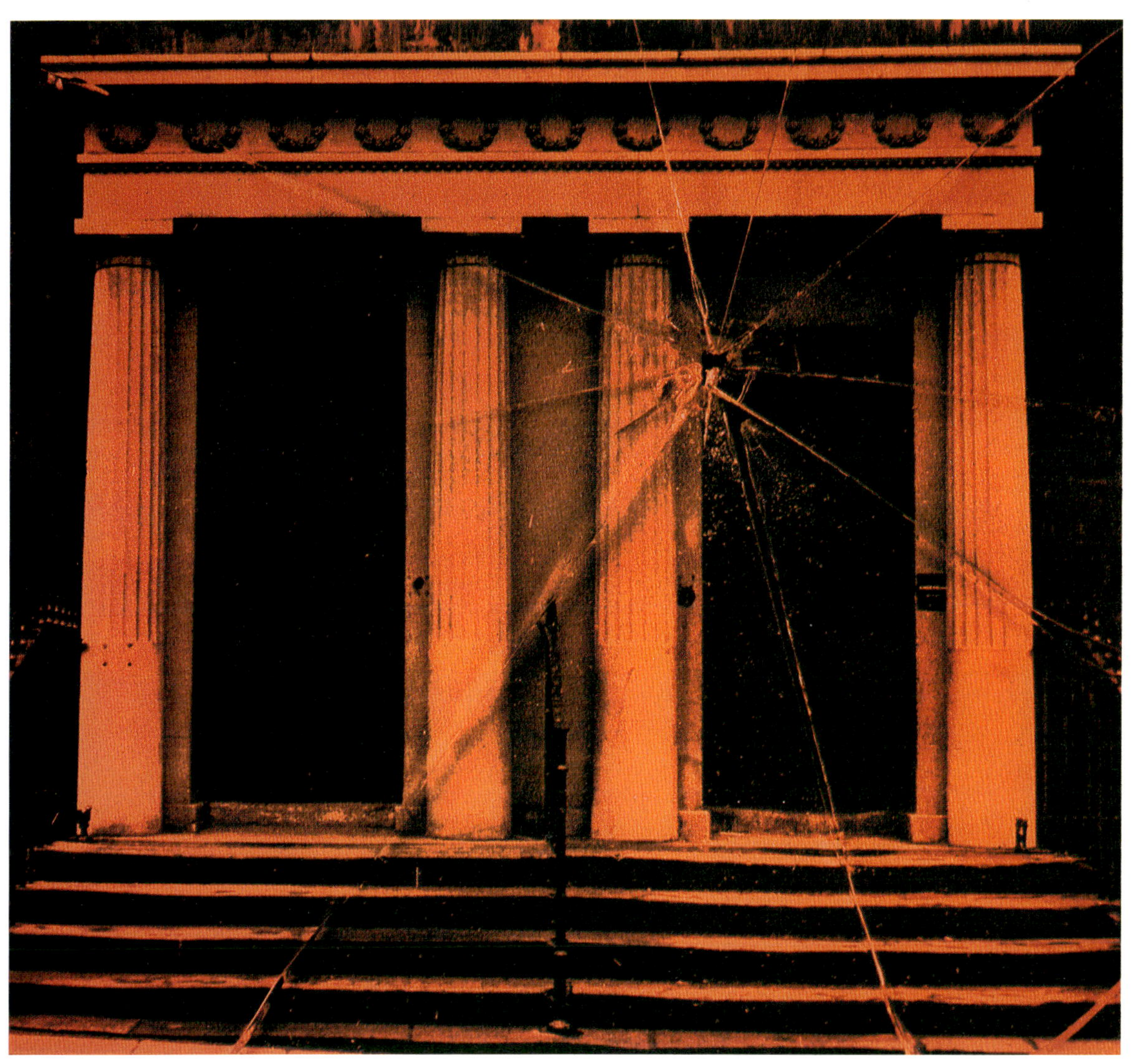

Jane Brettle (dis)Location 2 *cibachrome print from dyed, xeroxed silver-gelatin print*

LUIS GONZALEZ PALMA *Guatemala*

el Silencio de la Mirada

The Smith Art Gallery and Museum

DUMBARTON ROAD

STIRLING

UK PREMIERE

5 JUNE – 4 JULY

Luis González Palma appears courtesy of The Schneider-Bluhm-Loeb Gallery Inc., Chicago

Subsidised by the
Scottish Arts Council

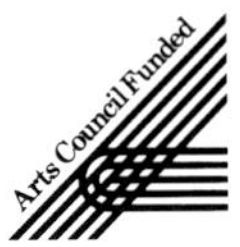

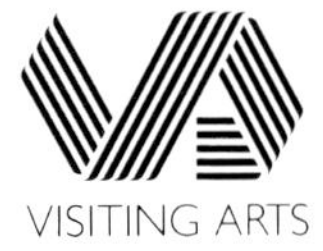

Pain, beauty and solitude dwell at the heart of Luis González Palma's work. Trained as an architect and living and working in Guatemala City, Palma's large, expressive photographic pieces take as their subject the indigenous Mayan people. His images are not photographic documents of contemporary existence, but mysterious icons which draw their visual language from the myths and traditions of the Maya. The Maya believe in a magical universe in which animals, plants and the earth itself are spiritually endowed. Today they are marginal people in their own land, but they have held onto their beliefs. As Luis González Palma explains, "The indigenous population of Guatemala accepted the Catholic religion (imposed by conquering Spaniards), as a sort of outside veneer, but kept their own religion as well. My work is a subjective approach to reality in Guatemala based on social conditions in the country as well as the solitude that is present in all human beings."

The large black and white photographs show contemporary Mayan and mixed-race Guatemalan people, transforming them by the addition of wings, roses, moons and skulls into something magical, and yet more close to the truth of their existence. The prints are overpainted with brown varnish or selectively toned sepia. Only the eyes and occasionally other small areas of the print retain their original whites and blacks. The umber overlay is reminiscent both of old photographs and of the earth from which their mystical world has sprung. The prints are mounted on large, distressed boards which the artist has made on site at the gallery. Although specifically Guatemalan in their visual language, these images evoke emotions that are universal. The critic A.D. Coleman expressed it thus: "There is something sweet about these images, but also something infinitely sad – like your grandparents' request that you serve as pall-bearer at their funerals."

It is only in the past two years that the reputation of Luis González Palma has begun to spread far and wide. In that time he has had a number of exhibitions in USA including *Persistence of Beauty, Persistence of Pain* at the Art Institute of Chicago. This exhibition marks his first showing in the UK.

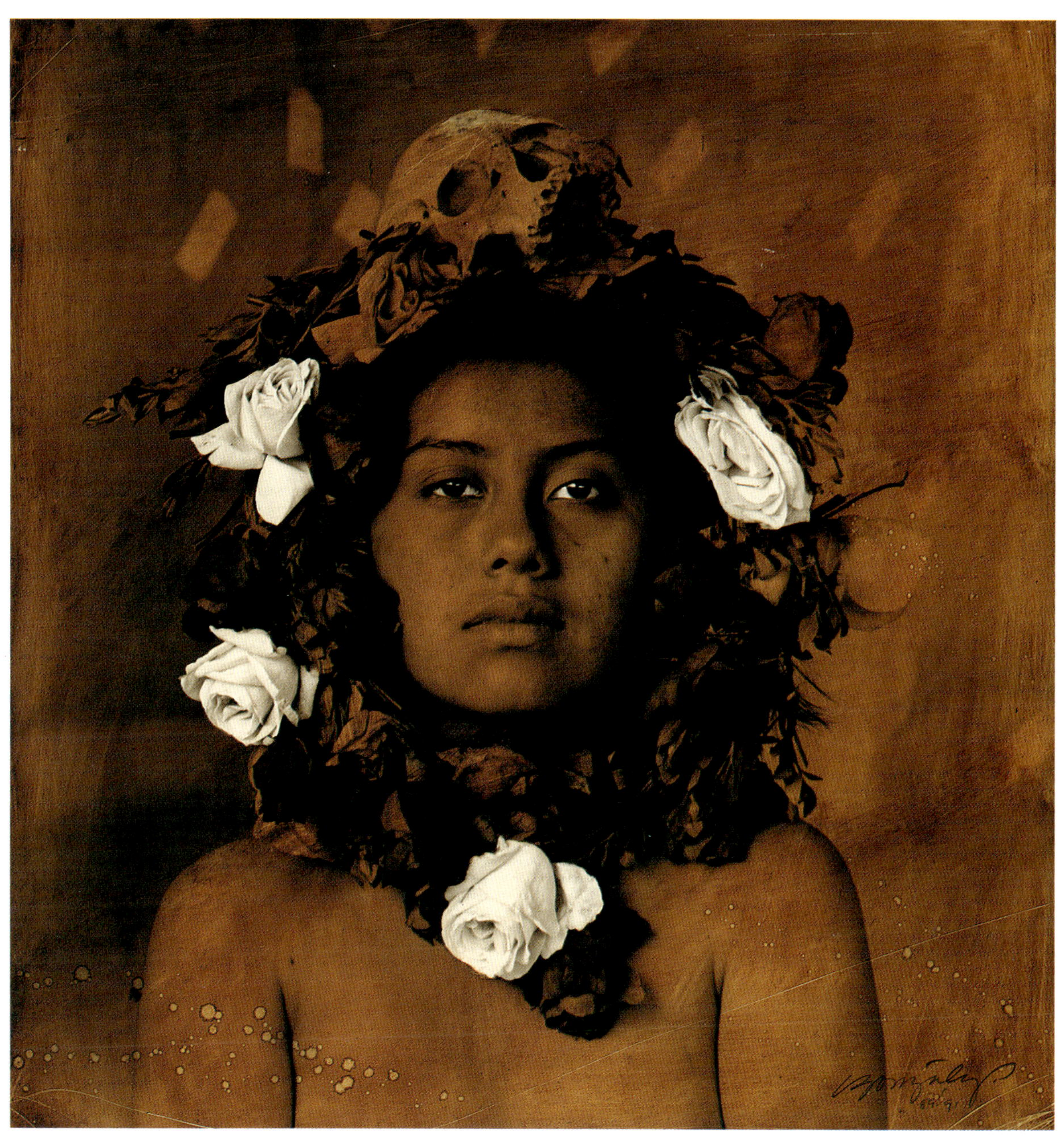

Luis González Palma Rosas (Roses) *mixed media*

PHOTOGRAPHY FROM LATVIA, LITHUANIA AND ESTONIA

Borderlands

Street Level Gallery at The Cottier

HYNDLAND STREET
GLASGOW

PREMIERE

5 JUNE – 4 JULY

Estonia

PEETER LINNAP

EVE LINNAP

HARALD LEPPIKSON

JÜRI LIIM

JÜRI OKAS

PEETER TOOMING

MART VILJUS

Lithuania

GINTARAS ZINKEVIČIUS

ALVYDAS LUKYS

REMIGIJUS TREIGYS

GINTAUTAS TRIMAKAS

SAULIUS PAUKSTIS

VYTAUTAS STANIONIS

Latvia

GVIDO KAJONS

VALTS KLEINS

INTA RUKA

ANDREJS GRANTS

The Baltic countries are 'borderlands' both geographically and psychologically. The status and psyche of the people have no doubt been influenced by population size and geographical location. These factors have turned Latvia, Lithuania and Estonia into an attractive object of conquest and have become an essential factor in shaping their cultural identity. There are many similarities as well as differences in the art and culture of these countries.

Throughout the long period of Soviet occupation, the Baltic people never fully integrated with the USSR, maintaining their own languages and culture. Unlike most of the rest of the Soviet Union, a distinction between – and parallel development of – State sanctioned and underground art did not really exist here: independent creative thought continued despite the external ideological pressure.

Borderlands brings together the work of seventeen contemporary photographers from these three countries. Rather than attempt a survey from the outside, Street Level invited Peeter Linnap, a photographer, teacher and curator based in Tallinn (Estonia), to curate the show. To properly represent the photography of Lithuania and Latvia, Linnap worked with the assistance of Gintautas Trimakas (Lithuania), and Valts Kleins (Latvia).

There has been much attention paid to the political situation in the Baltic States over recent years. It is now time to examine the photography of the Baltic States from a personal rather than a political viewpoint, looking at the effects of the recent changes on the artwork produced.

Sponsored by McGrigor Donald (Solicitors)

Subsidised by the
Scottish Arts Council

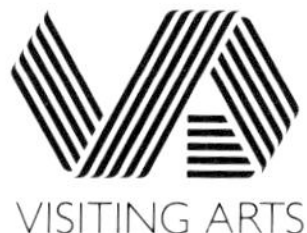

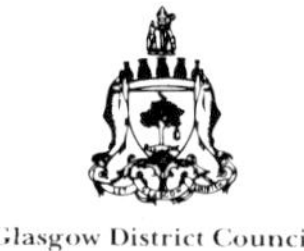

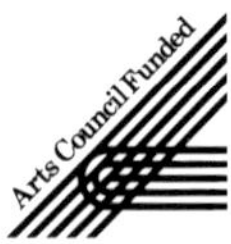

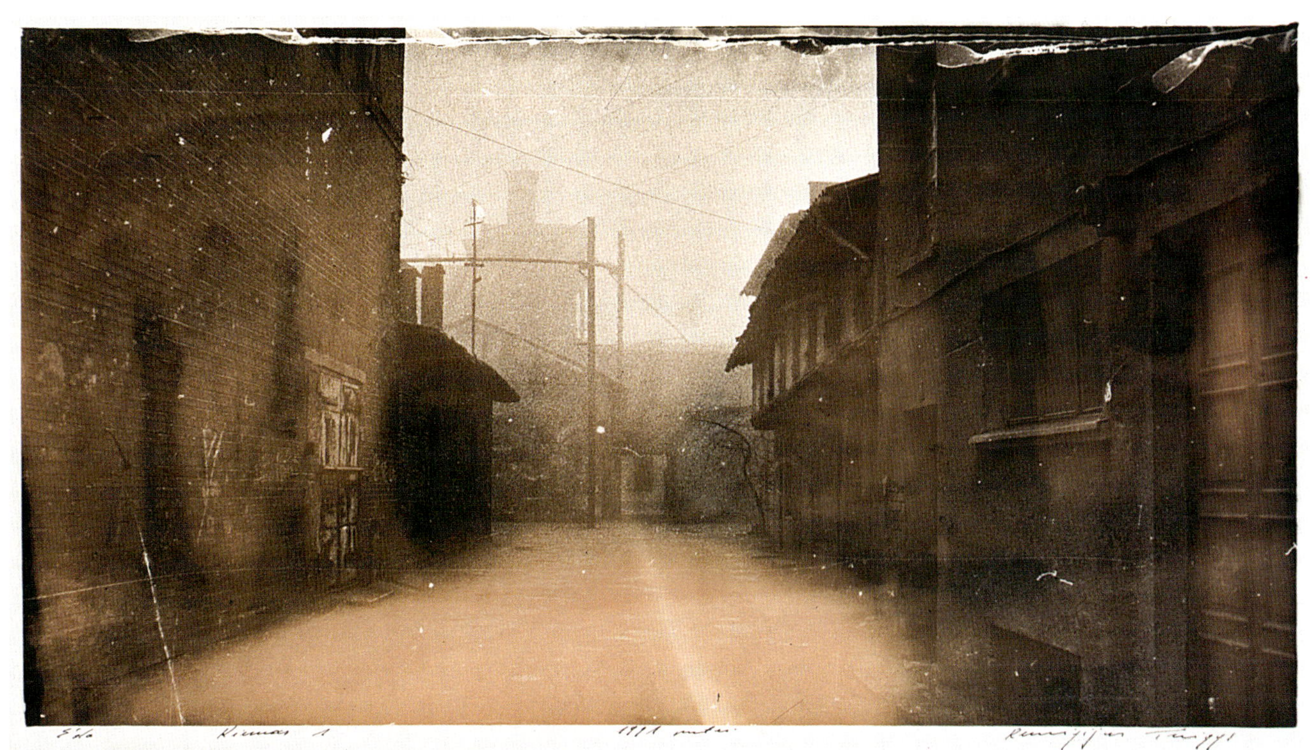

Remigijus Treigys Untitled *toned silver-gelatin print*

ALFREDO JAAR *Chile*
(Un)Framed

Tramway

25 ALBERT DRIVE, GLASGOW

PREMIERE

12 JUNE – 18 JULY

Alfredo Jaar is a Chilean-born resident of New York City whose photography-based installations focus on the relationship between the Developed and Developing worlds.

Jaar has exhibited widely in North and South America as well as Europe: his installation *La Géographie ça sert, d'abord, à faire la Guerre* was a major feature of the momentous *Magiciens de la Terre* exhibition in Paris in 1989 and his American one-person touring exhibition opened at the New Museum of Contemporary Art, New York in January, 1992. He had his first major show in this country last year at the Whitechapel Gallery, London.

Combining photography, architecture and theatre, Jaar's work examines the inextricable links that tie the so-called 'First World' to the 'Third World', exposing the iniquities in that relationship. For Tramway's theatre space, Jaar is creating a new installation *(Un)Framed*, which investigates particular political, social and geographical aspects of representation, in this case focusing on the Serra Pelada miners who work in the vast open-face gold mines of Brazil.

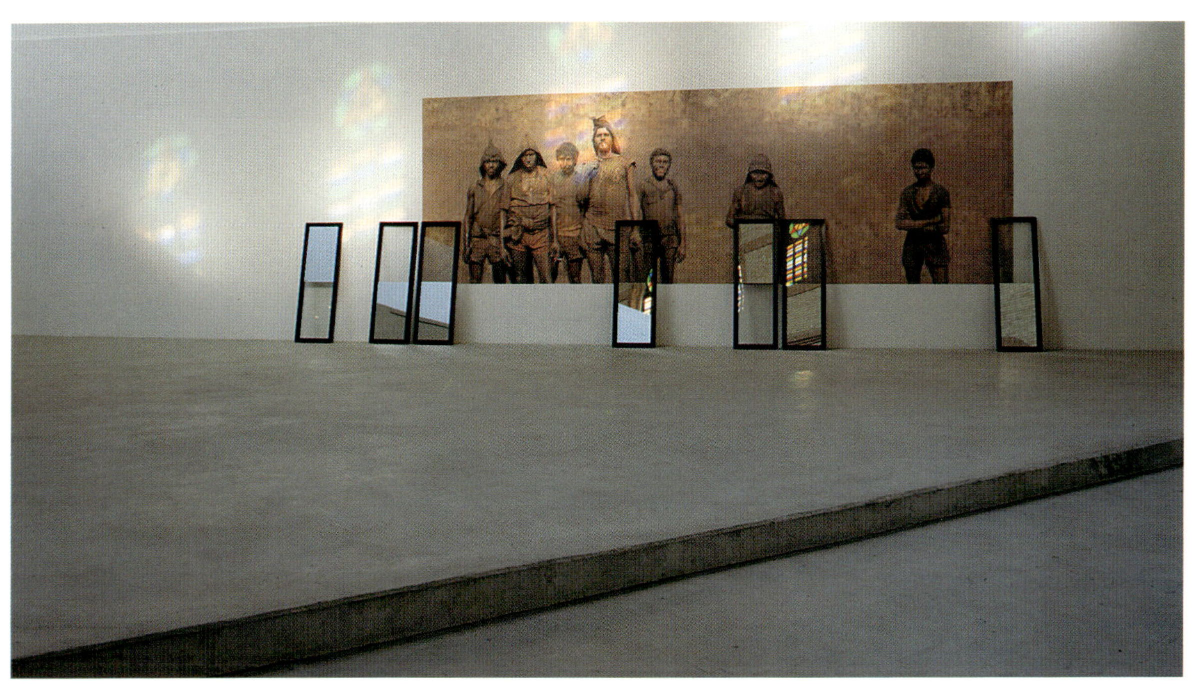

Alfredo Jaar (Un)framed *view of mixed media installation*

AFRICA GUZMAN *Spain*
Icasia

The Warehouse

61–65 GLASSFORD STREET
GLASGOW

UK PREMIERE

4 JUNE – 4 JULY

In Plato's philosophy, the term 'Icasia' (a Greek work which means imaginary) refers to the first stage of knowledge, which does not strictly mean knowledge, but 'opinion'.

Plato makes a distinction between the sensitive world and the intelligible one; the latter being considered the very Truth and its knowledge being the true one – Science.

The sensitive world consists of images, copies of this Truth. Beauty is a copy of Truth. A work of art is a copy of the copy: merely a shadow or reflection. This is what my photographs are.

In the Platonic system, photography belongs to the field of the Icasia, the world of darkness and shadows. My photographs are taken at night; the world of darkness is the furthest one from the Truth, from beauty, from 'light'.
Africa Guzman

Africa Guzman Tarragona *cibachrome print*

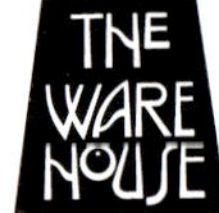

JOHN CLARIDGE UK

Warm in the Shadows · Cold in the Sun

Robert Burns Centre

MILL ROAD, DUMFRIES

4 JUNE – 4 JULY

Like his contemporaries, Bailey and Donovan, John Claridge tends to be known amongst photographers by his surname only. Claridge is one of those East End boys who made it to the Big Time in the sixties when the entire planet seemed to revolve around the swinging streets of London.

This exhibition of 60 photographs consists, not of his award-winning advertising shots, but the results of a personal project documenting the streets of his birthplace, the East End of London. Taken between 1959 and 1984, the photographs "... are to share with people an insight into what the East End meant to me ... there were lots of characters and a real community ... that finished as soon as they started putting up the tower blocks".

A Royal Photographic Society touring exhibition

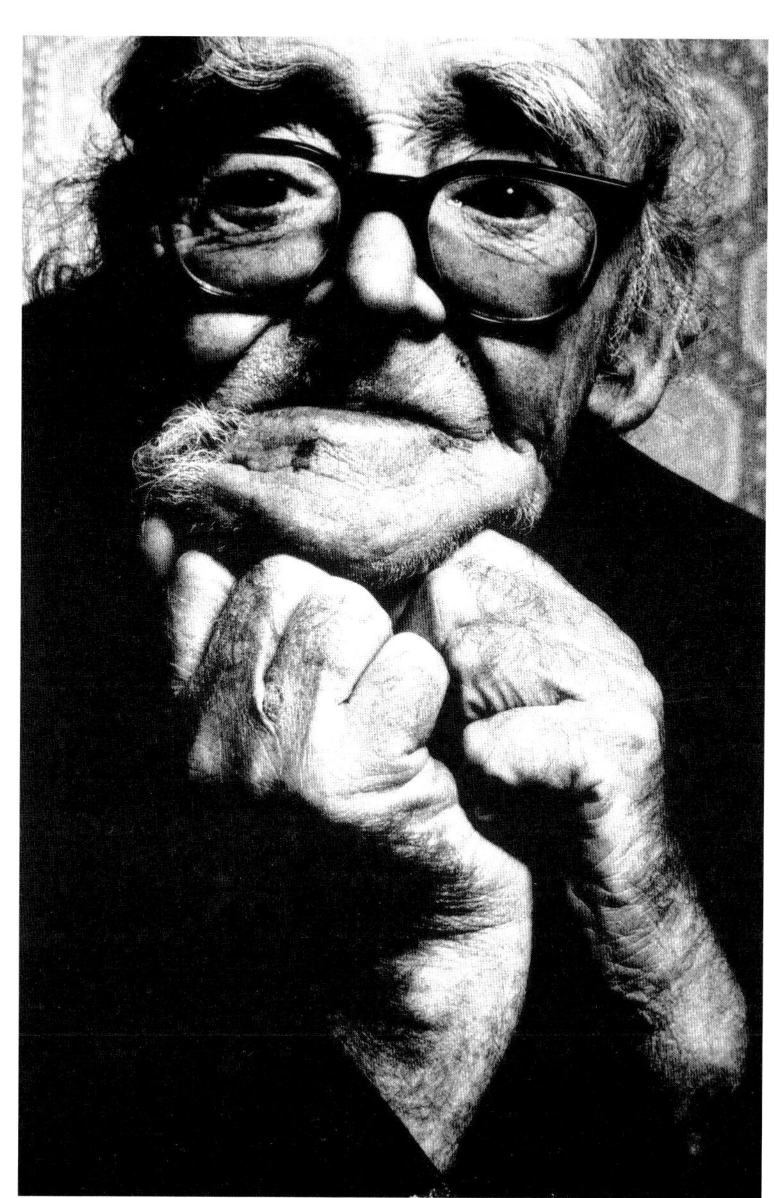

John Claridge Untitled *silver-gelatin print*

STAN DOUGLAS *Canada*

Hors-champs

Transmission Gallery

28 KING STREET,
GLASGOW

UK PREMIERE

8 JUNE – 3 JULY

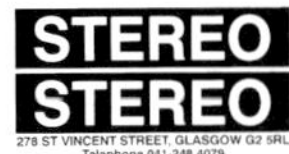

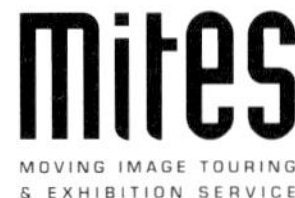

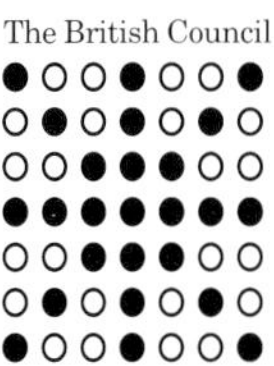

Produced at Centre Georges Pompidou by Musée national d'art moderne, Paris in the spring of 1992, Hors-champs *is dedicated to the people of South Central Los Angeles.*

What was typically known as 'The New Thing' in the United States and as 'Free Jazz' in Europe was an idiom of Afro-American music, characterized by simultaneous group improvisation and relative harmonic freedom. The music was generally associated with black nationalism in the U.S. — but, in France, during the late 1960's and early 1970's, the music acquired other connotations. For example, it was so popular among the Mai 1968 generation that audiences for Free Jazz concerts could number in thousands, and there were even festivals organised by the French Communist Party, which regarded the music as an ideal of social organisation.

Hors-champs presents the performance of four American musicians who either lived in France during the Free Jazz moment or who still reside there today: George Lewis (trombone), Douglas Ewart (saxophone), Kent Carter (bass) and Oliver Johnson (drums). The music they play is based on Albert Ayler's 1965 composition, *Spirits Rejoice*, and composed of four basic musical materials: a gospel melody, an attenuated call and response, a heraldic fanfare and *La Marseillaise*. Its proximity to the fanfare underlines the origin of the latter in military music, and, like many other national anthems, the recollection of its blood-thirsty lyric will remind one of the tacit content of myths of national identity.

Hors-champs was shot *en direct* in the style of an ORTF musical television production from the same era as Ayler's composition — notably those of Jean-Christophe Averty. Two video projections are simultaneously presented on recto and verso sides of a suspended wall. While one side of the screen shows a 'programme' montage of the two cameras, the other presents a simultaneous counter-narrative of everything that had been edited out, or relegated to the outside.
Stan Douglas

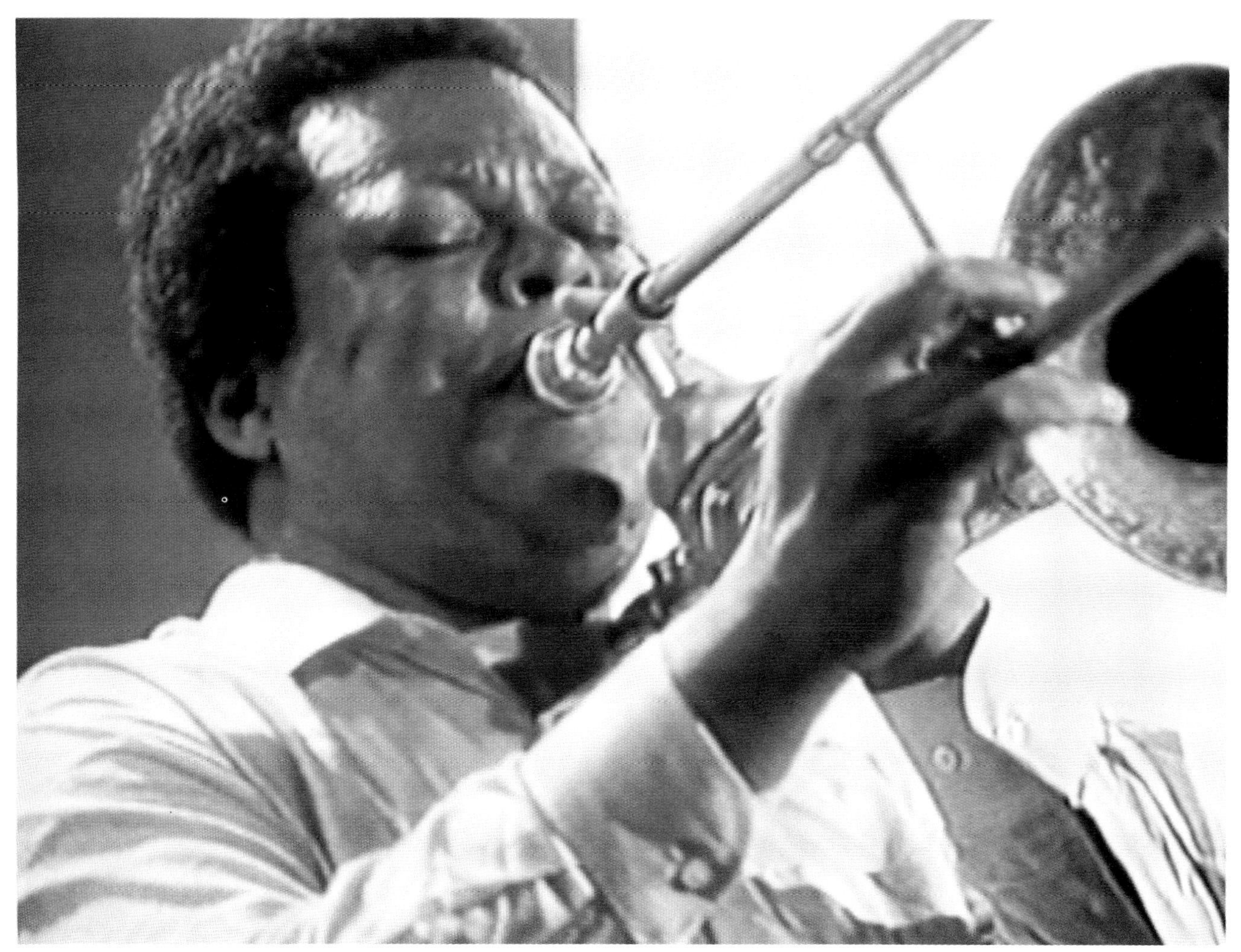

Stan Douglas George Lewis, trombone, *from* 'Hors-champs' *video projection*

EVGEN BAVCAR *France*

The Blind Photographer

The Dick Institute

ELMBANK AVENUE
KILMARNOCK

UK PREMIERE

26 JUNE – 24 JULY

Evgen Bavcar is something very unusual: he is a photographer and he is blind. Instead of recording the visible, Bavcar lends visibility to his photographs in the pictures he carries inside him of the past, of his dreams or his imaginings.

Evgen Bavcar has been blind for 36 years. He grew up in Slovenia, 27 kilometres from the Italian frontier. When he was eleven he stepped on a land mine. Within a few months he had lost his sight completely. With great effort he fixed in his memory the scenes that were gradually escaping him. He devoured picture books, and he impressed on his mind the faces of doctors and nurses.

When he began to take photographs, his blindness dictated the nature of his work. His starting point is not light but darkness. Working in the dark, he uses various light sources just as a painter uses brushes. He explores his subjects with light, recording them on film. "My eyes," says Bavcar, "are like the black box of the camera, and my other senses like the lens, with which I capture the outside world." The blind man outwits his blindness by using a camera as a substitute for the eye.

One of Evgen Bavcar's preferred motifs is his home country, the region around Ljubljana. He thus ensures his lasting possession of the only world he has ever really seen. For him, the park of Duino is a poetic revelation; it is the home of the angel: "Angels are like photons. They appear only to disappear, they are mediators between the visible and the invisible, between dark and light."

Esther Woerdehoff

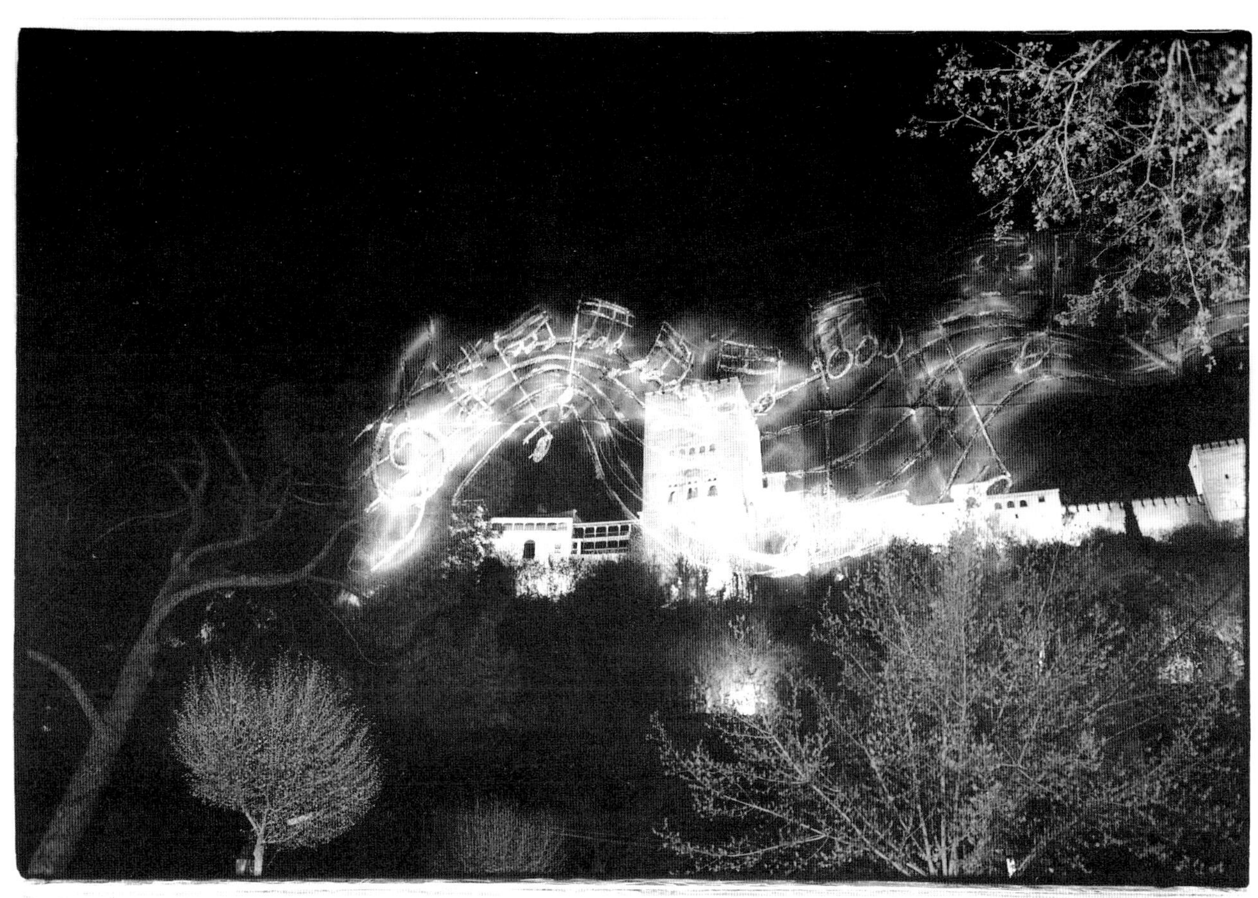

Evgen Bavcar Nostalgie *silver-gelatin print*

JAAKO HEIKKILÄ, RITVA TUOMI, JUKKA LEHTINEN JORMA PURANEN and JAPO KNUUTILA *Finland*

Second Nature

Gracefield Studios

28 EDINBURGH ROAD
DUMFRIES

UK PREMIERE

29 MAY – 27 JUNE

Second Nature draws on a very specific tradition in Finnish culture: the human body confronting and experiencing the landscape. Neither is, any longer, innocent. The human body is defined by its cultural environment and by the space it inhabits, just as the landscape is always already 'encultured', indeed created, by the human eye.

In his powerful work *Coming Home*, Jorma Puranen reinstates old portraits of Lapps found in the Museum of Ethnology in Paris within the landscape of Lapland. They are moving comments on the practices of colonialism, but also images that uncover and recover history.

Made on a tiny island in the Finnish archipelago, Japo Knuutila's photographs use fantasy to reflect the reality of island life. Members of the tightly knit community enact mysterious scenarios. Even the landscape seems to cooperate, unveiling its own dreams, secrets and layers of memory.

Jaako Heikkilä lives in northern Finland by the Tornio river on the border with Sweden. His images evoke the simplicity and serenity of this landscape. With few basic elements, the twilight of the midwinter day, ice and water, bodies wrapped in cloth, it is a restrained palette. He dreams the dream of humanity's unity with nature while documenting the landscape through the refracting lens of northern culture.

Ritva Tuomi takes a different, somewhat ironic approach. Here, mannequin dolls, idealized images of the young, beautiful and successful, inhabit a world of cosmetics and consumerism. But something threatens the idyll. There are cracks in the commercial perfection, flaws in the image.

Pursuing a similar theme Jukka Lehtinen's images of 'paradise' are more playful. Cut-out figures are placed in different landscapes – the beach, on the street, all in strange unnatural colours. The world of consumer leisure – paradise through artifice.

Subsidised by the
Scottish Arts Council

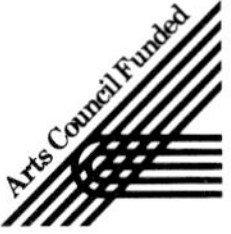

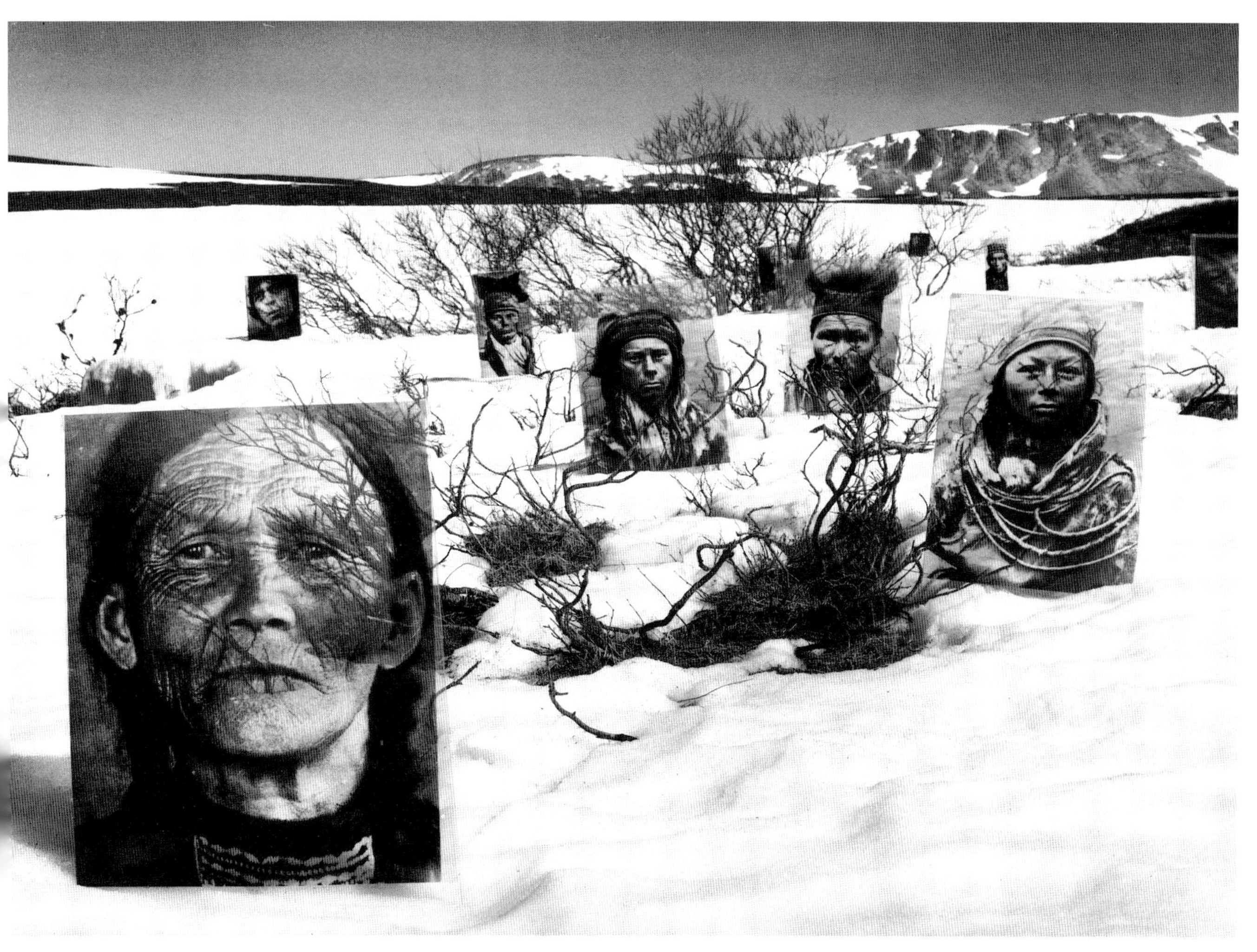

orma Puranen Untitled *silver-gelatin print*

PATRICIA MACDONALD UK

Salt • Sand

Art Gallery & Museum

KELVINGROVE, GLASGOW

PREMIERE

4 JUNE – 15 AUGUST

Salt • Sand is a personal exploration of the boundaries between familiar environments and patterns of life, and the unfamiliar: the 'other'. It begins with the idea of a familiar body of land and with the relationship of this to one's own body. Here the familiar body of land is the sub-continent of Europe.

From this centre, the images and accompanying quotations deal with the encounter of two distinct boundaries – with water, the oceanic edge, and with dryness and desert. The edge of the ocean, which is highly indented and not entirely fixed, with land and sea interpenetrating, is physically clearly defined; what lies on its other (oceanic) side is, however, hidden beneath the surface. The edge of dryness, subtly blending landscapes of erosion and diminishing greenness almost imperceptibly into the vast spaces of the true deserts, is much harder to locate exactly, both geographically and culturally. What lies beyond this dry boundary remains, apparently, clearly visible.

Each of these 'extreme' environments appears hostile to human life, but has nevertheless been traditionally associated with forces of great intensity and vitality, regenerative as well as destructive. This association persists, despite recent awareness that no environment remains any longer independent of human intervention. The work also deals with these paradoxes and the conflicting emotions associated with them.

Many of the colour images, some of which take the form of large banners, were made from the air (in collaboration with Angus Macdonald as pilot) at the oceanic edge or the desert margin. Others are intimate in both viewpoint and scale, functioning to locate the maker and viewer on one side or the other of the boundaries between familiar and unfamiliar, comfort and suffocation, freedom and unease, self and other.

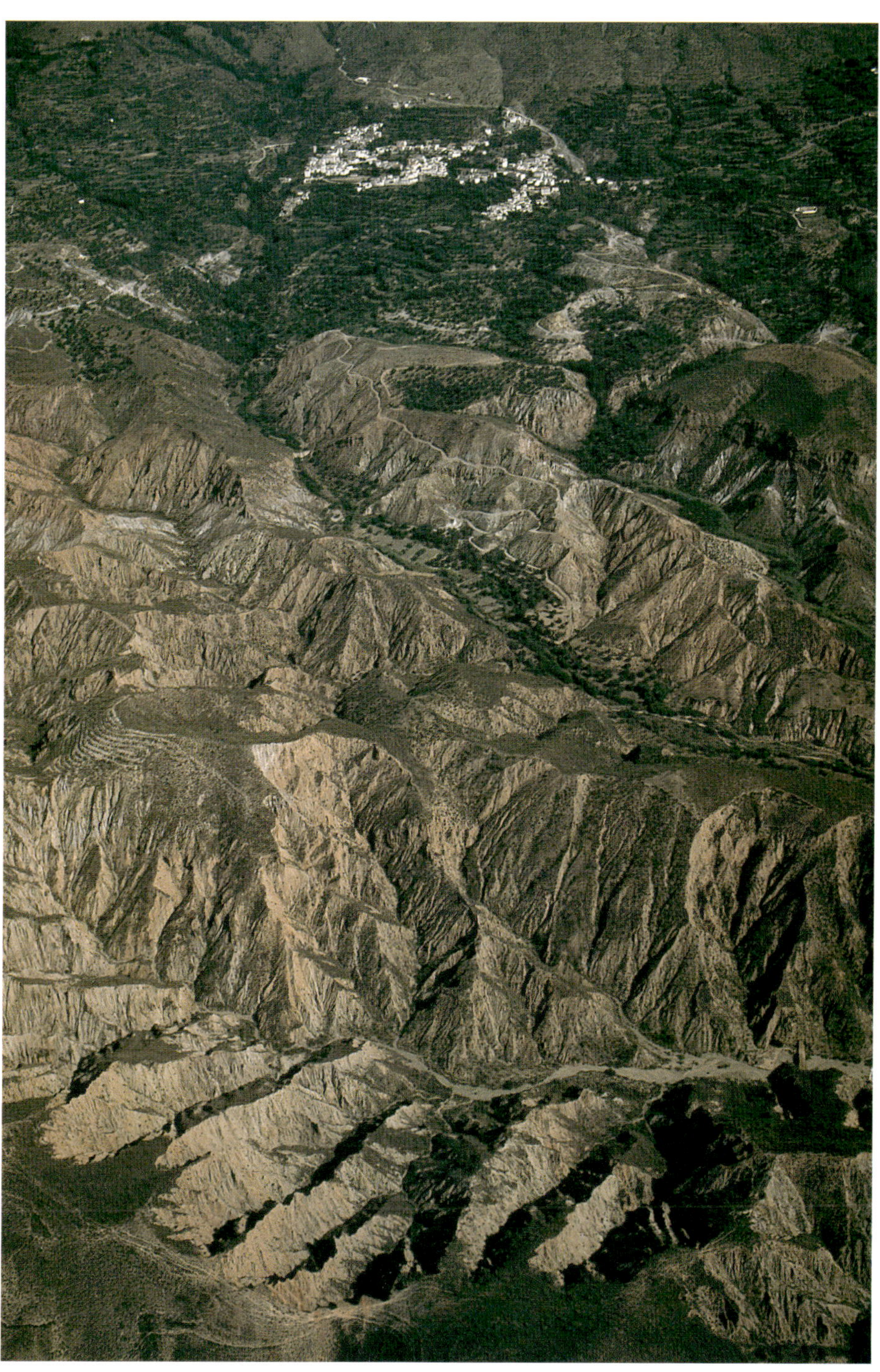

Patricia Macdonald with Angus Macdonald, pilot Eroding landscape on the edge of dryness *cibachrome print*

BARRY BERMANGE UK

Found and Lost Documents

Glasgow Film Theatre

12 ROSE STREET, GLASGOW

UK PREMIERE

4 JUNE – 4 JULY

With an archivist's eye for the aesthetic and historiographical value of discarded waste materials as a source of social documentary, Bermange has developed his disturbing portraiture: a language of marks and signs, of faces and forms in violent transition. The mute violence of his salvaged images runs parallel with prize winning international works in film, television, dramatic literature and the emerging acoustic arts which he helped to pioneer.

Born in London, Barry Bermange comes from a family of Polish and Ukrainian extraction. His photographic work conveys a perception of a world fragmented by violence and fear, inflicting pain upon itself then processing its wounds through the media. His *Found and Lost Documents* provide a new key to the influences of Bermange's fractured past and a new page in his own developing history.

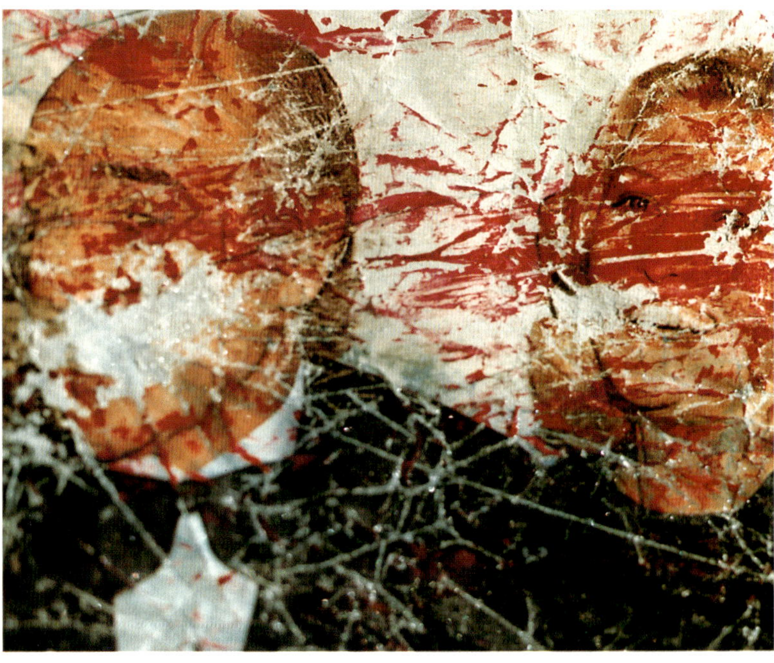

Barry Bermange Hollywood Interiors (2) *C-type print*

FROM THE EDGE
Photography in Printmaking

Glasgow Print Studio Gallery

22 KING STREET, GLASGOW

PREMIERE

5 JUNE – 26 JUNE

LUCY BYATT

ASHLEY COOK

JONATHAN CASSELS

PAUL CASSIDY

STUART DUFFIN

ELSPETH LAMB

ROB MULHOLLAND

AND OTHERS

In 1855, Alphonse Poitevin discovered and patented the process of applying albumen mixed with potassium bichromate, the first really successful method of photo-lithography. In the 1950's and early 1960's, during the Pop Art era, photographic screenprinting attracted many artists to exploit its flexibility and nature as a fast, and effective medium producing an enormous range of photostencil images in bold flat colour. At the Glasgow Print Studio from the mid 1970's onwards the techniques of photo-etching were pioneered by John Mackechnie and, through his research and practice in the art of full colour photo-etching, others developed their skills resulting in a diverse range of photo-related works.

All these processes continue to enjoy popularity amongst printmakers, as this exhibition demonstrates.

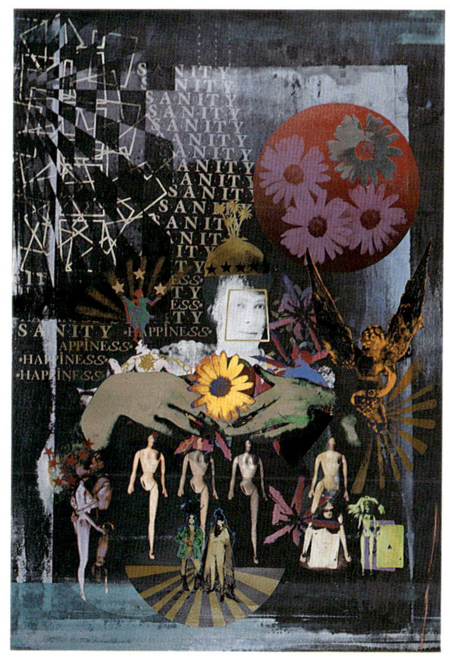

Ashely Cook Pure Hollywood *photo-silkscreen print*

ELSIE MITCHELL UK

Work from a Residency

Tramway

25 ALBERT DRIVE, GLASGOW

PREMIERE

12 JUNE – 18 JULY

Elsie Mitchell is a young Glasgow-based artist with a growing reputation for her innovative and poetic work in light-based media. This exhibition, which marks the culmination of a year spent as Artist in Residence for the South and South-East of Glasgow, features a number of installations and projects made in collaboration with a wide range of local people. Alongside this, Elsie Mitchell will show new work, made on her own, during the time of her residency.

This post of Artist in Residence has been funded by Scottish Arts Council and the South and South-East Area Management Committee of Glasgow District Council.

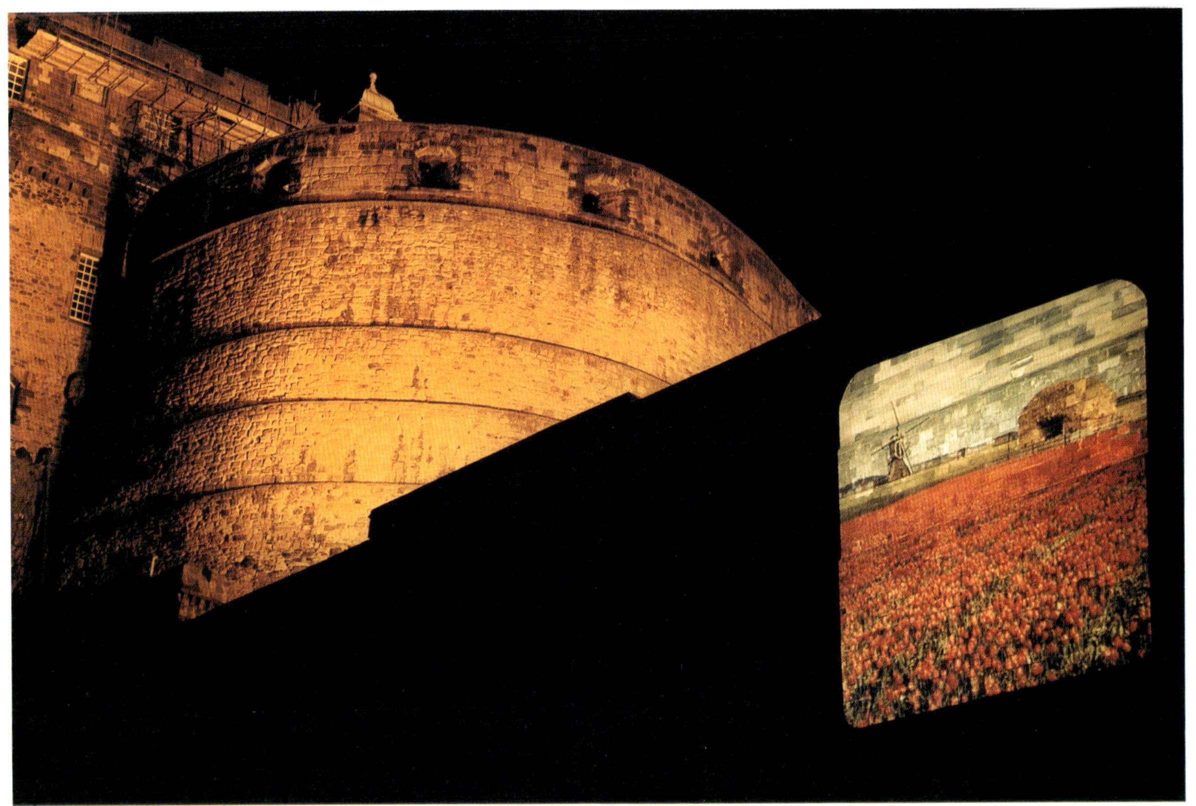

Elsie Mitchell with Gerard Scanlan Souvenir *(for Lux Europae, Edinburgh 1992) projection*

WOMANHOUSE UK

Tongue and Cheek

Women In Profile

5 DALHOUSIE LANE
GARNETHILL, GLASGOW

PREMIERE

28 JUNE – 19 JULY

Led by photographer in residence for Castlemilk, Nancy McFarlane, a group of women, who meet regularly at Womanhouse in Castlemilk, began this project by examining how they were affected by images of women in the media, whether they felt the pressure of expectation to conform and if they related directly to any of them.

The group then began to make photographic works. Four distinct areas were investigated using photography. The finished works, which examine personal biography, stress, pornography and internal dream worlds, were each approached in distinct photographic styles from documentary to abstraction, photo therapy and *mise en scene* photography.

Both Womanhouse and the photographer in residence post are funded by the Arts & Cultural Development Office, South-East Area Management Committee of Glasgow District Council.

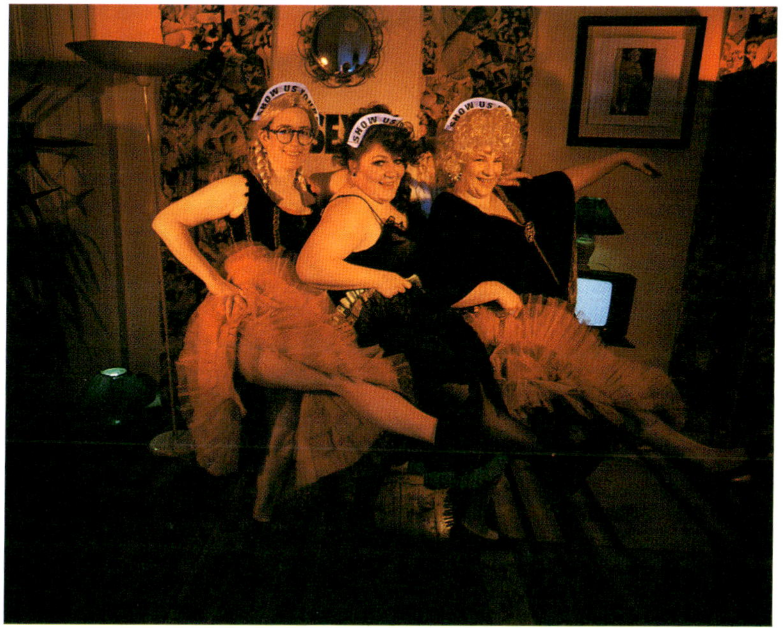

Nancy McFarlane Show us Yours *cibachrome print*

PHOTOGRAPHY FROM SINGAPORE
As I See It

Strathclyde Arts Centre

12 WASHINGTON STREET
GLASGOW

PREMIERE

4 JUNE – 4 JULY

This selection of work illustrates the current trends amongst Singaporean photographers. Its wide variety demonstrates a diverse talent and energy among the artists practising in this vibrant city.

Singapore does not have a long history of involvement in photography as an art form but in recent years, Singaporean photographers have established contacts all over the world and participated in a number of international exhibitions.

The exhibition has been made possible through the Singapore-Scotland Cultural Co-operation Programme which links Strathclyde, Scotland and Singapore and which started in January 1992. We look forward to making friends with fellow artists through the course of the exhibition.

Organised and sponsored by The British Council, Singapore and the National Arts Council, Singapore.

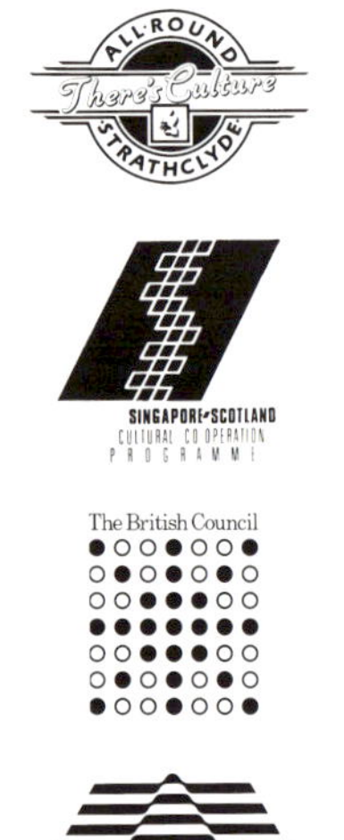

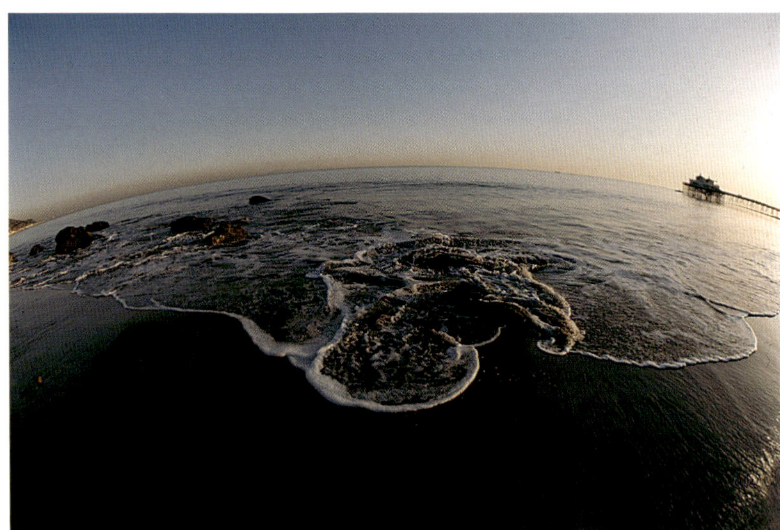

Teo Beng Tee Untitled *colour print*

NICK HOLMES UK

Watermarks

Carthouse Gallery

CALGARY, ISLE OF MULL

PREMIERE

4 JUNE – 4 JULY

This exhibition is supported by generous financial assistance from Lorn Arts and Crafts Association, Argyll and Islands Enterprise Ltd and Strathclyde Regional Council.

Watermarks are images of the transient interface between sea and shore – the manifest form of the dynamic interplay between the elements of water, air and earth – a process of continuous change. The rhythms of tidal ebb and flow are of an order whose magnitude is beyond representation, and yet the very laws of fundamental physics may be illustrated by a few particles of sand and by details of water. Any sense of harmony or of symmetry are human evaluations of a complex equation comprising wind speed, temperature gradient, water velocity, shore structure and time of day. The discovered detail calibrates a vast scale of natural order where the static reflects movement, and the small mirrors the large. Though views at the very edge, the photographs themselves are the watermarks at the very centre of our perception.

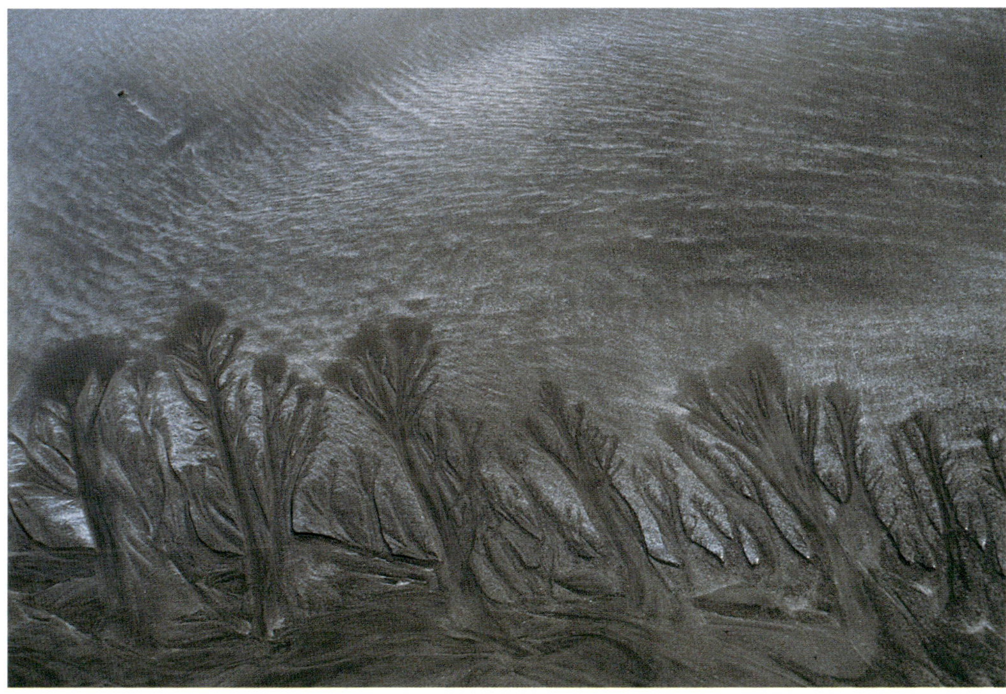

Nick Holmes Untitled *colour print*

NIGEL DICKINSON UK
Land Rights and Deforestation

Calder Glen Country Park Visitors Centre

STRATHAVEN ROAD
EAST KILBRIDE

PREMIERE

28 JUNE – 18 JULY

With the support of East Kilbride Arts Council and The Scottish Arts Council

In the face of overwhelming odds, South East Asia's indigenous peoples are fighting for survival. Their societies, culture and communal land rights are being undermined as national governments and multi-national investors reap huge profits at their expense. Sacred land providing the livelihood for native society, forest steeped in memories, mapped with hunting grounds and ancient burial sites, rich in history, each giant hardwood tree and mountain stream with its own song, can all be wiped out in a few moments. Nigel Dickinson's campaigning photojournalism reflects his commitment to grassroots advocacy and self determination. His work is published by Friends of the Earth, Survival International and The United Nations. The photographs are with 'Still Pictures'.

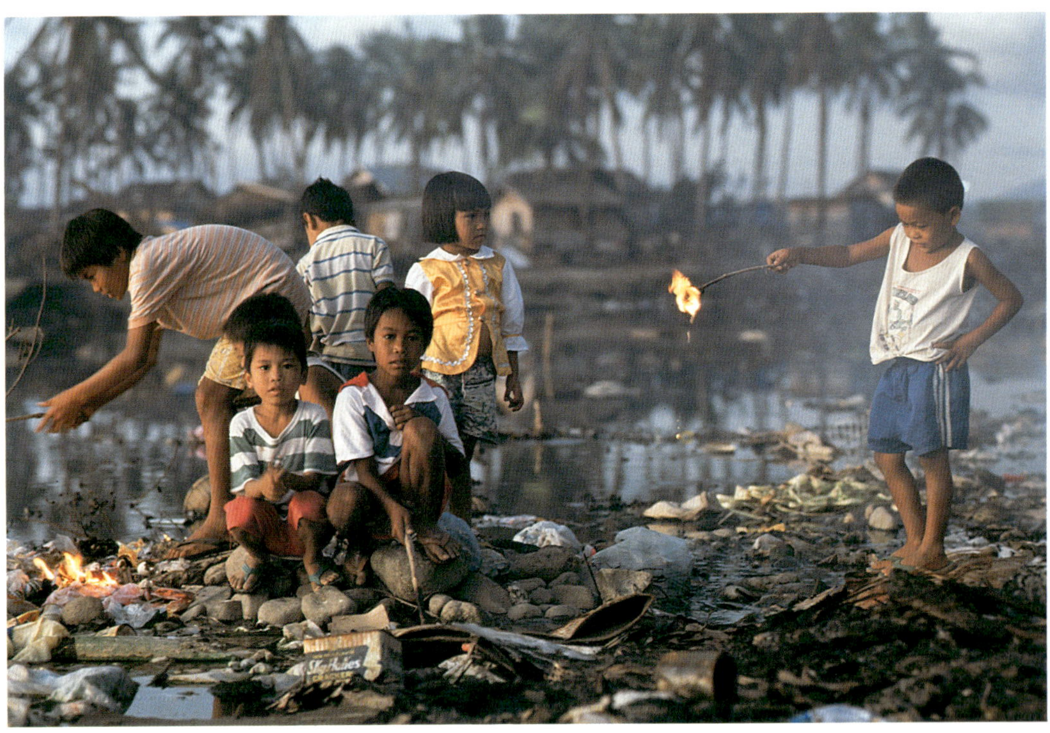

Nigel Dickinson Isla Verde survivors of flash flood, Leyte, The Philippines, 1991 *colour reversal*

BEATRIZ GRAU *Venezuela*
Spiritual Warriors

Royal Scottish Academy of Music And Drama

100 RENFREW STREET
GLASGOW

WORK IN PROGRESS

19 JUNE – 4 JULY

Forced into exile in 1959, the Tibetan people keep alive their identity, patiently waiting for the time when they will be able to recover their land. Concentrated primarily in India and Nepal, Tibetan refugees live in organised communities where they can secure food, shelter, medical help and a means of livelihood during their period of exile.

Aten, a Tibetan Kampa Warrior crossed the Jakpa La pass entering Nepal on the second moon of 1960:

"... Of the sixteen people who set out from my village, only four of us survived...I pray for my child, my wives and friends who died, and also for those living back in my unhappy land. That is all an old man can do now, pray ..."

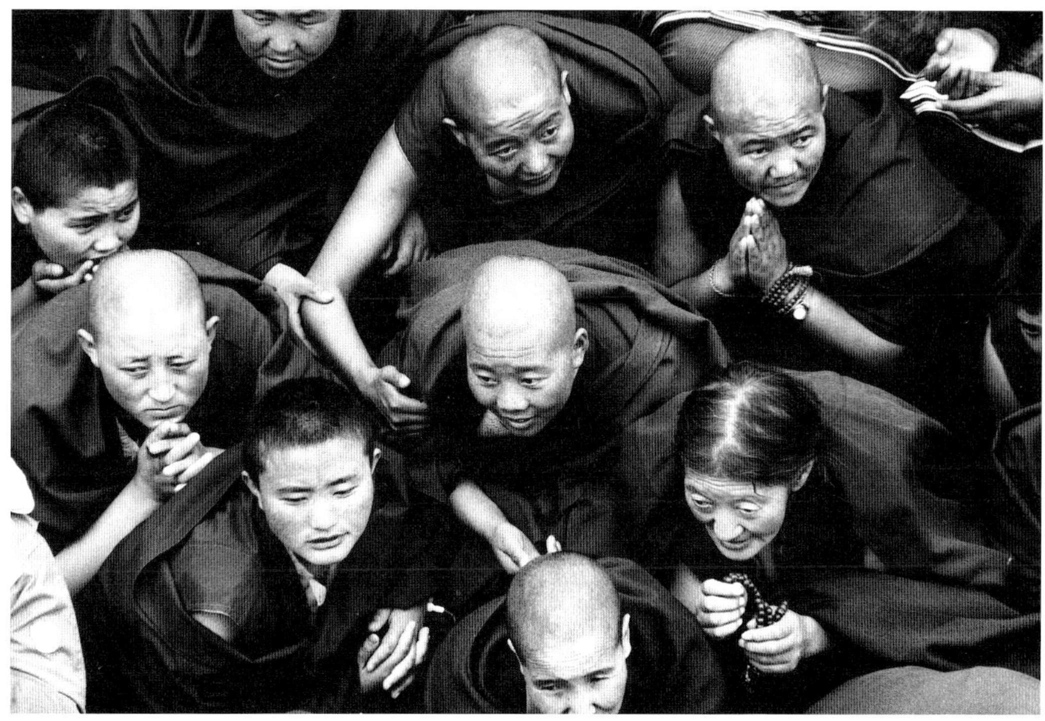

Beatriz Grau Nuns in Ceremony *silver-gelatin print*

HENRY BOND and LIAM GILLICK UK

Documents

Centre for Contemporary Arts

350 SAUCHIEHALL STREET
GLASGOW

PREMIERE

19 JUNE – 10 JULY

"We are part of a fascinating set of situations where the subject of the work is frequently presenting itself: when we attend news events, the participants know their role; a group of people are putting themselves on the line, preparing to be used or attempting to seduce you into passing on their information."

Henry Bond and Liam Gillick take photographs at press events. A photograph is then selected, framed and presented. Alongside each work is a quotation transcribed from a tape recording of statements made at the event.

Documents is a series of photographs that don't quite belong to any tradition or practice. Simultaneously personal and impersonal, they act on the border between different values – the value and supposed 'truth' of news reporting and the self-evident construction of the press event itself. At the same time, Bond and Gillick's photographs possess the action, composition and pleasure of 'good' photography.

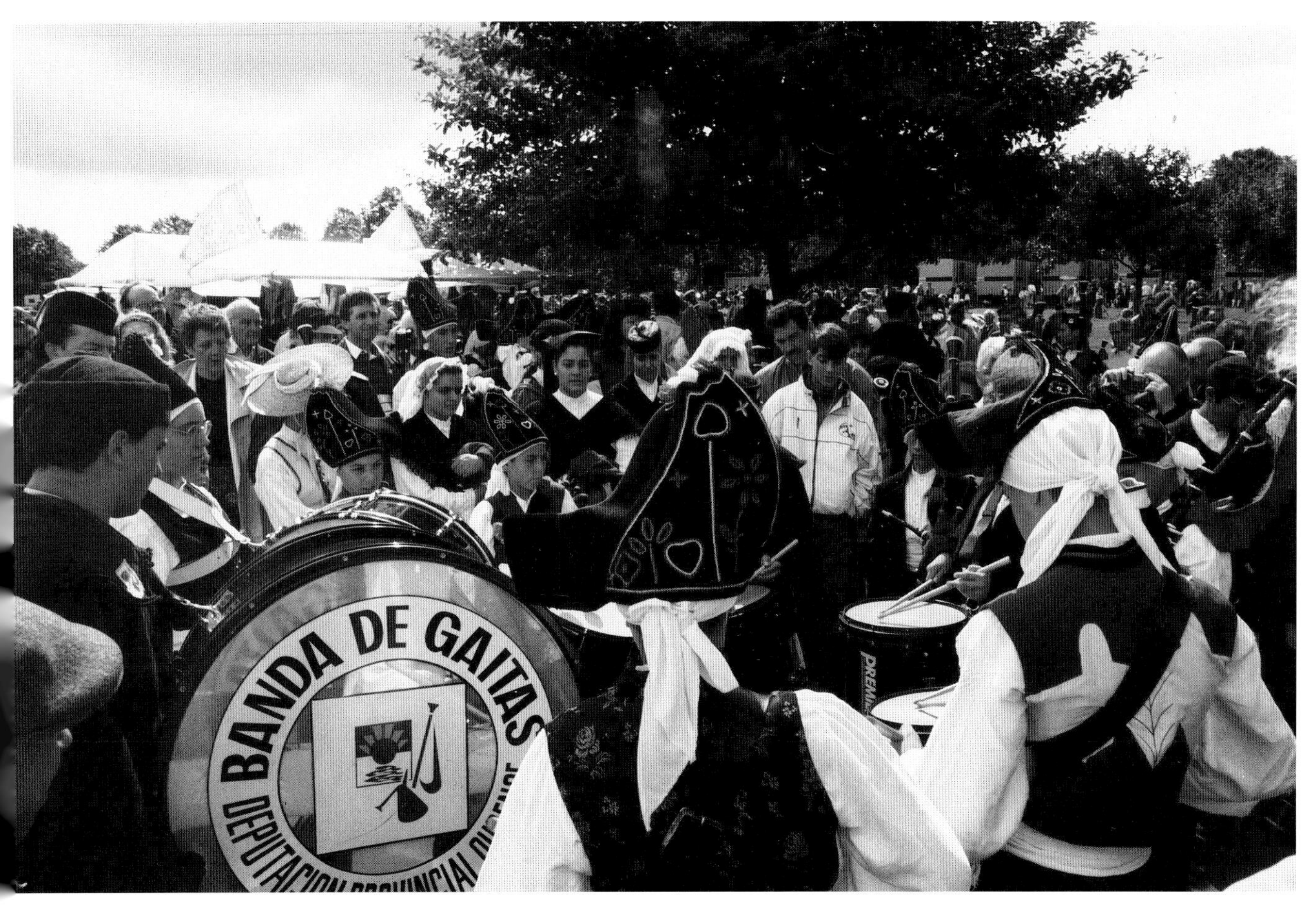

17 August 1991 Glasgow 10.00

World Pipe Band Festival, Bellahouston Park

Henry Bond and Liam Gillick *silver-gelatin print*

NETWORK PHOTOGRAPHERS UK
The Response to HIV

Cranhill Arts Gallery

18 KING STREET, GLASGOW

PREMIERE

4 JUNE – 4 JULY

There is something different about HIV and AIDS. If the aim of the photographers had been to explore the personal catastrophe of illness, there are many medical conditions that could have been documented – but unlike any other virus the medical and emotional battles of those living with HIV are underscored by unique social conditions. This exhibition is about how the whole of society is involved with the Human Immune Virus: its transmission, the provision of treatments, the support structures, the attitudes and, when the virus strikes closer to home, the emotion. A medical condition has become a social condition, and we are all required to form a response – whether by thought, action or even by attempting to hide.

The Response to HIV marks our entry to the second decade of AIDS care in Europe, and the exhibition is intended to reflect a more sophisticated public awareness of issues that extend far beyond identifying illness and attributing moral commentary. The use of documentary photography to explore the complex social and emotional responses to HIV challenges the perception of photojournalism as a simplistic record of illness: all too often documentary photography has been a tool for a negative commentary on AIDS, creating a modern iconography of victims.

Constructed in chapters, the exhibition directly tackles a range of subjects that includes sex, drugs, illness, grief, the gay response, impact on the family and much more. Many other themes are woven through these chapters to reflect different cultural responses, gender issues, educational processes and social shifts.

This is a team enterprise that has grown from the collaboration of two concerned groups: the Terence Higgins Trust (London's largest AIDS Service and Organisation) and Network Photographers (Britain's leading independent agency of documentary photographers), with funding from Levi Strauss Co. Ltd., the Arts Council of Great Britain and ABSA.

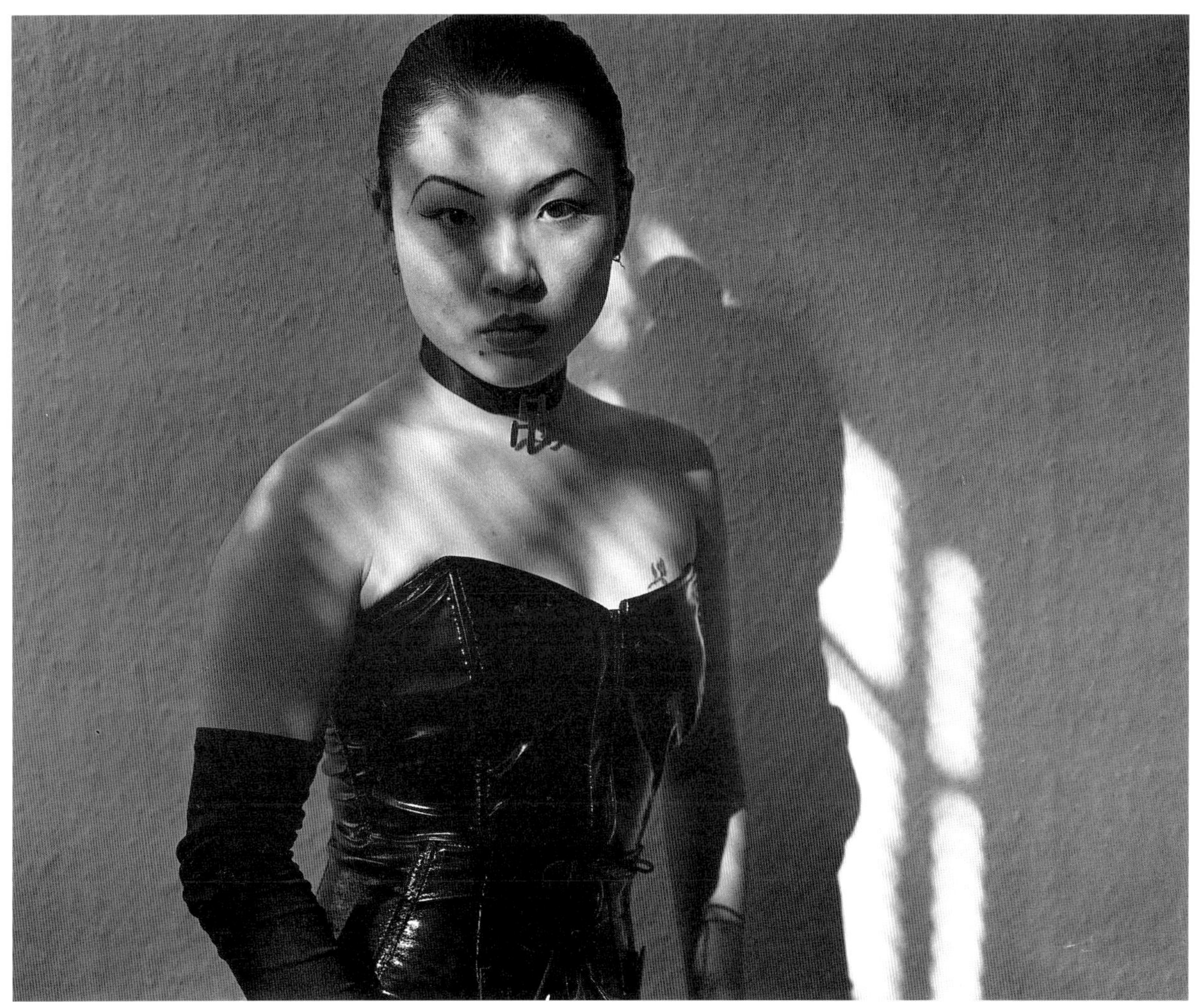

CAORI

It is one of the principles of fetish dressing that the body must be kept healthy. If you put these clothes on an uncared-for body you end up looking pretty silly. "The symbol is a Chinese symbol meaning 'hung', and when worn with fetish clothing it takes on a really aggressive meaning. People in my community respond very strongly – depending on what clothes I'm wearing at the time."

Denis Doran / Network Caori *silver-gelatin print*

ANNE ELLIOT UK
The Hazel MacLaren Portraits

Adshel sites throughout Glasgow

PREMIERE

14 JUNE – 11 JULY

Sponsored by Adshel

The portraits are placed around Glasgow in spaces which normally supply a captive audience with products, looks and lifestyles frequently purveyed by a characterless female protagonist. In contrast, the photographer's multiple images of a woman selling nothing, have a warmth and directness intended to reach women on their daily route through the city. They neither direct the viewer to act, nor detract from the viewed subject. Enjoyable in themselves, they are open-ended, allowing the viewer to attribute their own meaning, feeling and experience to them. They highlight the ability of still photography to portray people as timeless and individual.

The lighting of the photographs changes with location and time of day, echoing the realities affecting women's safety in public places.

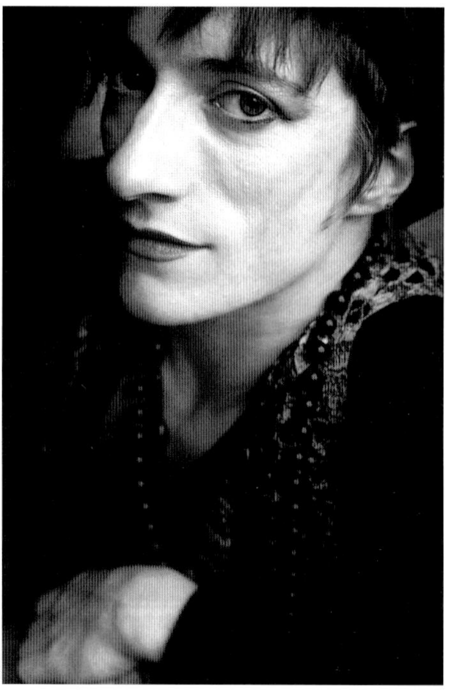

Anne Elliot Hazel MacLaren *silver-gelatin print*

PAUL McGUIGAN and ROBBIE KAVANAGH UK

Travels with my Aunt

Mitchell Theatre

GRANVILLE STREET
GLASGOW

4 JUNE – 4 JULY

SALVADOR BA

With writer James L. Smith, photographer Paul McGuigan has explored one of the most intriguing and exciting cities in Brazil. The exhibition includes an in-depth study of Salvador's historical centre, Pelourinho, described as the most beautiful favela in Brazil. The exhibition also includes a short film of Salvador which mixes stills with Super-8 footage.

TURKEY

Turkey, a predominantly Muslim country, is currently the subject of debate as to whether it can really be considered European and join the EC. Robbie Kavanagh's approach in photographing the country is more personal than journalistic. The photographs are counterpointed by small details relating to the content of the image and are accompanied by short texts.

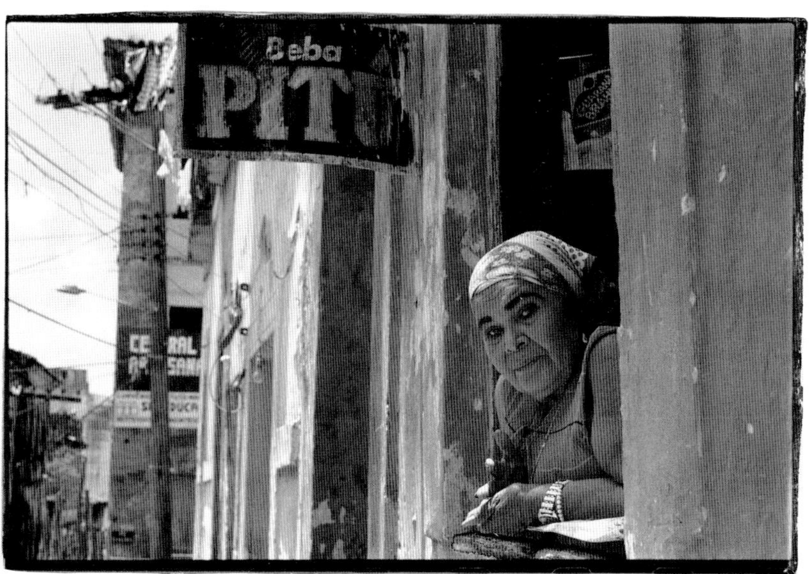

Paul McGuigan from 'Salvador BA' *silver-gelatin print*

CONTEMPORARY PHOTOGRAPHY FROM SLOVAKIA
Photography between Image and Vision

Ironworks Gallery

SUMMERLEE HERITAGE TRUST
WEST CANAL STREET
COATBRIDGE

PREMIERE

4 JUNE – 2 JULY

JOZEF SEDLÁK

MIRO ŠVOLÍK

MICHAL KERN

MATEJ KRÉN

DANIEL FISHER

PAVEL PECHA

VIKTOR HULÍK

TONO STANO

With financial support from the British Council in Bratislava and the Ministry of Culture of the Slovak Republic

The origins of Slovak photography are bound up with both the Czech and the Austro-Hungarian traditions. Before 1918, the Slovaks were ruled by the Austro-Hungarian monarchy whose aim was to create a single Hungarian identity for all the lands it possessed. Later, with the formation of the Czechoslovakian Republic, Slovakian photography developed in the shadow of the stronger Czech tradition and in the ideology of a unified cultural and political identity.

Against these odds however, individual Slovakian names have appeared throughout the history of 20th century photography: Kollár, Bluhová, Zsigmondiová, Marko, and later Kállay, Martinček, Štubňa and Borodáč. Very little of their work has been seen abroad, and then usually only under the banner of 'Czechoslovakian photography'.

Slovak photography in the seventies did much to enrich the field of conceptual art. Photography began to be recognized as equal to other branches of Fine Art, and a multi-disciplinary art practice began to emerge. This liberalisation broke the dominance of the documentary tradition and, by the end of the eighties, a number of artists were working in installation with integral photographic elements; *mise en scene* photography had gained a strong foothold; photography integrated with painting was well developed.

A specifically Slovak photographic identity is finally being established and nurtured. The Department of Photography was set up in the Academy of Fine Arts in Bratislava in 1990. Informed debate on photography continues in specialist arts periodicals such as *Profil* and *Vytvarny Zivot*. A Museum of Photography is to be established and artists are beginning to register with photographic organisations such as the Association of Professional Slovak Photographers. A new chapter is opening in the history of Slovakian photography.
from a text by Václav Macek & Simona Lábadyová

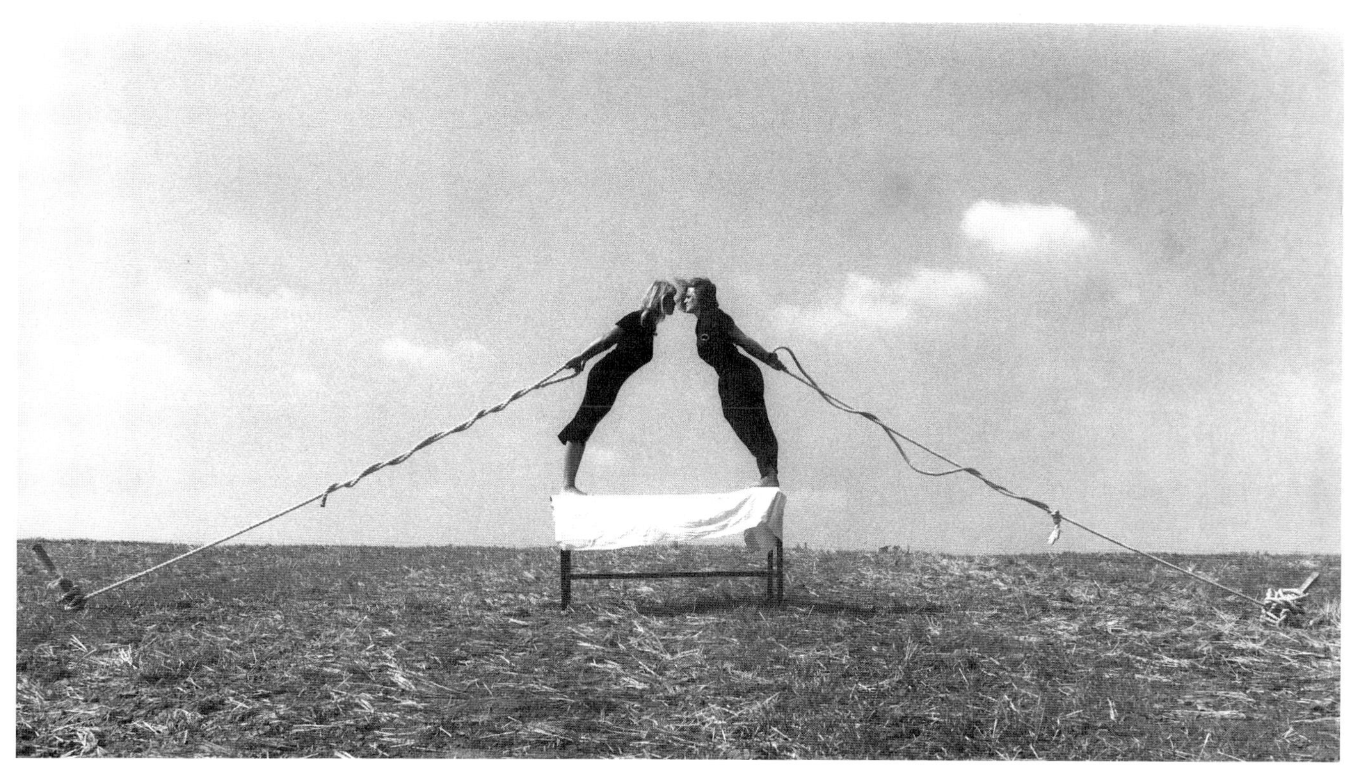

Pavel Pecha Untitled *toned silver-gelatin print*

Scottish Salon of Photography

Gracefield Art Gallery

EDINBURGH ROAD
DUMFRIES

29 MAY – 4 JULY

Castle Douglas Art Gallery

MARKET STREET
CASTLE DOUGLAS

29 MAY – 3 JULY

Stranraer Library

LONDON ROAD
STRANRAER

31 MAY – 30 JUNE

The *Scottish Salon* is believed to be one of the three oldest in the world and is the largest international photographic exhibition in the UK. The 76th Salon is being hosted in 1993 by one of Scotland's most successful amateur photographic societies, Dumfries Camera Club, and is expected to attract over 4,500 photographs from more than 50 countries. A distinguished panel of selectors will choose around 1000 prints and slides for exhibition during Fotofeis.

Entry to the Salon is open to everyone. The pictures, which come predominantly from amateur photographers, reflect the vision and experience of people from across five continents.

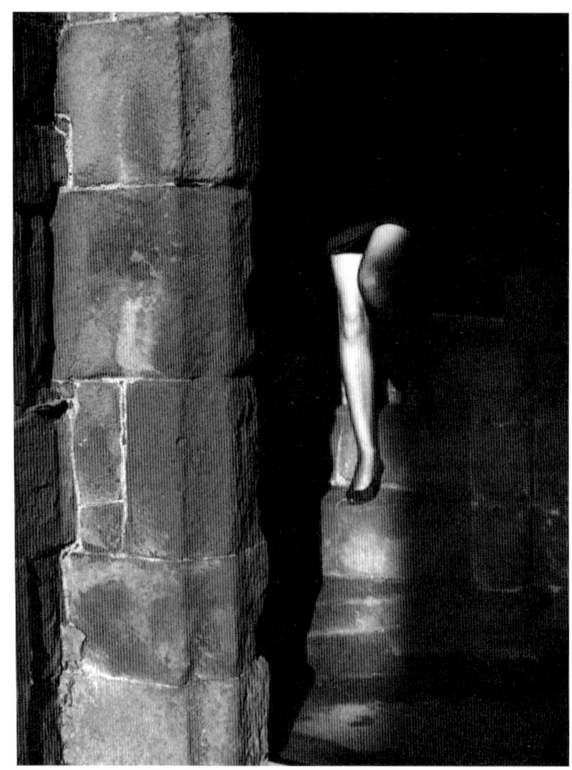

Dave Moyes Mystery Woman *silver-gelatin print*

EXPOSURE
Photographic works from the SAC Collection (1987–92)

Centre for Contemporary Arts

350 SAUCHIEHALL STREET
GLASGOW

19 JUNE – 10 JULY

Although a small exhibition, *Exposure* reflects the quality and ambition of photographic work made in Scotland over the past five years. It includes work by Raymond Moore, Owen Logan, Wendy McMurdo, Nathan Coley, Rory Donaldson, Jean Baird, Patricia Macdonald, Oladele Bamgboye, Calum Angus Mackay, and Frances Parker. However, these artists are not interested in the tired debates about photography's intrinsic distinctiveness, their primary concern (and indeed major contribution to contemporary art in Scotland) is the expression of ideas – how images can challenge and alter our perception of the world.

The works in this show, when not requested for exhibitions, are publicly accessible through the Collection's rental scheme. Hundreds of works in all media are circulated to public and private organisations throughout Scotland each year.

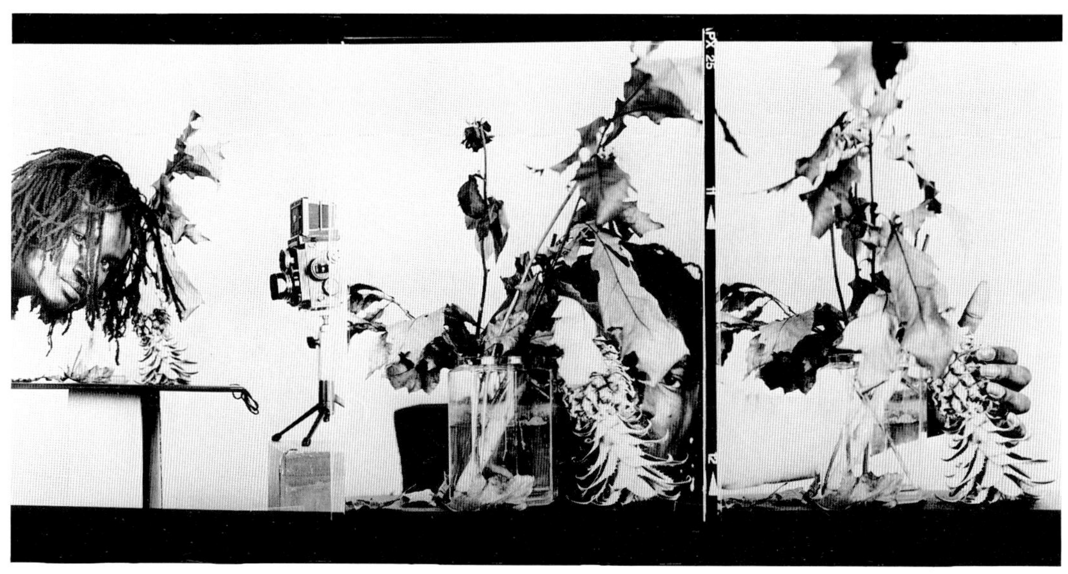

Oladele Bamgboye Berlin Bei Tag, Performance *silver-gelatin print*

OLIVER VAN HELDEN UK

Waterlands

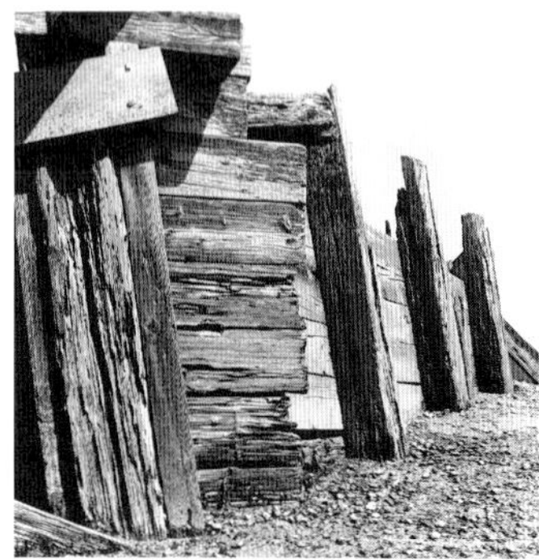

Oliver van Helden Untitled

Royal Scottish Academy of Music and Drama

100 RENFREW STREET
GLASGOW

PREMIERE

4 JUNE – 18 JUNE

Focusing on the tenuous hold humanity exercises over nature at the periphery of the land, this exhibition relates the natural world to the seaside economy with a study of a small town dependent upon its environment. The images focus on the winter desolation of the town and the vestiges of a culture that has largely ceased to exist.

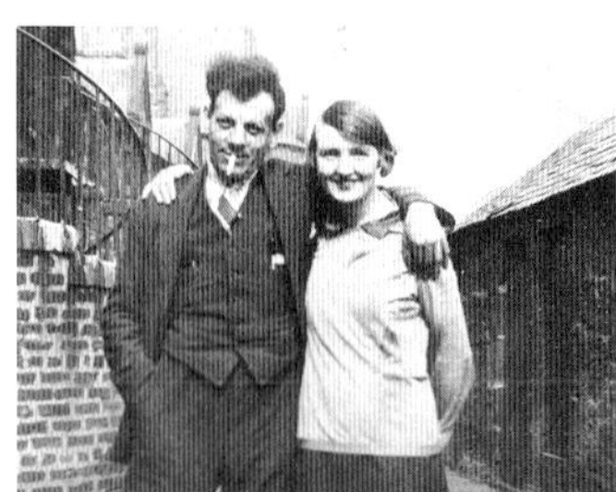

Anonymous Pals 1936, Kay Street, Springburn

SPRINGBURN

Families of the Fringe

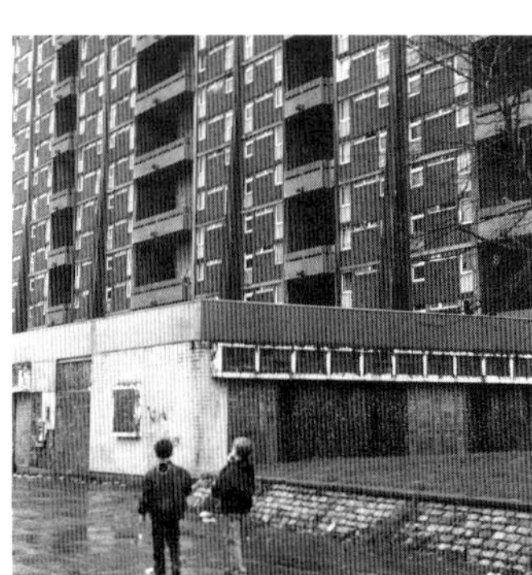

Queen Elizabeth Square Flats

Springburn Museum

ATLAS SQUARE, AYR STREET
SPRINGBURN, GLASGOW

4 JUNE – 4 JULY

Photographs, drawn from the local community, trace the development of domestic snapshots within Springburn and highlight the impact on photographic practice of changing apparatus (from the box brownie to the Polaroid) and shifting social attitudes. To emphasise how much of our interpretation of these photos is subjective, an exchange of material with a similar community overseas is planned.

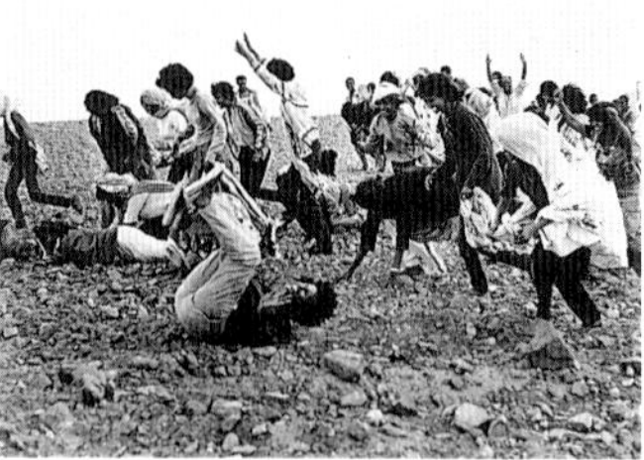

photograph from EPLF archive

CHRISTINA McBRIDE UK
Projecting Gorbals

The Queen Elizabeth Square Flats

QUEEN ELIZABETH SQUARE
OLD RUTHERGLEN ROAD
GORBALS, GLASGOW

PREMIERE

3 JULY, 10.30PM ONWARDS
THROUGHOUT THE NIGHT

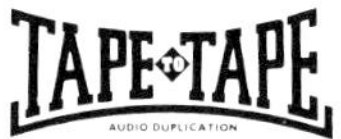

I was born and spent my childhood years in The Gorbals, my parents having moved from Donegal to Glasgow during the fifties in search of work. In the mid-seventies our building was demolished as part of The Gorbals Redevelopment Plan, with tenements replaced by multi-storey concrete blocks. This plan was executed in such a way that the shape and character of the once thriving community was obliterated.

Less than twenty years later, the Gorbals is undergoing another major transformation. The earlier Redevelopment Plan is a discredited failure; the award-winning Queen Elizabeth Square flats are to be blown up in the next few months.

My project – a series of large images projected onto the outside of this building – is intended as a focal point for both the community and the city at large; an opportunity to acknowledge and meditate upon the major changes which have taken place in this area over such a short period.
Christina McBride

JEAN WELSTEAD UK
The Women of Eritrea: Beyond the Trenches

Hillhead Library

348 BYRES ROAD, GLASGOW

PREMIERE

4 JUNE – 4 JULY

With thanks to the Sarah Noble Memorial Fund and the Welsh Arts Council

The thirty year war in Eritrea has been a powerful catalyst for the break-down of gender roles. The exhibition examines women's experiences behind the front lines and since liberation. Material has been gathered over seven years and includes photographs from the Eritrean People's Liberation Front archives. This exhibition comes at a time when Eritrea will be celebrating its first month of independence following the UN referendum on 25 April 1993. The artist would like to thank the various Eritrean organisations and individuals who have made this project possible.

EXHIBITIONS IN MOTHERWELL

Wishaw Library

KENILWORTH AVENUE
WISHAW

Motherwell Library

HAMILTON ROAD
MOTHERWELL

Craigneuk Community Centre

SHIELDMUIR STREET
WISHAW

Bellshill Cultural Centre

JOHN STREET, BELLSHILL

Viewpark Library

BURNHEAD STREET
VIEWPARK

4 JUNE – 4 JULY

LEWIS NAPIER

PAUL MCNALLY

GREATER SPRINGBURN PHOTOGRAPHIC GROUP

SANDY SHARP

BELLSHILL PHOTOGRAPHY GROUP

VARIOUS LOCAL ARTISTS

A variety of exhibitions, coordinated by Motherwell District Council Department of Leisure Services, foregrounds the work of local photographers whose subject matter ranges from portraits of Lanarkshire's prize racing pigeons, to documentary profiles of their own town and of the 1992 European City of Culture, Madrid. Also included is work that takes a more experimental approach to photography.

Following on from a series of workshops in photography initiated by Charlie Crawford, during a highly successful residency in 1992, a group of local artists also presents the fruits of six months work. The workshops continue to flourish involving people of all ages and abilities.

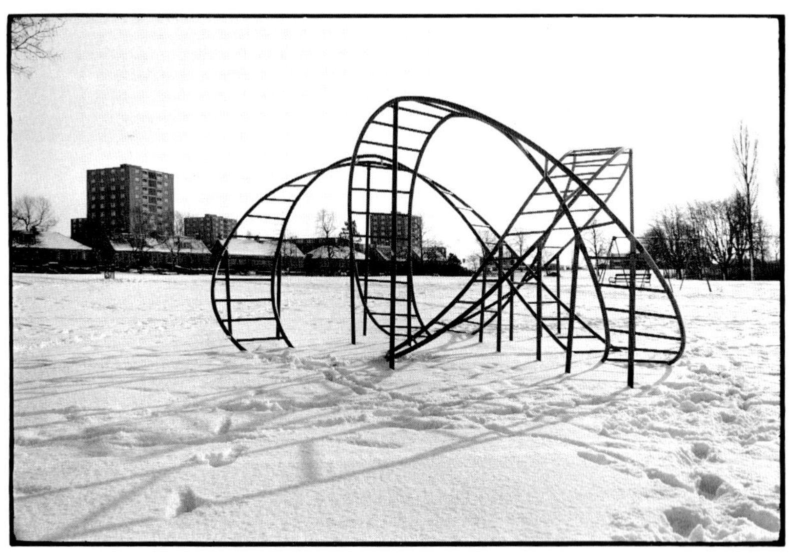

Sandy Sharp Children's Climbing Frame, Duchess of Hamilton Park *silver-gelatin print*

ROBERT HAMILTON UK
Shark Fishing in Govan

The Pearce Institute

840 GOVAN ROAD, GLASGOW

PREMIERE

4 JUNE – 4 JULY

At the Pearce Institute, a popular community centre in Govan, a small photographic studio has been set up within the building. Robert Hamilton invites local people in to sit for portraits, encouraging them to make full use of the props and sets he has gathered together. The popular public restaurant is the exhibition space with the work hung *ad hoc* as it is produced. This display should arouse vain passions in the clientele, encouraging yet more people to pose for portraits which reflect their aspirations.

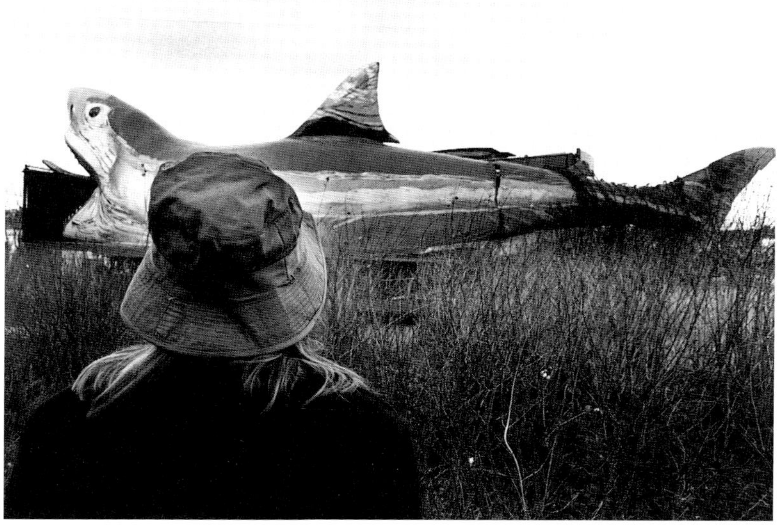

Robert Hamilton Shark Fishing in Govan *silver-gelatin print*

WIGTOWN
Photowalls

VENUES ACROSS WIGTOWN DISTRICT

LATE MAY – EARLY JULY

Five villages, each on the periphery of Wigtown District have created photographic billboards reflecting contemporary village life. The billboards will tour the participating villages during the festival. Meanwhile, young people in all four districts of Dumfries and Galloway, will be exchanging photographic imagery via the fax machine in a region-wide collaboration along the south-west edge of Scotland.

Feature Exhibitions

DAVID HATFIELD UK

A Collection of Birds' Eggs and Broken Spells

Inverleith House

WESTGATE
ROYAL BOTANIC GARDEN
ARBORETUM PLACE
EDINBURGH

5 JUNE – 1 AUGUST

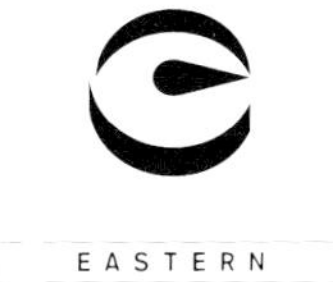

David Hatfield's new work, *A Collection of Birds' Eggs and Broken Spells*, stems from childhood memories of growing up in a rural community in the Yorkshire Dales. The title refers to the mixed perceptions of past events which co-exist in the artist's mind, those of the rational adult and those of the credulous child. The child, he says, "perceived the world as finite, and anything outside of the known became mythological. This was an innocent time [when] a mere coincidence became a sign".

The work is riddled with references to Hatfield's life-long passion for rural landscape and the wild creatures which inhabit it, (he is a former Peak Park Ranger). As one would expect from someone who has spent many years working with the land, his approach to it, though emotional, is unsentimental.

The work consists of photographs, text, *frottage*, impress printing and found objects. These elements are presented in large box frames which themselves become part of the work as the text on the glass casts shadows onto the mount below.

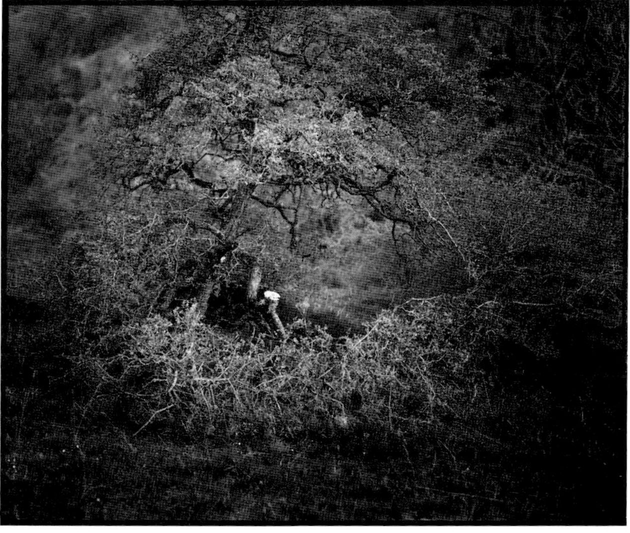

David Hatfield Detail from Bawson Pate Grey *silver-gelatin print*

DIRT ON THE LENS
Photography in Industrial Glasgow

Museum of Transport

KELVIN HALL
1 BUNHOUSE ROAD
GLASGOW

PREMIERE

28 MAY – 8 AUGUST

Within many collections around Glasgow lie huge quantities of dramatic and telling photographs depicting the city's industrial past and providing a dynamic representation of its industrial heritage. Curated by Andrew Patrizio, this exhibition critically examines the aesthetics that underlie these images and the kind of picture they give of industrial Glasgow.

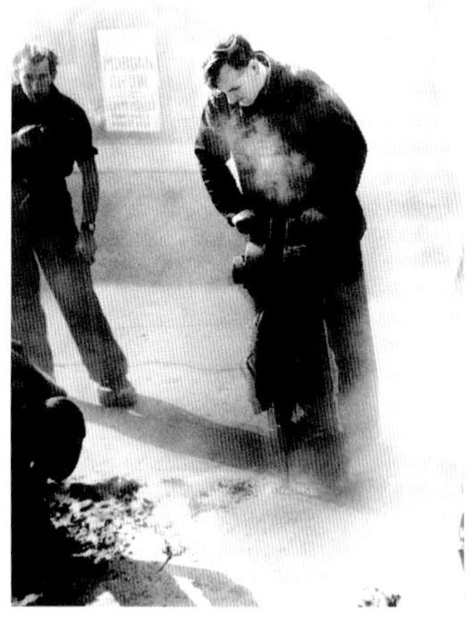

Alf Daniel Pneumatic Drill Operator, Glasgow, 1954 *silver-gelatin print*

Art Gallery & Museum

A Glasgow Album

KELVINGROVE, GLASGOW

PREMIERE

26 JUNE – 5 SEPTEMBER

The demolition of a church or old tenements, the closure of a long-established company: they may not make the headlines but their passing has an effect on the life of Glasgow. This exhibition of photographs drawn from the archives of the Social History Department of Glasgow Museums is a chance to preview tomorrow's history.

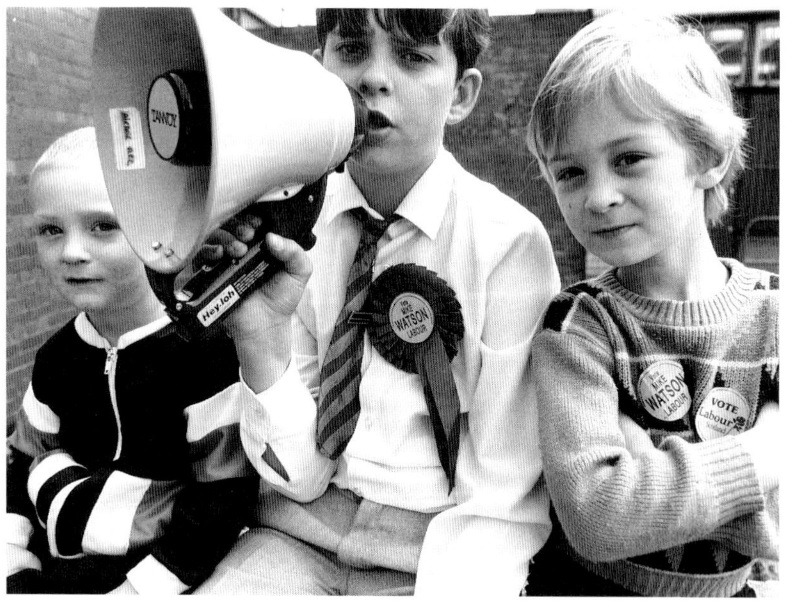

Unknown photographer Vote Mike Watson *silver-gelatin print*

GEORGE WALTON UK
Designer and Architect

Art Gallery & Museum

KELVINGROVE, GLASGOW

PREMIERE

10 JUNE – 19 SEPTEMBER

George Walton (1867 – 1933) is one of the most under-rated British designers of his era. This exhibition is the first to explore his varied and productive career. After establishing a flourishing decorating business in his native Glasgow, Walton moved to London in 1897. Starting with the design of the Photographic Salon Exhibition, he went on to become 'Decorator in Chief' to photographers, producing a series of lavish showrooms for the newly formed Kodak Company in the UK and on the Continent. He also produced advertising and packaging material for the wider photographic industry. His photographic commissions are explored through a reconstruction of his decorative scheme for the Eastman Photographic Exhibition of 1897. Through furniture, fabrics, stained glass, textiles and photographs the exhibition throws new light on Walton's work and the early years of the photographic industry.

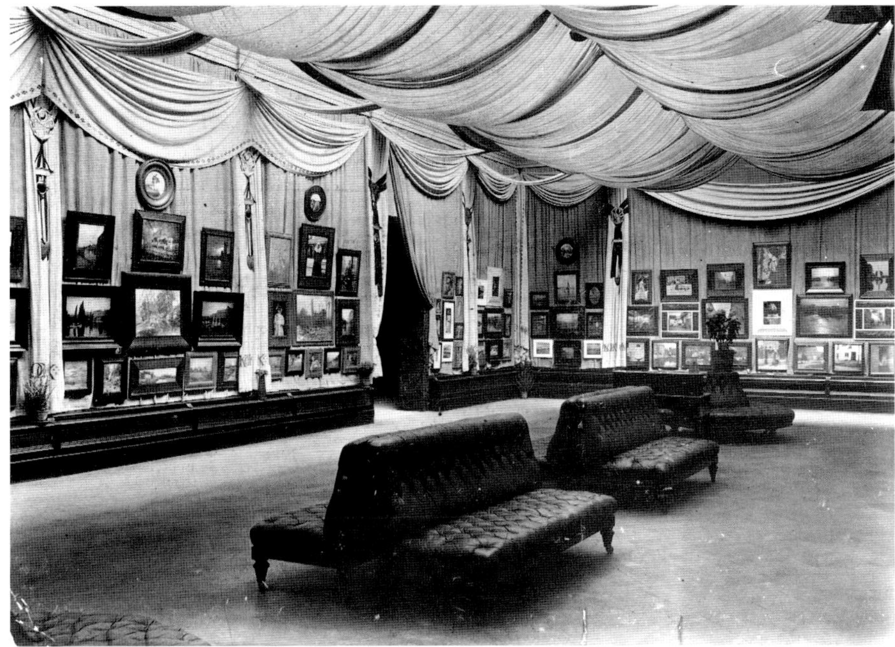

Eastman Photographic Exhibition, 1897 *decorated by George Walton*

CLACKMANNANSHIRE
Between the Ochils and the Forth

Alloa Museum and Gallery

SPEIRS CENTRE, PRIMROSE STREET, ALLOA

PREMIERE

4 JUNE – 4 JULY

Clackmannan District is found *Between the Ochils and the Forth* - the area has well defined boundaries. The hills and estuary provide dramatic and interesting subjects for local photographers W. Robertson, J. Hensby, I. Brown, A. Wilson, W. McConachie, L. Dyson Bruce, G. Sutherland and M. Lennon.

SKYE & LOCHABER
Through the Glass

An Tuireann Arts Centre

STRUAN ROAD, PORTREE, ISLE OF SKYE

PREMIERE

25 MAY – 19 JUNE

Through the Glass refers to the formation of a photographic image by the optic of a camera lens, but it also suggests the more complex view of reality which Alice found on her adventures through the looking glass. Bringing together work by artists from throughout Skye, this exhibition is testament to the vigour and diversity of photographic creativity in the western Highlands.

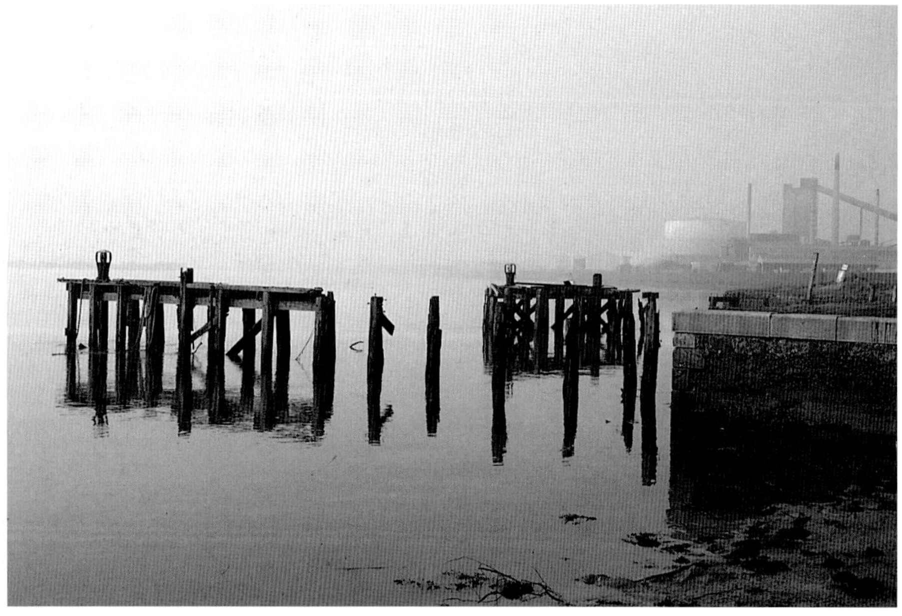

W. Robertson Ruined piers and Christian Nielsen's crane *(original in colour)*

DAVID BROWNRIDGE UK
Photographs

The Dick Institute

ELMBANK AVENUE
KILMARNOCK

26 JUNE – 24 JULY

These pictures were taken in the west of Scotland, around Irvine, the Garnock Valley and up into Paisley. That's in the central belt, the industrial bit where most Scots live. These are unromantic places, commonplace and often banal but as Ralph Waldo Emerson states:
"All things are engaged in writing their history...the ground is all memoranda and signatures, and every object is covered over with hints which speak to the intelligence."

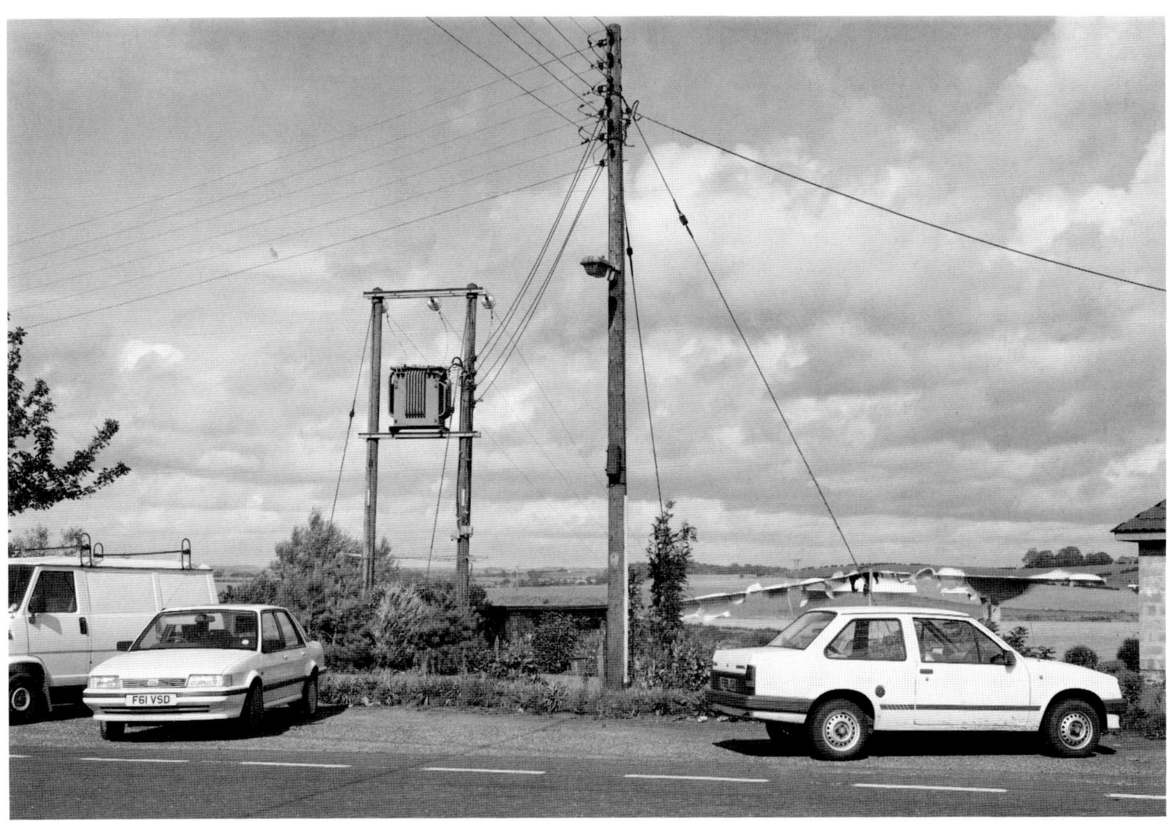

David Brownridge Cars and Powerlines, Drybridge *silver-gelatin print*

FOTOFEIS

Community and Education Programme

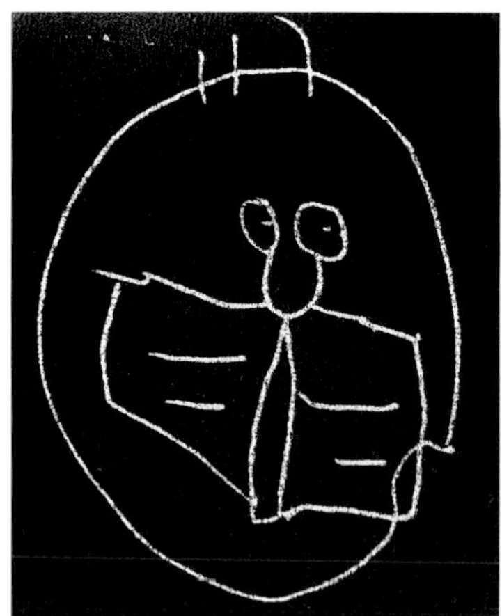

Elizabeth Jamaison Cat
This image was made by drawing on acetate and then using it as a photographic negative.

It has always been argued that photography is a truly democratic art form, accessible to all: after all, anyone can take a photograph. This is not to detract from the achievements of the acknowledged experts but merely to restate the obvious – in photography, unlike, say, painting or sculpture, there is rarely an enormous technical gulf between concept and execution: it is possible for the amateur, with no formal training, to produce an image with its own power, making its own statement.

It has been our intention to challenge the concept of exclusivity. By embracing an astonishingly wide range of photographic practice – from the documentary photographs of Owen Logan to the computer-generated images of Carol Flax; from the promotion of an internationally acclaimed artist such as Alfredo Jaar to the stimulation of a community arts project involving young people on the Powis housing estate in Aberdeen – Fotofeis breaks down the perceived distinction between 'high' and 'low' art both in the medium itself and in a wider context.

Part of our strategy at Fotofeis has been to empower through participation. We have overcome barriers to involvement by staging events, activities and exhibitions throughout the country, with no centre given more importance than any other. The venues too are diverse; ranging from traditional establishments such as museums, galleries, schools and community centres to rather more unusual sites like factories, hospitals, restaurants and public spaces. Throughout, our intention has been to attract as wide a variety of groups and individuals as possible – local and international, urban and rural, specialist and general. In this we have succeeded, as is demonstrated by more than one hundred exhibitions taking place in every corner of Scotland.

Another important part of the enabling process has been the development of an education and community programme which makes the Festival accessible to as wide an audience as possible.There are talks, seminars and conferences – where speakers from a range of disciplines, countries and backgrounds will discuss and exchange ideas with the audience. Practical and information-based workshops give participants the opportunity to explore techniques, processes and ideas relating both to the work of specific artists and to the themes of Fotofeis. Portfolio-viewings will allow photographers to discuss their work with invited curators and artists.

The opening up of artistic activity in new ways and to different audiences has generated a new debate. Dialogue has become an important word in the Fotofeis vocabulary, indeed a fundamental part of our ethos. Dialogue between individuals, communities and institutions has been established and we hope that this dialogue will continue throughout and beyond the Festival. Many specialised projects have this long-term aim in mind – the exhibition of work by children from Leith and Nepal coordinated by Kenny Bean, for example, which is showing at Leith Library (see page 56), and the artistic exchanges between the Baltic States and Glasgow which aim to strengthen links between these two, very different cultures.

Fotofeis Community Awards

As well as acting as a showcase for photography from all over the world, it was always our aim to involve local communities in the Festival. To make this possible, Fotofeis offered five grants of £500 to community groups for the production of work to be included in the programme. Applications were invited from groups across Scotland and one award was made in each of the four thematic areas of the country. Application was open to all members of the community, and a fifth award specifically offered to a group with special needs.

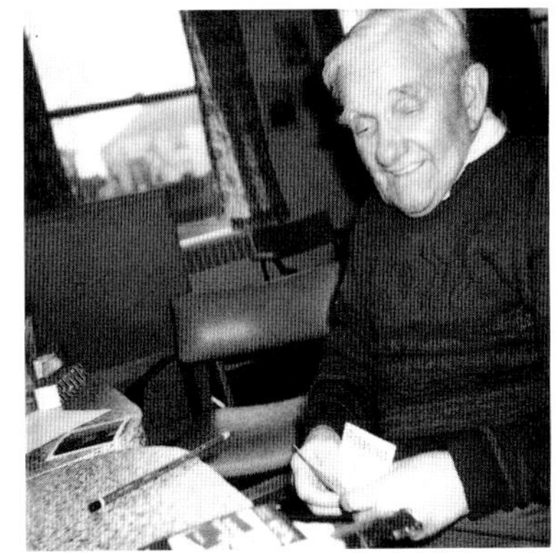

Rena Read
Tommy smiling
polaroid

POWIS: A CELEBRATION

The diversity and imagination of the winning entries is testament to the vigour of community arts activity in Scotland. Young people aged 15-24 from a housing project in Aberdeen, use photography, text and silkscreen printing in *Powis: A Celebration*, the finished results being printed onto posters, T-shirts and in a book.

WAY OF LIFE

The exhibition *Way of Life*, devised by the Bengali Cultural Association in Glasgow, explores changes in Bengali life in Scotland. Using archival and contemporary photographs, this exhibition presents a broad picture of the life and culture of the Bengali community in the city.

FAMILY TREES

In the border town of Peebles, *Family Trees* comprises full-sized photograms of individuals. These are then suspended from the ceiling of the Tweeddale Museum to form a forest of images, onto which are projected images from the family albums of local people. This unusual project, devised by Rachael Hunter at the Museum and Colin Cavers from Stills Gallery, Edinburgh, integrates the work of many individuals into a dramatic whole.

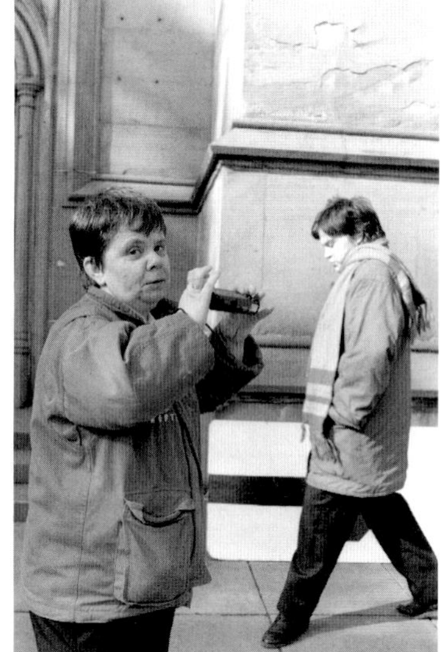

Linda Sheridan and Margaret Coull of the DARC Photography Group

LOCHABER CENTRE

At the Lochaber Centre in Fort William, a life-sized figure is created from many individual portraits. In this project up to 30 differently abled people are creating work using the photographic process and print making. The project has been structured so that no discrimination based on ability or physical appearance will affect an individual's participation.

DUDHOPE ADULT RESOURCE CENTRE

A group of people with learning difficulties from the Dudhope Adult Resource Centre in Dundee are creating a photo sculpture representing a part of Dundee (the Overgate) which has changed dramatically over the past 30-40 years. Photographic images, the spoken/written word, mixed media and personal memories are combined to convey the group's overall idea of this changing scene. As with many community projects the process of making the work is at least as important as the final product.

National Schools and Community Project

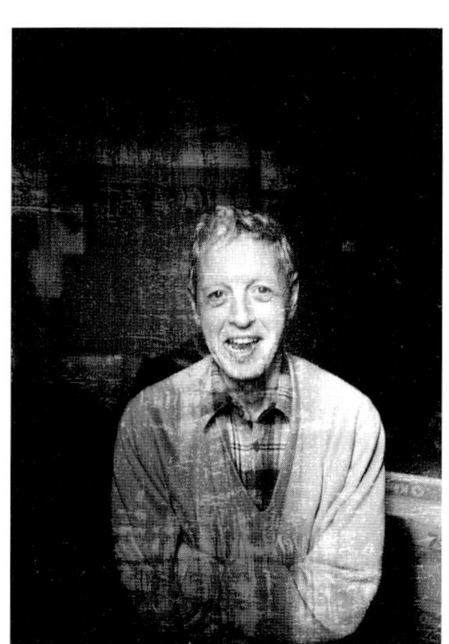

Charlie Otterson Martin Galin

As an integral part of the education programme, Fotofeis invited participation from schools and community groups who wished to share in the experience of producing work to be shown within the festival.

The remit was as wide as possible. Every school in Scotland which either had photography as part of its art department curriculum, or was interested in establishing it, could choose the theme of their geographic area or the national schools' theme of *Family*. Fotofeis themes fit sympathetically within existing course structures, containing elements which involve exploring various photographic techniques, not just to record or convey information, but to express personal ideas and feelings in ways which very often language cannot achieve.

The participating children are generally in secondary schools aged 14–17 years, although a few primary schools are taking part, for example in Fife. These schools are working independently from each other, with visits from Fotofeis' Education Team to facilitate and encourage the staff and pupils. Each region is having its own exhibition, which will run for the festival period and pupils are encouraged to view not only their own work, but that of other groups.

Strathclyde Regional Council took the original idea and developed it further, incorporating an equal number of Community Groups and schools into the project. Through special funding made available by the Council, Fotofeis has been able to allocate additional resources. The combined show from eight rural and urban secondary schools and eight community groups (all of whom have divergent skills and abilities), will be shown at the Strathclyde Arts Centre in Glasgow for the month long period of the festival. A brochure will describe the project from inception to exhibition. The groups involved people with mental or physical disabilities, young people in care, elderly groups in a long-stay hospital, and the Scottish Refugee Council, as well as the school children.

One of our major commitments is 'access to excellence'. Given the multiplicity of events and variety of exhibitions, we hope that schools who have not produced work this time will nevertheless become involved in Fotofeis through visits and discussions.

Underpinning the philosophy of Fotofeis is the belief that the visual arts should not be the preserve of the few but a source of creativity and inspiration for many. We are working with education departments throughout Scotland to make this a reality.

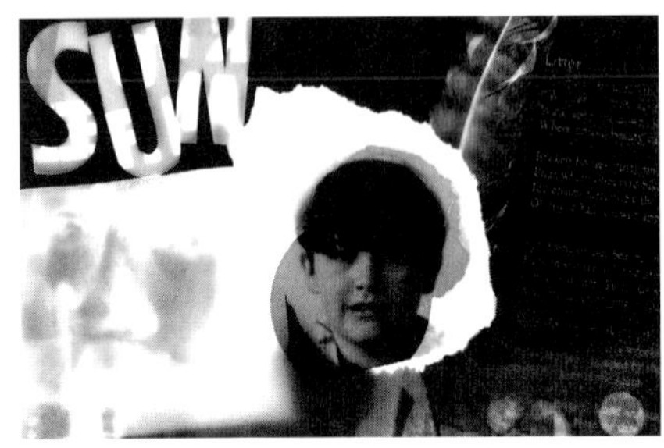

James McArthur James
photogram and photographic portrait

The range and diversity of community and education activities within Fotofeis is unusually wide. Some are referred to in the earlier sections of this catalogue, for example the Artlink project showing at The Collective Gallery, Edinburgh (see page 49) or *Looking in Reaching out* at An Lanntair which exploits new technology to link school children in Central London and the Isle of Lewis (see page 116).

There are many other examples. In Aberdeen, a *Photography Plus* project with City Moves, the dancer/choreographer Janice Parker and the photographer Mike Davidson will result in a piece of theatre involving slide projection and six dancers, some with special needs. The performance will be premiered at the Lemon Tree during Fotofeis. Elsewhere in Aberdeen, community groups are creating 360° photographs of the city which will be presented during the festival accompanied by words and music.

Building on the exhibition of photocopy art from the *Museo Internacional de Electrografia* in Cuence (Spain), a series of photocopy workshops will be held at venues across Highland Region. Run by members of the Photocopy Cooperative, London, these will allow local participants to explore the potential of these ubiquitous and immediate imaging machines.

In Drumchapel, a suburb of Glasgow, the newly refurbished Argo Arts Centre is the venue for a display of work produced by six young people from the area during a two week photography workshop.

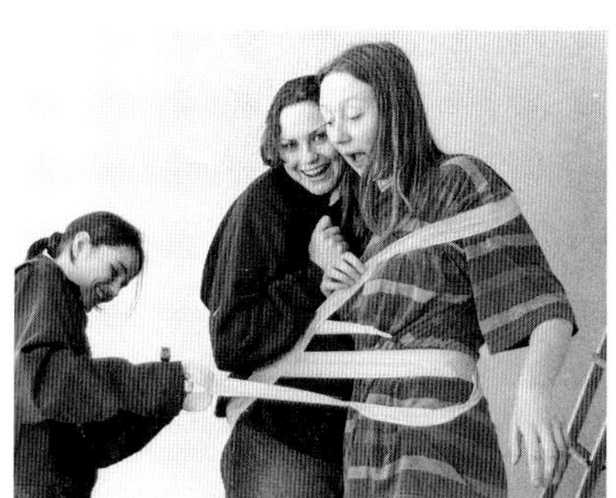

Elaine Cobb Balance

The debates surrounding the festival themes and exhibitions will be open to all through a programme of lectures, seminars, conferences and meet-the-artist events. Following the shifting focus of the festival, the education programme will highlight a new theme each week. Lectures will be held at the social centre in each area, with a weekly seminar or conference exploring the theme in more depth. Of particular interest is the two day conference, hosted by Highland Regional Council which will address the theme of *New Imaging*.

During this conference, leading artists, writers and academics from Europe and America (including Carol Flax, MANUAL, Sean Cubitt and Kathleen Rogers) will present an artistic, theoretical and philosophical overview of the new digital technologies and their impact on Art and Society. Through discussions, workshops and demonstrations, technologies such as electronic imaging, computer generated imaging, telecom transmission of art and Virtual Reality will be explored. In the light of the advent of ISDN lines to the Highlands and the increased access to telecommunications and new technology, the conference will examine the potential for artists to create work and communicate with the rest of the world using fax and computer / modem links.

Art Buses and Tours

Outreach is an important part of our education programme. During the festival, buses housing travelling galleries will tour outlying regions of Scotland offering groups the opportunity to view a range of international and local work, and to participate in practical workshops and discussions. Tours between venues, for example across Fife, will allow the public to meet some of the exhibiting artists and to draw parallels and comparisons between the range of exhibitions.

Through an ambitious, multi-faceted education and community programme, Fotofeis hopes to generate a greater involvement in, and an enjoyment and understanding of photography and its related media.

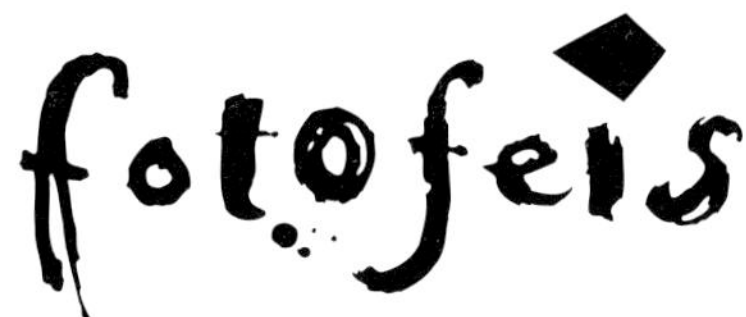

GRATEFULLY ACKNOWLEDGES
THE GENEROUS ASSISTANCE OF THE FOLLOWING
FUNDERS, SPONSORS AND DONORS:

The Scottish Arts Council

THE SCOTTISH ARTS COUNCIL

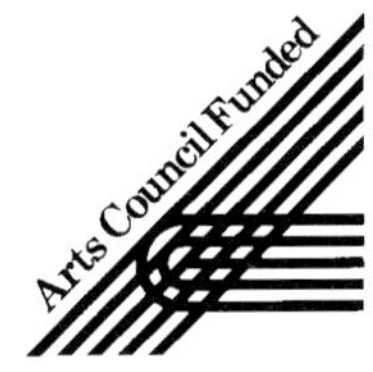

THE ARTS COUNCIL OF GREAT BRITAIN

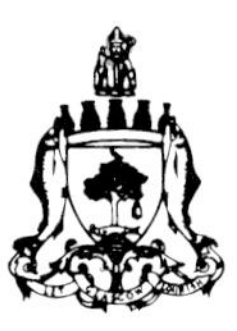

GLASGOW CITY COUNCIL

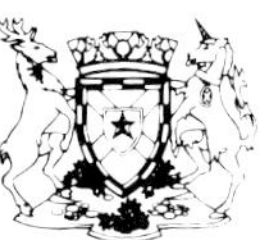

HIGHLAND REGIONAL COUNCIL

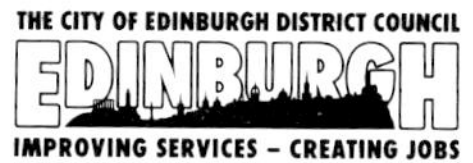

CITY OF EDINBURGH DISTRICT COUNCIL

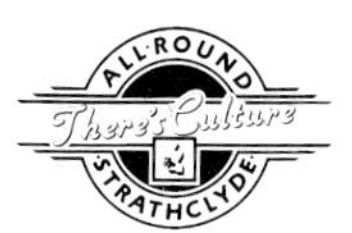

STRATHCLYDE REGIONAL COUNCIL

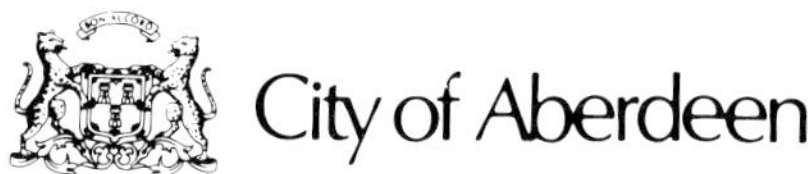

CITY OF ABERDEEN DISTRICT COUNCIL

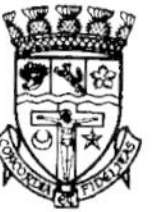

INVERNESS DISTRICT COUNCIL

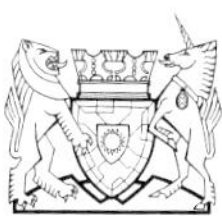

LOTHIAN REGIONAL COUNCIL

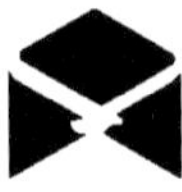

HIGHLANDS AND ISLANDS ENTERPRISE

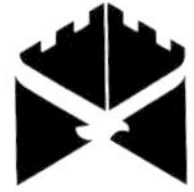

INVERNESS & NAIRN ENTERPRISE

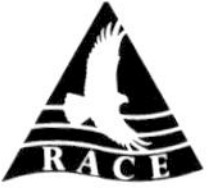

ROSS & CROMARTY ENTERPRISE

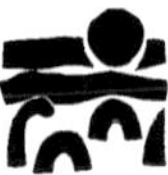

INVERNESS & NAIRN TOURIST BOARD

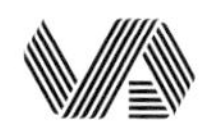

VISITING ARTS

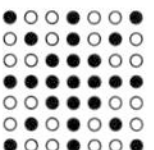

THE BRITISH COUNCIL

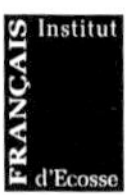

INSTITUT FRANÇAIS D'ECOSSE

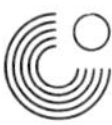

GOETHE-INSTITUT

THE ESMÉE FAIRBAIRN CHARITABLE TRUST

THE RUSSELL TRUST

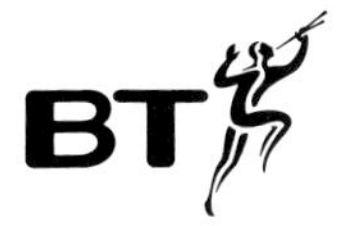

BRITISH TELECOM

Canon

CANON

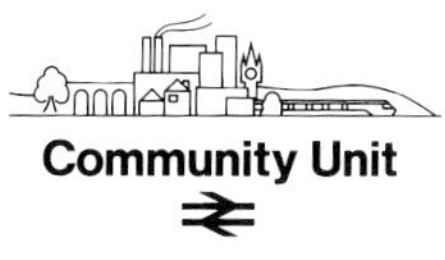

BRITISH RAIL

FOREST ENTERPRISE, INVERNESS

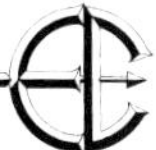

THE EASTGATE CENTRE, INVERNESS

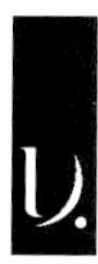

UNITED DISTILLERS

NORBORD-HIGHLAND LTD

TAYBURN STRATEGIC DESIGN

ARTWORK ASSOCIATES

SUMMERHALL PRESS

ROBERT HORNE PAPER

SCOTWORK

Fotofeis would like to thank Moyra Peffer of Whyte & Mackay Group PLC, who has been advising on the development of a press/publicity strategy. The placement was arranged through Business in the Arts.

Acknowledgement

Fotofeis has involved the combined efforts of many individuals and organisations. To all those who have been involved, to all those who have so freely offered help and advice, who have given their time, their encouragement and their expertise, we give our sincere thanks. You know who you are, without you this would not have been possible.
Take a bow!